Schenker Studies

Schenker Studies

edited by
Hedi Siegel

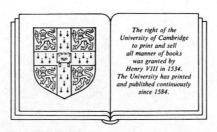

The right of the
University of Cambridge
to print and sell
all manner of books
was granted by
Henry VIII in 1534.
The University has printed
and published continuously
since 1584.

Cambridge University Press

Cambridge
New York   Port Chester   Melbourne   Sydney

Published by the Press Syndicate of the University of Cambridge
The Pitt Building, Trumpington Street, Cambridge CB2 1RP
40 West 20th Street, New York, NY 10011, USA
10 Stamford Road, Oakleigh, Melbourne 3166, Australia

First published 1990

Printed in Great Britain at the University Press, Cambridge

British Library cataloguing in publication data
Schenker studies
1. Music. Analysis. Theories of Schenker,
Heinrich, 1868–1935
I. Siegel, Hedi
781

Library of Congress cataloguing in publication data
Schenker studies / edited by Hedi Siegel.
   p.   cm.
Includes index.
ISBN 0–521–36038–2
1. Music – Theory – Congresses. 2. Schenker, Heinrich, 1868–1935 –
Congresses. I. Schenker, Heinrich, 1868–1935. II. Siegel, Hedi.
MT6.S457 1989
780 – dc19 89–467 CIP

ISBN 0 521 36038 2

in memoriam
Felix Salzer
(1904–1986)

CONTENTS

The following works of Heinrich Schenker will often be cited by title alone. Complete bibliographic information is given below, with the abbreviated form appearing in bold type.

Counterpoint, Books I and II, a translation of *Kontrapunkt* by John Rothgeb and Jürgen Thym, edited by John Rothgeb (New York: Schirmer Books, 1987).

Erläuterungsausgabe *der letzten fünf Sonaten Beethovens* (Vienna: Universal Edition, 1913–20); new edition, revised by Oswald Jonas (Vienna: Universal Edition, 1971–72).

   Op. 109, published 1913; revised edition, 1971.

   Op. 110, published 1914; revised edition, 1972.

   Op. 111, published 1915; revised edition, 1971.

   Op. 101, published 1920; revised edition, 1972.

   (Op. 106 was never published.)

Five Graphic Music Analyses, republication of *Fünf Urlinie-Tafeln* (Vienna: Universal Edition, 1932; New York: David Mannes Music School, 1933), with a new introduction and glossary by Felix Salzer (New York: Dover, 1969).

Free Composition (*Der freie Satz*), translated and edited by Ernst Oster (New York: Longman, 1979).

Der freie Satz, Volume III of *Neue musikalische Theorien und Phantasien* (Vienna: Universal Edition, 1935); second edition, edited and revised by Oswald Jonas (Vienna: Universal Edition, 1956).

Harmonielehre, Volume I of *Neue musikalische Theorien und Phantasien* (Stuttgart: Cotta, 1906; reprint edition, Vienna: Universal Edition, 1978).

Harmony, a translation of *Harmonielehre* by Elisabeth Mann Borgese, edited and annotated by Oswald Jonas (Chicago: University of Chicago Press, 1954; reprint edition, Cambridge, Mass.: M.I.T. Press, 1973).

Kontrapunkt, Volume II of *Neue musikalische Theorien und Phantasien*: Book I (Stuttgart: Cotta, 1910); Book II (Vienna: Universal Edition, 1922).

Das Meisterwerk *in der Musik*: *Jahrbuch* I (Munich: Drei Masken Verlag, 1925); *Jahrbuch* II (Munich: Drei Masken Verlag, 1926); *Jahrbuch* III

(Munich: Drei Masken Verlag, 1930); reprint edition, three volumes in one (Hildesheim: Olms, 1974).

Der Tonwille: Issues 1–10 (Vienna: A. Gutmann, 1921–24; later republished in three volumes by Universal Edition).

PREFACE

In March of 1985, an event took place at The Mannes College of Music in New York which would indeed have surprised Heinrich Schenker, the man to whose work the event was dedicated. That event was a three-day symposium, attended by a large group of musicians from many regions of a country not highly regarded by Schenker. He had made a prediction in 1921, as he wrote the opening essay of his series *Der Tonwille*, that the people of the United States "would not attain the intellectual and moral qualifications needed for them to take part in achieving a higher goal for humanity." Yet at the symposium, musicians were meeting to hear papers, read largely by native-born Americans, which gave proof of a profound understanding and imaginative application of Schenker's ideas.

This book grew out of that symposium; its essays are based on papers read during those three highly stimulating days. It is hoped that some of the excitement felt by the participants will be captured on its pages. For the symposium, which was initiated as a commemoration of the fiftieth anniversary of Schenker's death, became a celebration of the widespread recognition Schenkerian thought has received in the English-speaking world. The achievement and continuing growth of this recognition, not only in America, but now in Great Britain as well, is documented in the last section of this book, "Schenker Studies Today."

The largest number of contributions is contained in the book's second section, "Analytical Studies." This emphasis reflects the main tradition of Schenkerian teaching as well as the central focus of Schenkerian thought, for Schenker's approach grew out of his own analytical study of individual works of music – out of his search for the underlying principles that govern them all.

The first section of the book, "Historical Studies," brings together five rather diverse essays. Included are studies of Schenker as a historical figure; two focus on his own pursuits – his work with musical manuscripts and thorough-bass theory – and one explores the philosophical basis of his ideas. Also included are two articles that extend Schenker's theories and apply them to the study of music history.

The organization of the book loosely follows the schedule of the symposium. Some of the papers were considerably altered before publication in this volume while others remain essentially the same as the conference presentation. It was not practical to reproduce extensive examples from the musical works discussed; thus the reader is asked to consult the appropriate scores. A few introductory remarks have been added to each section, with selected bibliographic information given in the notes.

It was appropriate that the first conference devoted exclusively to Schenker's ideas was held at The Mannes College of Music, the first (and for many years the only) school of music to offer theory and analysis courses based on Schenkerian principles. The symposium – from its inception to its present form as a published book – was made possible by the inspired and untiring work of the Mannes administrators, staff, and theory faculty, especially Mannes's President, Charles Kaufman, and Robert Cuckson, the school's Dean at the time the symposium took place. Faculty members Carl Schachter, Larry Laskowski, and David Loeb served on the symposium's advisory committee; they, together with committee members Charles Burkhart and Saul Novack, took on the difficult task of selecting the conference program, thus assuring the high quality of the essays in this volume. Special thanks go to Eric Wen, on Mannes's faculty at the time of the symposium but now based in London, for his work as a member of the selection committee and for his help in transatlantic communication with the publisher. A great debt is owed to Penny Souster for her perceptive guidance; she and her colleagues at Cambridge University Press made this book a reality. As the book approached its final form, others gave valuable help: I am grateful to Channan Willner for his advice and continuing interest, to James Hatch, Linnea Johnson, Elizabeth Salvie, and Frank Samarotto for their watchful checking of proof, and to Deborah Kessler for preparing the index with exceptional care. Finally, I owe very special thanks to Deborah Griffith Davis, the Mannes Librarian, for the expert assistance she offered unstintingly at every stage in this book's preparation.

Felix Salzer served as honorary chairman of the advisory committee, but he was too ill to attend any of the symposium's sessions. However, he was surely present in the thoughts of the participants. There were few who did not owe some aspect of their Schenkerian knowledge directly to him, to one or more of his students, or to the articles and books he had written or had guided into print. And this is no doubt true of many who will read this book. To its contributors, this volume represents a Festschrift published in his honor, and we fondly dedicate it to his memory.

Hedi Siegel
Hunter College,
The City University of New York

Introduction

The five studies in this section point to some of the directions Schenkerian historical research has taken in recent years. Schenker himself is the subject of the first three essays; they take their cue from his own interests or from influences upon his thought. John Rothgeb's article focuses on Schenker's deep concern for the study of composers' autographs, on his recognition of the importance of such study for the analysis and informed performance of music. Another of Schenker's life-long preoccupations – and a formative influence on his theories – was the discipline of thorough bass. His primary interest was in the theories of C. P. E. Bach, but he also turned his attention to a thorough-bass manual attributed to J. S. Bach, and this is the subject of Hedi Siegel's essay. William Pastille looks outside the area of music for an important influence on Schenker's ideas – the scientific thought of Goethe.

The articles by David Stern and Saul Novack take Schenker's approach beyond areas he himself developed. As is well known, Schenker's own studies are of eighteenth- and nineteenth-century music. David Stern applies Schenker's theories to the music of the Renaissance, shedding light on the history of voice leading and its relation to structure. Saul Novack's essay is based on this kind of extension of the traditional Schenkerian repertory, an extension initiated by Felix Salzer but carried through in a large measure by Novack himself. Here Novack undertakes a survey of the history of tonality viewed in the perspective of Schenker's concept of structural levels – foreground, middleground, and background.

At the 1985 Schenker Symposium, two papers were read that extend the application of Schenker's ideas toward the twentieth century – James Baker's "Schenkerian Analysis: Key to Late-Romantic Extended Forms," and Roy Travis's study of Benjamin Britten's *Death in Venice*. These papers are not part of this volume because they were destined for publication elsewhere.[1] They join the considerable number of studies exploring the pre- and post-Schenkerian repertory that have appeared in this decade. In his third bibliographic article on Schenkerian research, covering the period 1979–84, David Beach provides a comprehensive list under the heading "Extensions of Schenker's Theories" and devotes an entire section of the valuable essay that precedes his listings to a discussion of this literature.[2] He also fully documents the investigation of historical aspects of Schenker's thought; the writings he lists under the heading "Historical Research" include discussions of the philosophical basis and historical significance of Schenker's theories.

A further area of activity – which is only minimally represented within this book – has been the preparation of English translations of the writings of Schenker himself. Beach supplements his list of Schenker's own writings (he includes available reprints and translations) with a discussion of projected translations.[3] Some of these have now been published, most significantly the translation of *Kontrapunkt* by John Rothgeb and Jürgen Thym.[4] Translations of Schenker's shorter essays continue to appear; these include the annotated translations by Ian Bent of two Scarlatti analyses from *Das Meisterwerk* published in *Music Analysis*.[5] In addition, extracts from Schenker's personal papers have been published (in German); Hellmut Federhofer's recent biographical study contains important material pertaining to Schenker's ideas both within and outside the field of music, much of it in quotations from letters and diaries.[6]

It is hoped that this sketch of current work will direct the reader toward the growing field of historical Schenker studies.

Notes

(Selected bibliographic information on Schenkerian historical studies)

1. The material presented by James Baker is included in his book, *The Music of Alexander Scriabin* (New Haven, 1986). An expanded version of Roy Travis's paper has been published as "The Recurrent Figure in the Britten/Piper Opera *Death in Venice*," *The Music Forum*, Vol. 6, Part 1 (New York, 1987), pp. 129–246.
2. David Beach, "The Current State of Schenkerian Research," *Acta Musicologica* 57/2 (1985), pp. 275–307. The first two articles in Beach's series are "A Schenker Bibliography," *Journal of Music Theory* 13/1 (1969), pp. 2–37, reprinted in *Readings in Schenker Analysis*, ed. Maury Yeston (New Haven, 1977), pp. 275–311; and "A Schenker Bibliography: 1969–1979," *Journal of Music Theory* 23/2 (1979), pp. 275–86.
3. Beach, "The Current State of Schenkerian Research," Appendix I and pp. 281–82. A list of Schenker's works is included in the translations available from Schirmer Books in New York: Schenker's *Free Composition* (1979), *J. S. Bach's Chromatic Fantasy and Fugue* (1984), and *Counterpoint* (1987), as well as Jonas's *Introduction to the Theory of Heinrich Schenker* (1982). The bibliography of Ian Bent's *Analysis* (London and New York, 1987) has an extensive entry for Schenker, with a list of primary sources as one of its separate sections. The other sections of the entry, as well as large portions of the book itself, provide much important information that pertains to Schenkerian historical studies, including the extension of Schenker's theories.
4. At the 1985 Schenker Symposium, Irene Schreier reported on her translation of Schenker's *Die Kunst des Vortrags*; this and Heribert Esser's edition of the German text have not yet appeared as of this writing.
5. "Essays from *Das Meisterwerk in der Musik*, Vol. I (1925)," trans. Ian Bent, *Music Analysis* 5/2–3 (1986), pp. 151–91. The translations, which are of Schenker's essays on the Scarlatti Sonatas in D minor and G major, and of an important short theoretical section, are prefaced by Bent's article "Heinrich Schenker, Chopin and Domenico Scarlatti" (pp. 131–49).

6. Hellmut Federhofer, *Heinrich Schenker: Nach Tagebüchern und Briefen in der Oswald Jonas Memorial Collection* (Hildesheim, 1985). See also William Pastille's review of Federhofer's book in the *Journal of the American Musicological Society* 39/3 (1986), pp. 667–77, which begins with a comprehensive account (giving bibliographic details) of recent Schenkerian writings on historical issues.

Schenkerian theory and manuscript studies: modes of interaction

John Rothgeb

My purpose in this article is to provide a general notion (for those who have not already studied it in depth) of the character of Schenkerian work with manuscript materials. I shall concentrate chiefly on Schenker's own work and on that of Oswald Jonas, who, among Schenker's pupils, was the one who specialized early and extensively in such studies. I shall try to indicate along the way how those aspects of Schenkerian theory that are most uniquely Schenkerian can contribute special insights to the interpretation of manuscripts.

Under "manuscripts" are to be included two fundamentally different classes of materials: (1) autograph manuscripts of finished compositions, and (2) sketches and working drafts. These categories overlap in some cases; in particular, documents of the first category very frequently embody elements of the second, in the form of revisions, in which case the autograph manuscript takes on additional significance similar to that of a sketch.

Let us for the moment leave aside such revisions and consider the significance of an autograph score *qua* autograph score. The first and most obvious benefit it provides is in establishing a definitive text. Although Schenker was well aware that autographs could not be regarded as absolutely definitive in all cases, he considered them in general far more important than any other type of source. In his essay on Beethoven's "Eroica" Symphony he prefaces a discussion of a copy of the symphony revised in Beethoven's hand with the following words:

The manuscript of the Third Symphony has thus far not come to light; but neither the first print of the parts or the score, nor even the copy revised by Beethoven, can substitute for it. Unfortunately, a copy of a Beethoven work always presents a picture completely different from that of the master's own script, which shapes the content even for the eye in a way that is persuasively and convincingly artistic.[1]

It is well known that Schenker's editions of Beethoven's piano sonatas were among the first to adhere closely to manuscript sources. His edition was the first, for example, to follow Beethoven's own notation in a case such as measure 16 of the Sonata Op. 101 (Example 1a), where all previous

---

1. Schenker, "Beethovens dritte Sinfonie," *Das Meisterwerk* III, p. 86. The translations given in this article are mine.

Exmaple 1. Beethoven, Sonata Op. 101, first movement

(a)

(b)

(and many subsequent) editions present the notation as in Example 1b. In his *Erläuterungsausgabe* of Op. 101, Schenker explains as follows:

> In measure 16 the notation of the autograph had to be restored; it had been lost already in the original edition and can no longer be found in any other edition: I refer to the notation of the eighth-note group in the upper staff (instead of in the bass), which automatically communicates to the most casual glance the secret of the line, the continuation of g#¹ of the downbeat by the last eighth-note g#¹.[2]

Oswald Jonas elsewhere cites the same example and comments still more precisely: "It is as though the handwriting wished to demonstrate the origin of the composed-out third e–g# from the third e–g# of the right hand. The left hand thus directly continues the content of the right."[3] The reference to composing-out makes this a specifically Schenkerian interpretation of the orthography.

The last part of Schenker's comment quoted above on the revised copy of Beethoven's "Eroica" suggests another characteristic of autograph scores to which special attention has been directed by both Schenker and Jonas. In the preface to his Op. 101 edition, Schenker writes:

> Recently I saw Chopin's autograph of the Scherzo in E major, Op. 45 – extremely delicate and neat, like everything from that master's hand, and prepared in such a way that there could be no question concerning the master's exact wishes. The original edition also confirms the authority of the manuscript, and yet: even in such a rare agreement between manuscript and first print, the former nevertheless exhibits several brilliant pen-strokes that speak directly to the eye and lead reliably to important insights. . .[4]

And further, concerning the autograph of Brahms's Op. 117:

> Although the first printing is in general to be credited only with the best fidelity, in the manuscript, nevertheless, certain other features, even very important ones, are to be found, which the first printing was unable to reproduce.[5]

Schenker may have had in mind such features as that shown by the handwriting in measure 6 of Beethoven's Piano Sonata Op. 81a (see Plate 1). The orthography of the *sf* followed by decrescendo strongly

2. Schenker, *Erläuterungsausgabe, Op. 101* (1972 edn), p. 23.
3. Oswald Jonas, "Musikalische Meisterhandschriften," *Der Dreiklang* 2 (May 1937), p. 58.
4. *Erläuterungsausgabe, Op. 101* (1972 edn), p. 6.
5. *Ibid.*

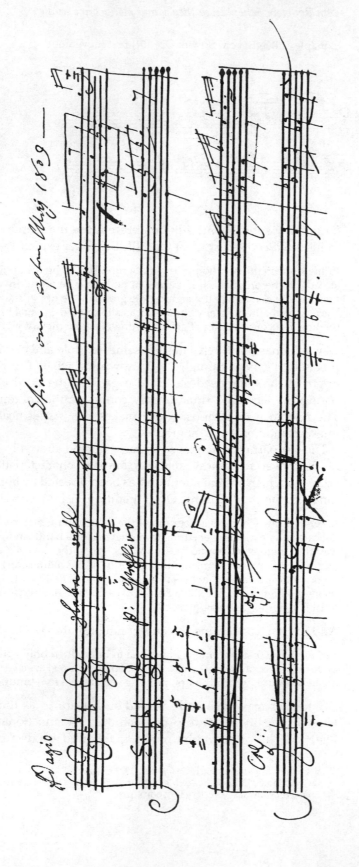

Plate 1. Beethoven, Sonata Op. 81a (from the first page of the autograph)

suggests a deliberate singling-out of the third-progression d²–eb²–f²: it is these tones above all that answer, within the newly achieved dominant harmony, the descending third g¹–f¹–eb¹ of the beginning.[6] What is particularly interesting here is that the autograph shows a feature of such subtlety that it *cannot* be reproduced in any printed edition, yet which is deeply suggestive for performance and understanding of the passage.

Sketches and drafts are a different matter entirely. They are seldom of importance for establishing a correct text, although a notable exception exists in the case of the notorious a♯ at the end of the development of the "Hammerklavier" Sonata.[7] Schenker describes and comments, sometimes rather extensively, on sketches in his analytical studies of Beethoven's Fifth and Ninth Symphonies, as well as in the *Erläuterungsausgaben* of the last piano sonatas. There has been much debate recently about the significance of sketches – in particular, it has been disputed that sketches for a given work can be invoked as an aid for understanding the finished work itself. To the extent that such an objection is valid, however, it does not apply to Schenker's work. The benefit of sketch study, from a Schenkerian perspective, has been summarized by Oswald Jonas as follows:

> It seems to me that the cardinal point of such investigations is to answer the following question: what were the artistic necessities that guided Beethoven's musical instinct? If we follow the course of evolution of any individual work with this in mind, the insights we derive will have a general artistic value; indeed, only through their generality will they have a special value for us.[8]

The sketches, then, provide information not about the finished work, but about the principles that guided its formation.

It would far exceed the scope of this paper to undertake a detailed appraisal of even a single series of sketches; but a clear idea of Schenker's approach to the study of revisions in general can be gained from a brief examination of his commentary to his facsimile edition of Beethoven's "Moonlight" Sonata.[9] The autograph manuscript under consideration incorporates numerous revisions discussed in some detail by Schenker.[10] Part of the sixth page of the facsimile is reproduced in Plate 2. Beethoven's alterations to the third measure (measure 56 of the first movement) are of interest, and Schenker comments as follows:

---

6. This passage was shown to me by Oswald Jonas, who did not, however, write about it, so far as I know.
7. A sketch reproduced by Nottebohm, in which Beethoven writes in figured-bass figures, establishes the authenticity of the a♮ beyond all question, as Schenker remarks in a footnote to his edition.
8. Jonas, "Zur Betrachtung Beethovenscher Skizzen," in "Beethoveniana," *Der Dreiklang* 6 (September 1937), p. 151.
9. Beethoven, *Sonate Op. 27, Nr. 2*, facsimile edition with an introduction by Schenker (Vienna, 1921).
10. Schenker also reproduces and comments on three independent sketch pages for the final movement.

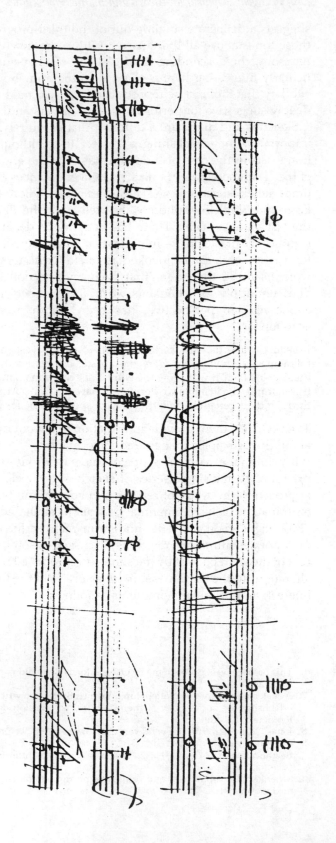

Plate 2. Beethoven, Sonata Op. 27, No. 2 (from the autograph of the first movement)

Beethoven's first plan is to introduce the final cadence already at this point [Example 2].

Example 2

But since the prominence of the last section [the coda] would certainly have suffered considerably, he alters his approach to include a richer scale-degree progression: I–IV–VII–III–VI–II–V–I. An obstacle is presented, however, in that he first continues to write the bass of measure 56 in the form of two half notes; this yields an overly harsh collision between the half notes of this measure and the quarters of measure 57 [Example 3].

Example 3

Thus in order to mediate between the two rhythms and to motivate the quarter notes, he writes a quarter note in measure 56 for the second half note. And now a particularly inspired detail: to establish clearly that the so-achieved quarter note is to be related only to the following quarters and not to the preceding dotted half, he expressly links the latter back to the second half of measure 55 by means of a legato slur [Example 4].[11]

Example 4

It is clear that Schenker here speaks to several "artistic necessities" (and the specific technical means used to satisfy them): the necessities for (1) appropriate weighting of formal sections; (2) avoidance of a sharp rhythmic disjunction where it could serve no larger purpose; and (3) above all, clarity – that is, avoidance of an ambiguity that could only become an unresolved enigma.

It is curious that Schenker, writing in 1921, makes no mention of the fact that measure 58 of the movement (the last measure of system 1 in Plate 2) was obviously inserted after the surrounding measures 57 and 59 were written. Measure 58 serves several purposes, of which one of the most important could have been explained convincingly in the light of Schenker's developing voice-leading theory – indeed, by a particular example that he included in *Free Composition*. First, measure 58 obviously restores a desirable rhythmic equilibrium in that it once again mediates

11. Introduction to the facsimile edition, p. iv. Schenker's interpretation of the purpose of the legato slur is given credence by the fact that the motion from F♯ to D♯ under circumstances such as are present here would not ordinarily call for a portamento treatment; indeed, the "applied-dominant" relationship of the D♯ ⁶₅ chord to the following E triad, which gives the former an appoggiatura-like significance, might of itself have suggested the opposite procedure – that is, a fresh articulation of D♯ followed by a slur to E.

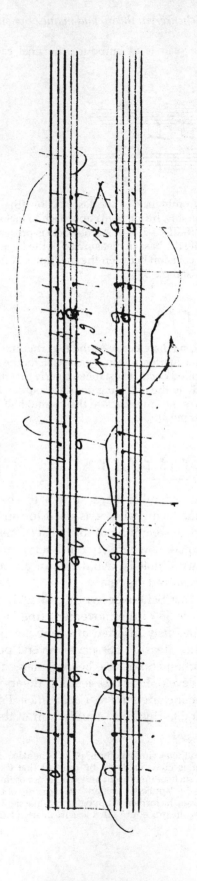

Plate 3. Beethoven, Sonata Op. 27, No. 2 (from the autograph of the Allegretto)

between the quarter-note motion of measure 57 and the essentially stationary outer voices of measure 59 by providing a composed retard. But beyond this, the f#[1] of measure 58 furnishes a stepwise continuation of the descending motion of the upper voice initiated in measure 56: because it is inevitably heard as continuing through e[1] and d#[1] of measure 59, it completes the descending octave-progression of which Schenker was fully aware as he wrote Figure 54/3 of *Free Composition* (Example 5).[12]

Example 5. Beethoven, Sonata Op. 27, No. 2, first movement, measures 55ff.
(from *Free Composition*, Figure 54/3)

By establishing closure, this alteration contributes also to the "prominence of the last section" and thus to formal equilibrium.

While we are on the subject of the "Moonlight" Sonata, let us consider also Plate 3, from the Allegretto (the last system on the eighth page of the facsimile). This excerpt begins with the first complete measure after the double bar and repeat sign (measure 17 of the movement). Schenker comments on the characteristic lengthening of slurs in the left-hand part, but he does not mention the erasure in the penultimate measure of the example. Beethoven first worte a $\frac{4}{2}$ chord over g♭, with the bass continuing g♭–f–c; this would have preserved the sixth-relationship of the upper voices. But the alteration introduces the important low c in a stronger way (by a third-progression) and moreover provides a third (enlarged) statement of the turn motive that has been prominent in the bass (here as e♭–d♭–c–d♭).

A uniquely Schenkerian insight into a passage from Beethoven's "Pastorale" Symphony enables us to interpret some of Beethoven's sketches for the work as documentation of his creative process. Schenker did not write about the sketches themselves, but an example in *Free Composition* (Figure 119/8) reveals a certain artistic tour de force in the finished

Example 6. Beethoven, Symphony No. 6, first movement
(from *Free Composition*, Figure 119/8)

12. Figure 54/3 of Schenker, *Free Composition*, is reproduced in Example 5 by permission of Schirmer Books, a division of Macmillan, Inc.

composition (see Example 6).[13] The motive marked "a" in measures 11–12 of the theme is fantastically enlarged in measures 275ff., as shown in the right-hand portion of Schenker's example. The F major sonority of measures 279ff., in spite of its length, has exactly the same meaning as the fifth designated "cons.p.t." on the left: it intervenes between IV and V and provides consonant support for a passing tone.

Let me take a moment to amplify this example, which appears without further comment under the rubric "repetition by enlargement," and to place it in the context of Schenker's theory of tonal organization. In Part 6 of *Counterpoint*, under the subtitle "Bridges to Free Composition," he writes:

. . .my efforts [in identifying such bridges] will be primarily directed to establishing the laws of a polyphonic passing event (*Durchgang*) such as arises for the first time in the context of combinations of species, and to demonstrating how these passing events, rooted in fundamental laws, tend even in the combined species toward an independent setting, which is characteristic of them in free composition as well, although there in greater variety.[14]

The origin of such a polyphonic passing event is shown in Example 7. In Example 7a, we see what Schenker would call an *Ur*-phenomenon: the

Example 7

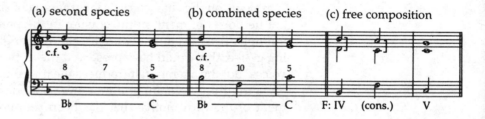

topmost voice moves through a regular passing dissonance in a three-voice setting of the pure second species; in Example 7b, in a setting of the combined species, the passing tone is joined by another second-species voice (the lowest) that transforms it into a consonance. The newly acquired consonant support does not in the least obliterate our impression of a succession of just two harmonies: Bb–C. The formation in Example 7c, no longer bound to a cantus firmus, oversteps the limits of species counterpoint; it is typical of free composition. The two upper voices move in parallel sixths at the upbeat, with the result that the inner voice anticipates the octave of the coming C harmony. In measures 11–13 of the "Pastorale" Symphony, the two upper voices of Example 7c are inverted for motivic reasons (the primary passing tone, a, now appearing as an

---

13. Figure 119/8 of *Free Composition* is reproduced in Example 6 by permission of Schirmer Books, a division of Macmillan, Inc.
14. Schenker, *Counterpoint* II, p. 176.

inner voice), and the upper-voice succession d²–c² of measure 11 continues to the passing seventh, bb¹, of measure 12.[15] Example 8 may sup-

Example 8. Beethoven, Symphony No. 6, first movement

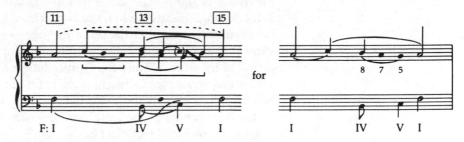

F: I　　　IV　V　I　　　　　　I　　　IV　V　I

plement Schenker's example as an explanation of the F major chords in both measure 22 and measures 279ff.; the brackets between the staves indicate parallelism.

What Beethoven accomplished in measures 279ff., then, was not only to integrate a moment of the most profound formal consequence – the beginning of the recapitulation – into an enlargement of an established motive, but to associate inextricably that moment and the F major sonority it delineates with an event of quintessential musical transience: a *passing tone.*

It is not surprising that the extant sketches for the "Pastorale"[16] reveal that Beethoven spent considerable effort on this problem. The sketches have been described and interpreted by Philip Gossett, who writes the following about this unique fusion of development and recapitulation:

Example 1 [our Example 9] gives a harmonic outline of the definitive retransition (mm. 247-79). An eight-measure phrase derived from the opening group appears

Example 9

8 mm.　8 mm.　　　　8mm., etc.

sequentially in the strings in A major, in D major, passing through G major to C major, where played by the entire orchestra it addresses the tonic. Instead of resolving, it dissolves into Bb major, the subdominant. The winds disappear, fortissimo fades to piano, and Beethoven eases us into the *tonic* recapitulation [emphasis added] via the subdominant. The subdominant plays a key role throughout this movement. The opening melody implies a I–IV–I progression,

15. If the context did not require us to hear the F major chord of measure 11 as passing in this strictly contrapuntal sense, the 5–5 outer-voice succession in measures 11–12 would sound really crude.
16. These are divided today between the British Museum and the Stiftung Preussischer Kulturbesitz in West Berlin. See Alan Tyson, "A Reconstruction of the Pastoral Symphony Sketchbook," in *Beethoven Studies*, ed. Alan Tyson (New York, 1973), pp. 67–96.

soon after realized harmonically (mm. 9–11). . .The rare subdominant approach to the recapitulation . . . is both relevant and peculiarly appropriate for the world of the *Pastorale*.[17]

Gossett's description is not lacking in insight; he is on the right track in his choice of the words "eases us into" and in his reference to measures 9–11 (although his attention there is restricted to the presence of subdominant harmony to the exclusion of the upper voice). But in his view, the story of the beginning of the recapitulation appears to be finished at the arrival of measure 279 and the "tonic" harmony.

Beethoven's accomplishment is really far greater than Gossett imagines. Schenker has shown us just what it truly is in his example from *Free Composition*, and his theory gives us a way to understand its precise, organically musical, technical basis.

Schenker's greatest contribution to manuscript study, then, is probably not his own relatively sparse writings about manuscripts, however valuable they may be. It is rather his service in suggesting to the musical ear a wider range of possibilities for the interpretation of musical content than anyone had dreamed of before. Schenker gives us at least the possibility of understanding what the composer *has* in fact accomplished; only with such understanding can we follow the cryptic hint provided by manuscripts of what the composer sought, and why.

17. Philip Gossett, "Beethoven's Sixth Symphony: Sketches for the First Movement," *Journal of the American Musicological Society* 27/2 (1974), pp. 252–53.

A source for Schenker's study of thorough bass: his annotated copy of J. S. Bach's *Generalbassbüchlein*

Hedi Siegel

In the Introduction to *Der freie Satz*, Schenker outlines a plan of instruction which would, in his words, "provide a truly practical understanding" of the concept of organic coherence. This plan calls for three stages of instruction: (1) "in strict counterpoint (according to Fux–Schenker)," (2) "in thorough bass (according to Johann Sebastian Bach and Carl Philipp Emanuel Bach)," and (3) "in free composition (according to Schenker)."[1] The first and third stages are implemented by Schenker himself in *Kontrapunkt* and *Der freie Satz*. But no published work appeared during Schenker's lifetime that provides a guide to the second stage: instruction in thorough bass according to J. S. Bach and C. P. E. Bach. It is clear that Schenker was not thinking of his own *Harmonielehre*. He did not think of harmony as a preparatory study at all; he viewed it as a matter for rather advanced speculation. It was his belief that "the study of harmony ought to be concerned only with the psychology of the abstract scale step,"[2] and that harmonic theory could "never. . .simply take the place of figured-bass theory."[3]

But Schenker did write a work that implements the second stage of his plan and exactly fits his description of a figured-bass study – a monograph with the title "Von der Stimmführung des Generalbasses" (The Voice Leading of Thorough Bass). Part of Schenker's early work on *Der freie Satz*,[4] this study was never published. It exists in manuscript form, in the hand of Schenker's wife (with corrections inserted in Schenker's hand; like *Der freie Satz*, it was written down by Jeanette Schenker from her husband's dictation). It is dated 29 August 1917 on the manuscript's last page. More than one typescript appears to have been made from the manuscript. The introductory section appeared in print shortly after Schenker's death; it was published in 1937 in *Der Dreiklang*.[5]

1. Schenker, *Der freie Satz*, p. 15; the translation is from *Free Composition*, pp. xxi–xxii.
2. Schenker, *Harmonielehre*, p. 226; the translation (slightly altered) is from *Harmony*, p. 176.
3. Schenker, "Von der Stimmführung im Generalbass," *Der Dreiklang* 3 (June 1937), p. 76. The translation is from John Rothgeb, "Schenkerian Theory: Its Implications for the Undergraduate Curriculum," *Music Theory Spectrum* 3 (1981), p. 146.
4. See Oswald Jonas's Preface to *Free Composition*, p. xvi; see also the footnote provided by the editors of *Der Dreiklang* to Schenker, "Von der Stimmführung im Generalbass," p. 75.
5. *Der Dreiklang* 3 (June 1937), pp. 75–81. The article will hereafter be referred to as *Generalbasslehre*, Chapter 1, §1 (*Der Dreiklang*). The title of the article, "Von der Stimmführung im Generalbass," differs slightly from the title of the study as given in the typescript: "Von der Stimmführung des Generalbasses." A translation of the complete study will be published in Vol. 6, Part 2, of *The Music Forum* (in preparation).

In his valuable discussion of Schenker's unpublished study on thorough bass, John Rothgeb speaks of Schenker's expansion and reorganization of thorough-bass theory so that it takes harmonic theory into account – specifically the concept of the harmonic scale degree and, implicitly, the idea of composing-out. We learn that Schenker provides thorough-bass theory with an internal system; unlike eighteenth-century thorough-bass theorists, he organizes the various configurations according to conceptual categories.[6]

In spite of the originality of his study, Schenker did not think of it as mainly an exposition of his own theories. He wrote in the opening section:

Of course the presentation of thorough-bass theory required a change in my past procedures. Since I needed to present a theory other than my own, it would be preferable that I immediately draw upon the words and examples of the two greatest authorities on this subject. It had previously been my custom to refer to the opinions of others. . .under the heading of "literature," but in this case the theories of others became the *main* theories. Thus it is my purpose – and this is no mean task – to elucidate these theories in their own right as well as in connection with my ideas.[7]

For this reason, Schenker's thorough-bass study contains a large number of references. By far the majority are to C. P. E. Bach's *Versuch über die wahre Art das Clavier zu spielen*.[8] Schenker had made a preliminary study of the *Versuch*, known as his "Kommentar." As he worked his way through Part II of the treatise, he appears to have dictated his thoughts on Bach's treatment of various topics. This commentary exists in the form of a separate manuscript in Jeanette Schenker's hand, with corrections added by Schenker.

A much smaller number of references in Schenker's study are to an instruction book reputed to be by J. S. Bach – to what Schenker called Bach's *Generalbassbüchlein*. But their smaller number does not, I think, diminish their significance, as I hope to show in my discussion of these references and their source.

It is quite natural that Schenker's study includes fewer references to J. S. Bach than to C. P. E. Bach: J. S. Bach's writings on thorough bass are not nearly as comprehensive as those of his son, and they are far less voluminous. They were available to Schenker in a single source – the thorough-bass instructions published by Spitta in the Appendix to his biography of Bach.[9] Schenker had fifty or so pages of Spitta's Appendix bound separately; they make up a slim black leather-bound volume.[10]

6. Rothgeb, "Schenkerian Theory: Its Implications for the Undergraduate Curriculum," pp. 145–46.
7. *Generalbasslehre*, Chapter 1, §1 (*Der Dreiklang*), p. 77. Translations from Schenker's thorough-bass study are mine unless otherwise indicated.
8. See C. P. E. Bach, *Essay on the True Art of Playing Keyboard Instruments*, trans. and ed. William J. Mitchell (New York, 1949).
9. See Philipp Spitta, *Johann Sebastian Bach*, 8th unaltered edn (Wiesbaden, 1979), Vol. 2, pp. 913–50 (Anhang B, XII). The original edition of Vol. 2 appeared in 1880.
10. Spitta's supplementary musical examples (see *Bach*, Vol. 2, Beilage, pp. 1–20) are bound

Its brown paper wrapping bears the title "Seb. Bach / Generalbass" (written in Jeanette Schenker's hand). Schenker habitually referred to it in the diminutive – he called it a "Büchlein," a "Heftchen," or a "Werkchen."[11] This small volume is of value because it contains copious annotations in Schenker's own hand. We can therefore be present, so to speak, as he turns its pages and studies its contents.

A discussion of Schenker's annotations in the *Büchlein* and their relation to his study of thorough bass should perhaps be prefaced by a brief survey of the *Büchlein's* provenance, its contents, and Schenker's thoughts on thorough bass. Though I shall draw mainly on Schenker's unpublished study, I shall also refer briefly to some of his other writings.

In the opening section of his thorough-bass study, Schenker expresses his regret at having been wholly dependent on Spitta's transcription of the *Büchlein's* source; he had made every effort to gain access to the manuscript but had not succeeded.[12] Spitta gave a description of the manuscript, identifying only the hand of Johann Peter Kellner, to whom he ascribed the title page and some corrections (these are now thought to be in the hand of Carl August Thieme, who studied at the Thomasschule in Leipzig).[13] The manuscript's title, which bears the date of 1738, is "Vorschriften und Grundsätze zum vierstimmigen spielen des General-Bass oder Accompagnement" (Precepts and Principles for Playing Thorough Bass or Accompanying in Four Parts), intended for use by Bach's "Scholaren in der Music." Schenker may not have been aware of Spitta's later identification of Friedrich Erhardt Niedt's *Musicalische Handleitung* as Bach's direct source for the material in the early chapters.[14]

The similarity to Niedt's treatise, as well as the fact that the manuscript is not in Bach's own hand, have cast doubt on its authenticity. Recently discovered external evidence seems to confirm its origin in Bach's circle of students. But because the settings do contain errors, it is thought that Bach perhaps wrote or dictated only the bass lines and the figures, and

with the pages from the Appendix. The volume was owned by Felix Salzer, as were the manuscript and a typescript of the *Generalbasslehre*; I am much indebted to Mrs. Hedi Salzer for continuing to make these materials available to me.

11. Hereafter referred to as the *Büchlein*.
12. *Generalbasslehre*, Chapter 1, §1 (*Der Dreiklang*), pp. 75–76. The manuscript Spitta transcribed is now in the Bibliothèque du Conservatoire Royal de Musique in Brussels (Ms. No. 27.224). A full description of the manuscript is given in Johann Sebastian Bach, *Neue Ausgabe sämtlicher Werke*, Supplement: *Bach-Dokumente*, Vol. 2, ed. Werner Neumann and Hans-Joachim Schulze (Kassel, 1969), No. 433, pp. 333–34 and opposite p. 400 (facsimile of the title page).
13. See Hans-Joachim Schulze, "'Das Stück im Goldpaier' – Ermittlungen zu einigen Bach-Abschriften des frühen 18. Jahrhunderts," *Bach-Jahrbuch* 64 (1978), pp. 39–41; and Schulze, *Studien zur Bach-Überlieferung im 18. Jahrhundert* (Leipzig, 1984), pp. 125–27.
14. Spitta had not as yet made this identification when he published his biography of Bach; it does not appear in his description of Bach's writings on thorough bass given in Vol. 2, pp. 599–602. Two years after the publication of this volume, Spitta published an article entitled "Bachiana: Der Tractat über den Generalbass und F. Niedt's 'Musicalische Handleitung,'" in the *Allgemeine musikalische Zeitung* 17/16 (19 April 1882), cols. 241–45; the article was reprinted in Spitta's collection, *Musikgeschichtliche Aufsätze* (Berlin, 1894), pp. 121–28. The information given in the article was, however, incorporated into Clara Bell and J. A. Fuller-Maitland's English translation of Spitta's *Bach* (New York, 1952; reprinted from the 1889 edn), Vol. 3, p. 120.

that he never corrected the realizations.[15] Schenker himself was aware of these problems and wrote that "the obvious errors and missing accidentals all require that the work be approached with great caution." But he did accept it as an authentic work by Bach, and said that he considered it "a welcome supplement" to C. P. E. Bach's *Versuch*.[16]

Bach's treatise actually consists of two separate sets of instructions. The first, called "Kurtzer Unterricht von den so gennanten General Bass" (Brief Instruction in So-called Thorough Bass), presents rules similar to those found in Bach's Notebook for Anna Magdalena of 1725. The second set, "Gründlicher Unterricht des General-Basses" (Detailed Instruction in Thorough Bass), is much longer and more comprehensive, and takes up all the rest of the *Büchlein*. Schenker made very few annotations in the opening pages; he focused on Bach's specific rules and their fully realized four-voice illustrations. One type of annotation in the margins – figured-bass numerals written in red pencil and enclosed in large square brackets – seems to have been made for the purpose of indicating for Schenker himself the subject matter of each rule or example. Since he often includes references to the treatment of each figure in other chapters and sections, these annotations provide us with a kind of table of contents and index of the most important sections. The rules are organized according to what Schenker (when speaking of C. P. E. Bach's *Versuch*) characterized as a "mechanical succession of figures."[17] Here the succession is roughly 6, 7, 9, 11; figures containing each of these intervals (as measured up from the bass) are considered in turn. Then many of the same figures are taken up again in two sets of increasingly more complex examples. Two final sections present four-part chord sequences (given without realizations) and cadential formulas.[18]

The chief external feature of Bach's figured-bass realizations is that, with one small exception, they consistently maintain a four-voice texture. Schenker does not regard these four-voice settings as representative of Bach's own highly artistic improvised accompaniments; rather, he considers them "preliminary" and "primitive" models,[19] which "establish a minimum, geared for the average performer."[20] This view recalls Schenker's discussion in his Preface to *Kontrapunkt*, where he makes a distinction between "thorough bass" and "accompaniment," characterizing four-voice

15. See J. Schreyer, "Bachs Generalbasslehre," *Bach-Jahrbuch* 3 (1906), p. 136, and the discussion between F. T. Arnold and Schreyer, *Bach-Jahrbuch* 6 (1909), pp. 153–162, especially Arnold's comments on p. 153. See also Alfred Mann, "Bach and Handel as Teachers of Thorough Bass," in *Bach, Handel, Scarlatti: Tercentenary Essays*, ed. Peter Williams (Cambridge, 1985), pp. 250–51.
16. *Generalbasslehre*, Chapter 1, §1 (*Der Dreiklang*), p. 78.
17. *Generalbasslehre*, Chapter 1, §1 (*Der Dreiklang*), p. 79. The translation is from Rothgeb, "Schenkerian Theory: Its Implications for the Undergraduate Curriculum," p. 145.
18. These final sections of the "Gründlicher Unterricht," as well as the entire "Kurtzer Unterricht," are translated in *The Bach Reader*, ed. Hans T. David and Arthur Mendel (New York, 1945), pp. 392–98.
19. *Generalbasslehre*, Chapter 1, §1 (*Der Dreiklang*), p. 78.
20. The quotation is from Chapter 1, §5, of Schenker's unpublished study "Von der Stimmführung des Generalbasses," hereafter referred to as *Generalbasslehre* (unpublished).

figured-bass realizations as "a didactic tool. . .for learning the art of accompaniment."[21]

Throughout his thorough-bass study, it is Schenker's practice to contrast J. S. Bach's four-voice settings with C. P. E. Bach's more subtle and refined alternation of three, four, or five voices. But he sees no inconsistency between the realizations provided by father and son. He reminds us of C. P. E. Bach's statement:

It is best to begin with four-part accompaniment and establish its foundations. Those who learn this style thoroughly will find it easy to go on to others.[22]

Schenker adds these comments:

He [C. P. E. Bach] explicitly indicates the ultimate purpose of a purely four-voice execution, namely, to acquaint students with the difficulties of the various distributions and progressions. He expressly acknowledges that a four-voice texture by its nature gives rise to awkward progressions; this, specifically, should be noted by the student.[23]

This description is entirely applicable to the four-voice settings of the *Büchlein*.

Schenker's acquaintance with the *Büchlein* dates at least as far back as *Harmonielehre*, and it was there that he first expressed his view that Bach's thorough-bass realizations – preparatory studies in four-voice writing though they were – manifest the prolongations of basic progressions characteristic of free composition. This view is absolutely central to Schenker's thorough-bass theory. *Harmonielehre* contains an example that is drawn from Bach's *Büchlein* (Example 1).[24]

The first nine measures of this example are reproduced in *Harmonielehre*.[25] Schenker is comparing them with a I–V–I–IV–V–I progression in a simple four-voice setting, as given in Richter's *Lehrbuch der Harmonie*, a popular harmony text of his day.[26] After characterizing this kind of progression as "a logical misfit, which does not belong either in the theory of harmony or in the theory of counterpoint,"[27] Schenker goes on to contrast it with

---

21. Schenker, *Kontrapunkt* I, p. xxviii; the translation is from *Counterpoint* I, p. xxviii.
22. C. P. E. Bach, *Essay on the True Art of Playing Keyboard Instruments*, pp. 176–77. C. P. E. Bach's words are echoed by one of his father's most notable students, Johann Philipp Kirnberger: "It is best to begin with four voices, because it is not possible to write for two or three voices perfectly until one can do so for four voices." See Kirnberger, *The Art of Strict Musical Composition*, trans. David Beach and Jürgen Thym (New Haven, 1982), p. 159.
23. *Generalbasslehre* (unpublished), Chapter 1, §5.
24. *Büchlein*, Cap. 10, Exemplum 6. See Spitta, *Bach*, Vol. 2, p. 928; English edn, Vol. 3, p. 328. This and subsequent examples from the *Büchlein* include my transcriptions of Schenker's annotations (most of which are too faint to reproduce photographically). The examples themselves are those given in Spitta's Appendix, with the original soprano clef for the right-hand part changed to treble clef.
25. *Harmonielehre*, p. 230, Example 175; *Harmony*, p. 179, Example 140.
26. Ernst Friedrich Richter, *Lehrbuch der Harmonie*, 23rd edn (Leipzig, 1902), p. 20, Example 24, quoted in Schenker, *Harmonielehre*, p. 224, Example 174; *Harmony*, p. 175, Example 139.
27. *Harmonielehre*, p. 227; *Harmony*, p. 176.

Bach's figured-bass realization (see Example 1). He provides the following description:

What do we see in this example? A bass line, showing rich rhythmic articulation. Its development could constitute part of a living composition; in other words, this bass line provides more than the outline of scale degrees shown in the Richter example. The bass notes are supplied with figures, indicating intervals. And what is the meaning of the upper parts? They are constructed partly in accordance with strict contrapuntal rules, partly in free style. Viewed together, bass line and voice leading take on the appearance of a free composition, of a piece that stands on the threshold of reality.[28]

Example 1. From Bach, *Generalbassbüchlein*, Cap. 10,
            with Schenker's annotations transcribed

Exemplum 6.

Wann $\frac{6}{4}$ oder $\frac{4}{2}$ oder $\underline{2}$ oder $\underline{4}$. über einer Note stehet, so muß der *Bass* allezeit durch die vorhergehende Note liegen, und $\frac{4}{2}$ wird in die rechte Hand genommen und *resolviret* meistens in $\frac{6}{5}$ wenn der *Bass* einen halben oder gantzen Thon zurück steiget.

In his study of thorough bass, Schenker emphasizes the relationship of figured-bass settings to free composition, as in the following representative statements:

Thorough bass is. . .a truly organic part of a composition.[29]

In truth we are faced with a finished two-voice composition, to which we should offer only such inner voices as are dictated by the outer voices.[30]

However, a figured-bass exercise is naturally quite different from an actual free composition, for even when the inner voices are realized, it is far from being a true keyboard solo. . .[31]

Thorough bass shares with free composition, of which it is an organic part, the intertwining of harmonic degree and voice leading that constitutes the essence of free composition.[32]

Primary to thorough bass – and equally primary to free composition in general – is the process of composing-out, whereby a larger melodic entity is governed by a single sonority.[33]

In reading the opening paragraphs of Bach's *Büchlein*, Schenker heavily underlined the following words, which either gave rise to or confirmed the thoughts quoted above:

. . . der General Bass ein Anfang ist zum componiren (thorough bass is the beginning of composition).[34]

The annotations Schenker made in Bach's *Büchlein* are so plentiful and informative that they provide us with the equivalent of a commentary on the work. The most arresting indications are the long slurs, added stems, Roman numerals at harmonic degrees, and capped Arabic numbers above the top-voice line – all familiar from Schenker's graphs of complex compositions. What is remarkable here is that Schenker chose to apply them to settings he himself characterized as somewhat primitive exercises. They provide clear evidence that he saw them as examples of the process of composing-out.

We shall see that he also carefully examined each setting for the practical aspects of figured-bass realization. His annotations emphasize the details of voice leading; this emphasis is also evident throughout his thorough-bass study. It bears out the passage from *Der freie Satz* quoted at

reads as follows in the original: "eines Stückes, das schon an der Schwelle der Wirklichkeit steht." The view expressed in this quotation is echoed in *Der freie Satz*, where Schenker strongly recommends that, as a first step in the study of Bach's bass motions, one should "attempt to ascertain the linear progressions implied in [the] seemingly simple basses" of the *Büchlein*. See *Free Composition*, p. 75, §210.

29. *Generalbasslehre*, Chapter 1, §1 (*Der Dreiklang*), p. 81.
30. *Generalbasslehre* (unpublished), Chapter 1, §2.
31. *Generalbasslehre* (unpublished), Chapter 1, §6. Here Schenker is careful to point out the difference between the upper voice of a figured-bass accompaniment and the truly composed-out principal voice of a complete composition.
32. *Generalbasslehre* (unpublished), Chapter 1, §3.
33. *Generalbasslehre* (unpublished), Chapter 1, §2.
34. *Büchlein*, opening of Cap. 5. See Spitta, *Bach*, Vol. 2, p. 917; English edn, Vol. 3, p. 319 (translation altered slightly).

the beginning of this article – that the concept of organic coherence requires "a truly practical understanding." Thus an understanding of thorough bass, with its empirical focus on what Schenker called the "purely musical-technical"[35] aspects of composition, is seen as an important prerequisite for a deeper and broader understanding. Some of these detailed annotations are shown in Example 2.[36]

Example 2. From Bach, *Generalbassbüchlein*, Cap. 8,
with Schenker's annotations transcribed

Regula 3.

Wenn über einer Note stehet die Zahl 6. so bedeutet es die *Sext*. das ist ich muß von den *Fundament* oder Note ob welcher sie stehet anfangen zu zehlen, und den 6ten *Claven* anschlagen. Zu solcher wird entweder die *Tertz* oder *Sext* verdoppelt bißweilen die *Octav* darzu genommen zu mahl wenn *immediate* eine Note folgt und mit $^6_5$ bezeichnet ist. *e. g.*

The various combinations of the figures 8, 6, and 3 entered under the bass refer to the rules of doubling stated in the text above the example:

> With [the interval of the sixth] may be played either the third or the doubled sixth, and sometimes the octave, especially when a note with the indication $^6_5$ follows immediately.[37]

Schenker's characteristic shorthand notation for doubling summarizes this rule in the left margin: $^6_{33}$ $^{66}_3$ $^8_6$. In the next to last measure, the bracket under the 6–$^6_5$ ascending bass motion is drawn in red pencil and calls attention to the last part of this rule: the use of the doubling $^8_6$ at a 6 that is followed by a $^6_5$. Schenker seems to have gone through the *Büchlein* for the purpose of finding illustrations of the doubling and the voice leading used at this motion; the same kind of red bracket is found on many pages (for instance, the bracket under measures 2–3 of Example 3).

Another very specific annotation seen in Example 2 is Schenker's correction of a misprint in the second chord, in which he substitutes d[1] for the erroneous f[1]. His annotation in the margin may be translated as: "f obviously a slip of the pen, stands for d." This is only one example of numerous errors Schenker found in the *Büchlein*.

The tone-connecting lines found between the first two chords of measure 2 (in the right-hand part) represent a different type of annota-

35. *Generalbasslehre*, Chapter 1, §1 (*Der Dreiklang*), p. 81.
36. *Büchlein*, Cap. 8, Regula 3. See Spitta, *Bach*, Vol. 2, p. 920; English edn, Vol. 3, p. 321.
37. *Ibid*. (translation altered slightly).

tion: lines that are used to point out similar motion to a fifth or to an octave (as is the case here) or even the actual presence of parallel fifths and octaves.

In Example 3,[38] we see an annotation that belongs in a new category: markings that call attention to specific figured-bass progressions or numerals (many of which Schenker's study discusses at considerable length, as interpreted by both J. S. Bach and C. P. E. Bach).

Example 3. From Bach, *Generalbassbüchlein*, Cap. 8,
with Schenker's annotations transcribed

Regula 7.

Wann *Secund* und *Quart* ($\frac{4}{2}$) über einer Note stehet so wird <u>ordent-lich</u> die 6 auch darzu genommen wenn es gleich nicht darüber stchet.

$\left.\begin{smallmatrix}6\\4\\2\end{smallmatrix}\right\}$ wird <u>allezeit frisch angeschlagen</u> wann das <u>Fundament</u> liegen <u>g</u>eblieben,

$\left.\begin{smallmatrix}6\\4\\2\end{smallmatrix}\right\}$ *resolvirt* sich aber $\frac{6}{5}$ wenn der *Bass* in ein halbes *Intervallum* rückwärts geht, wie aus folgenden Exempel zu sehen ist

The arrow under the figure 6 in measure 1 is cued to the arrow in the margin, and Schenker's note "6=$\frac{6}{5}$" refers to the following observation, found in his chapter on the chord of the seventh and its inversions:

J. S. Bach, unlike C. P. E. Bach, repeatedly uses the figure 6 to mean $\frac{6}{5}$. . .[39]

Schenker gives some page and measure numbers referring to instances of such use in the *Büchlein*; his annotations confirm these and point to many further illustrations.

Schenker's bracketed numerals in the margin summarize the rule given above the example; it pertains to the figure $\frac{4}{2}$ and the motion $\frac{6}{2}$–$\frac{6}{5}$. He also gives the reference "vergleich (compare) E.6 (Exemplum 6)" – our Example 1 – which illustrates basically the same rule as the one given here. Indeed, Example 1 and Example 3 begin in the same way.

Oswald Jonas included this same example in an article he published in the issue of *Der Dreiklang* that contains the introductory section of Schenker's thorough-bass study. Jonas's general view of figured-bass realizations is in accord with Schenker's, and so is his view of the broad motion in this example. His comments read as follows:

38. *Büchlein*, Cap. 8, Regula 7. See Spitta, *Bach*, Vol. 2, p. 922; English edn, Vol. 3, p. 323.
39. *Generalbasslehre* (unpublished), Chapter 6, §6.

The process of composing-out brings to life even the simplest and most elementary exercises in figured bass. . .[Here] the A triad is composed out in the bass – an achievement that brings this exercise very close to a real composition.[40]

He illustrates his point by connecting the bass tones a, c, e, and the final low A with slurs.

Returning briefly to Example 2, we see that Schenker entered the figures 3 4 4 3 under the next to last measure. In this case the figures refer to the intervals above the prevailing bass tone, the dominant G. As he went through the *Büchlein*, Schenker seems to have been alert to the reappearance of this progression; his annotations invariably call attention to its presence. Example 4 shows how it is introduced.[41]

Example 4. From Bach, *Generalbassbüchlein*, Cap. 8, Regula 8,
with Schenker's annotations transcribed

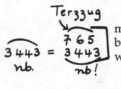

Wo *Cadentz Clauseln* stehen als die ͞3 ͞4 ͞4 ͞3 / ͞7 ͞6 ͞5 oder auch ͞3 ͞4 ͞4 / ͞7 ͞6 ͞4 so nennet man selbige *Syncopationes* weil sie gleichsam verbunden und verwickelt, biß weilen werden sie auch einfach 3 4 4 3 gesetzt aber doch völlig gespielet wie folgt

Schenker again summarizes the rule in the margin: 7–6–5 over 3–4–4–3 is to be played even if only 3–4–4–3 is notated. He twice adds the indication "Nb" to call attention to the neighboring function of the 4. He also characterizes the 7–6–5 motion as a "Terzzug," a melodic progression through a third.

In the important chapter on the *Stufe* in Schenker's study of thorough bass, he explains, under the heading of "broader harmonic entities," that a single scale degree may sometimes be represented by a series of thorough-bass figures. Referring to his discussion of 3–4–4–3 motion in *Kontrapunkt* II,[42] he now speaks specifically of the fact that a 3–4–4–3 progression pertaining to a single bass tone may be expressed in the most diverse figures, and that examples may be found in the *Büchlein*. He prom-

40. Oswald Jonas, "Die Krise der Musiktheorie," *Der Dreiklang* 3 (June 1937), p. 74. (My translation omits Jonas's reference to a second example and thus alters the original slightly.) Some of the ideas he expresses (pp. 67–74) recall those in the section entitled "Kritik der bisherigen Theorie" (Critique of Previous Theories) of Jonas's *Das Wesen des musikalischen Kunstwerks: Eine Einführung in die Lehre Heinrich Schenkers* (Vienna, 1934); see the translation by John Rothgeb, *Introduction to the Theory of Heinrich Schenker* (New York, 1982), pp. 122–28. These ideas were taken up again in Jonas's Introduction to Schenker's *Harmony.*
41. *Büchlein*, Cap. 8, Regula 8. See Spitta, *Bach*, Vol. 2, p. 922; English edn, Vol. 3, p. 323.
42. *Kontrapunkt* II, pp. 251–52; *Counterpoint* II, p. 261.

ises the reader a "schöne Tafel" (beautiful set of examples), but since none is actually given, the annotations in the *Büchlein* itself must serve as our only source.[43]

Schenker tells us that these illustrations are found in the set of supplementary examples in the *Büchlein*. The first of these is shown in Example 5.[44] The section is introduced by the heading: "To give further enlightenment, the following examples have been written out."[45] In describing these settings Schenker writes that they present "alternatives and liberties that reflect a bolder approach to voice leading than in the foregoing pages."[46] The opening measures of the first example contain annotations that show Schenker considered them illustrations of two 3–4–4–3 progressions (see Example 5).

Example 5. From Bach, *Generalbassbüchlein*, "Mehrere Erleuchterung. . .," No. 1, with Schenker's annotations transcribed

Schenker refers to these same measures in Chapter 1 of his study, where they serve to illustrate his point that thorough-bass figures are incapable of expressing certain relationships.[47] It happens that he reprinted these measures in the second *Jahrbuch* of *Das Meisterwerk*, as part of his "Forseztung der Urlinie-Betrachtungen." They are printed with almost the same annotations that are seen in the *Büchlein*, and are used to illustrate the same point, which is now expressed more explicitly. The passage in *Das Meisterwerk* reads as follows:

. . .even thorough bass, whose aim and purpose it is to provide the continuo player with figures that express every detail of the voice leading, is forced to ignore certain events, since no figured-bass notation can be found or given that will not mislead the player.

And he goes into more specific detail in explaining measures 1–2:

Bach would hardly venture to designate the d¹ [at the last quarter of measure 1] as a 9; in fact there is no ninth here at all, only a tied note in the inner voice, which

43. Schenker, *Generalbasslehre* (unpublished), Chapter 2, §7: "Von grösseren Stuteneinheiten."
44. *Büchlein*, "Mehrere Erleuchterung zu geben sind folgende Exempel ausgesetzet worden," No. 1. See Spitta, *Bach*, Vol. 2, p. 930; Englisn edn, Vol. 3, p. 330.
45. The translation of the heading is from *The Bach Reader*, p. 390.
46. *Generalbasslehre*, Chapter 1, §1 (*Der Dreiklang*), p. 79.
47. *Generalbasslehre* (unpublished), Chapter 1, §7.

bears no vertical relationship to the neighboring tone in the bass. The four sonorities I have connected with a slur constitute the neighboring motion ↓3̲–4̲–4̲–↓3, taking place above the bass tone D, which itself is extended by a neighboring motion.[48]

This clarifies Schenker's annotations in the *Büchlein* – his designation of the two bracketed passages (shown in Example 5) as 3–4–4–3 over a single scale degree even though the thorough-bass figures do not express this motion. In the margin, he explicitly states that the progression contains neighboring chords (Nebennotenharmonien) and that the figures actually stand for something else: "statt $\frac{5}{3}$ 4 4 3." The next annotation in the margin refers to measures 1–2: "at V$\frac{5}{3}$: $\frac{6}{4}$ combined with a neighboring motion in the bass." And he adds "compare p. 950," a reference to the *Büchlein*'s final section on cadences, which includes the cadential formula 3–4–4–3.[49] (The remaining annotation in the margin, $\frac{7}{5}$, summarizes the general subject matter of this example, which primarily illustrates various uses of the seventh chord.) In the example itself, the annotations "Nb" pinpoint the neighboring motions in the bass, and the words "Quintlage" and "Terzlage" indicate the positions of the fifth and the third that characterize the principal chord of each progression.

Many other progressions bear similar markings, including the one shown in Example 6.[50]

Example 6. From Bach, *Generalbassbüchlein*, "Mehrere Erleuchterung. . .," No. 6, with Schenker's annotations transcribed

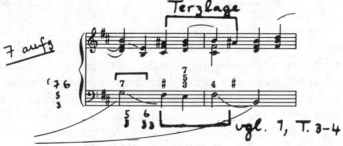

Here Schenker adds the reference "compare [No.] 1, measures 3–4" – a reference back to the passage given in our Example 5 (No. 1 of the set of supplementary examples in the *Büchlein*) with its similar "Terzlage."

Returning now to Example 1, we see that Schenker's markings include

48. Schenker, *Das Meisterwerk* II, pp. 27–28 (my translation). Schenker may have marked this passage with the direct purpose of preparing it for publication in *Das Meisterwerk* II. This would mean that these annotations were made around 1926, twenty years after those that may date from the time of *Harmonielehre*. Schenker seems to have returned to the *Büchlein* frequently throughout his life; many of the markings appear to have been retraced, once in red pencil and once in black. His diary indicates that he showed the *Büchlein* to Furtwängler in 1932, during an after-dinner conversation. See Hellmut Federhofer, *Heinrich Schenker: Nach Tagebüchern und Briefen in der Oswald Jonas Memorial Collection* (Hildesheim, 1985), p. 128.

49. "Die gebräuchlichsten *Clausulas* [sic] *finales*." See Spitta, *Bach*, Vol. 2, p. 950; English edn, Vol. 3, p. 347. See also *The Bach Reader*, p. 398.

50. *Büchlein*, "Mehrere Erleuchterung. . .," No. 6. See Spitta, *Bach*, Vol. 2, p. 930; English edn, Vol. 3, p. 330.

almost every type of annotation I have discussed, along with a few others. In the left margin, Schenker uses red pencil to note down the example's general subject matter: "2, 4, $\frac{4}{2}$, $\frac{6}{4}$." The reference "compare Chapter 8, Rule 7" is to the rule included in Example 3. The wording of that rule is similar to the text given at Example 1, which reads:

When $\frac{6}{4}$ or $\frac{4}{2}$ or 2 or 4 are placed over a note, the bass must always be held from the preceding chord. $\frac{4}{2}$ is played by the right hand and usually resolves to $\frac{6}{3}$, with the bass descending a semitone or a whole tone.[51]

Commenting on this in the margin, Schenker writes: "nicht immer, je nach Stufen." He perhaps means to say that $\frac{4}{2}$ does not always ("nicht immer") resolve to $\frac{6}{3}$; its resolution is determined by the scale degrees involved ("je nach Stufen"). This comment reflects an important statement Schenker makes in his study, that "the theory of scale degrees becomes a latent, supplementary component of figured-bass theory,"[52] and in fact reflects the approach to thorough bass evident throughout the study.

When Schenker turns to the example itself, he adds analytic slurs and a few Roman numerals. I shall briefly describe the detailed annotations that are shown in Example 1.

In measures 8–9, he takes note of the doubling: $\frac{8}{3}$ and 33 are marked at the 7–6 series. In measures 3 and 10 he marks the $\frac{5}{3}$ doubling that initiates two sets of fifths (which I shall discuss below). A misprint is corrected: In measure 9, the c^1 shown at the second half note in the inner voice represents a correction in Schenker's hand; it is written on top of the printed d^1. (The c^1 appears as a tacit correction in this example as it is printed in *Harmonielehre*.) In measures 1, 3, and 10 Schenker calls attention to Bach's frequent use of the figure 6 to represent $\frac{6}{3}$; in measure 1 this occurs at a $\frac{4}{2}$ to $\frac{6}{3}$ succession, in measures 3 and 10 the $\frac{6}{3}$ concludes a 7–6 suspension.

Many of the markings pertain to voice leading. In measure 2, a line connects the inner-voice augmented second, f^1–$g\sharp^1$; Schenker places a question mark under the motion and in the left margin. He perhaps intended to include this example in his thorough-bass study, where there is a reference to a missing "Tabelle" that would illustrate the following comment:

The four-voice texture of J. S. Bach's exercises compels him – like it or not – to write dissonant horizontal intervals such as the augmented second. . .[53]

Rather heavy lines are used three times to point out parallel fifths. In measure 3 and in measures 10–11, Schenker marks the motion from a diminished fifth to a perfect fifth; in measure 3 he adds a question mark both in the music and next to his indication "5–5" in the margin, where he also adds an exclamation point. He may have been thinking of C. P. E. Bach's words on descending fifths of this kind:

51. *Büchlein*, Cap. 10, Exemplum 6. See Spitta, *Bach*, Vol. 2, p. 928; English edn, Vol. 3, p. 328 (translation altered slightly).
52. *Generalbasslehre* (unpublished), Chapter 2, §1. The translation is from Rothgeb, "Schenkerian Theory: Its Implications for the Undergraduate Curriculum," p. 146.
53. *Generalbasslehre* (unpublished), Chapter 3, §3.

Two open fifths of different quality may be played in succession. . .but a diminished fifth may succeed to a perfect fifth only out of necessity, and preferably not in the outer parts.[54]

The parallel fifths Schenker marks in measure 11 are both perfect fifths; perhaps he felt their effect was somewhat lessened by the fact that the second fifth marks the beginning of a new motion – a separation of the fifths may be indicated by the vertical line he drew between the staves. In measures 8 and 14, similar motion to an octave is indicated; and in measure 2, consecutive octaves by contrary motion are marked in the outer voices. I should stress that Schenker's markings indicate only that he was taking note of Bach's voice-leading procedures, not that he was censuring them in any way. We might recall what he said about this example in *Harmonielehre*: "the upper parts. . .are constructed partly in accordance with strict contrapuntal rules, partly in free style."

In measures 5 and 9, the brackets in heavy pencil show parallel octaves that are mitigated by intervening motion. The bracket and the annotation in the margin indicate that other such avoided octaves are to be found in specific measures of Nos. 4, 6, and 3 of the supplementary examples. The chapter on parallel octaves and fifths in Schenker's thorough-bass study has a reference to an example showing "the means by which Bach avoids parallel octaves."[55] The example is missing; marked passages such as these in the *Büchlein* now permit its reconstruction.

Finally, at the cadence, the bracket under the lower staff marks the motion 7–6–5 over 3–4–4–3, with the bass note A placed in parentheses to show that E is the main tone over which the motion takes place.

I have attempted to show how the annotations Schenker made in the *Büchlein* directly supplement his study of thorough bass. Gratifying as it is to find annotations in Schenker's hand that correspond exactly to examples and references given in the study, it is of even greater importance to find annotated passages that are *not* specifically mentioned – for they clarify parts of the study that would otherwise remain obscure. I have presented only a very small sampling of a few categories of annotations: general indications in the margins; slurs, stems, and numerals showing large-scale motion; shorthand notation pertaining to practical matters such as doubling; correction of misprints; symbols calling attention to specific figured-bass progressions; lines or brackets in heavy pencil pointing up voice-leading procedures; and brackets that single out a specific broad neighboring motion. There are other types, and many more examples of each type than the ones I have presented here. I hope that even these few examples have conveyed the overwhelming impression I receive each time I open Schenker's copy of the *Büchlein* – of the unbelievable care, thoroughness, and brilliant insight Schenker lent to this small document.

54. See C. P. E. Bach, *Essay on the True Art of Playing Keyboard Instruments*, p. 200, §§21–22. Schenker cites and discusses these and succeeding sections of the *Versuch* in Chapter 4, §2, of his unpublished *Generalbasslehre*. See also *Free Composition*, p. 56, §160.
55. *Generalbasslehre* (unpublished), Chapter 4, §1.

Music and morphology: Goethe's influence on Schenker's thought

William Pastille

To say that Schenker was influenced by Goethe is, in a sense, to state the obvious. What educated, German-speaking person born in the nineteenth century did not learn about Goethe's writings, his life, and his achievements while in school? In an engaging trilogy entitled *Discovering the Mind*, Walter Kaufmann showed that many great German thinkers of the last century and the early part of this century were steeped in Goethe's life and work. Kaufmann also believed that Goethe's ideas – and more important, his personality – contributed significantly to the formation of such prominent intellectual figures as Hegel, Nietzsche, Freud, Adler, Jung, Heidegger, and Buber.[1] Like these prominent writers, Schenker too was fully conversant with Goethe's work.[2] But could Goethe's influence have had much of an effect on Schenker's work? Could Goethe, whom Schenker himself considered musically untalented,[3] have contributed anything to Schenker's complicated musical theories?

Some scholars have already detected enough similarities between Goethe's and Schenker's ideas to answer these questions in the affirmative.[4] What is particularly interesting about these points of similarity is that they arise from consideration of Goethe's *scientific* work, which is not nearly so familiar to modern scholars as his literary work. This essay allies itself with those who have detected Goethe's influence in Schenker's work, and it attempts to provide more evidence than has hitherto been brought forth to show that the fundamental principles of Goethe's epistemology and scientific methodology were assimilated by Schenker, and that a Goethean interpretation of Schenker's musical ontology can help to explain some puzzling aspects of his thought.

---

1. Walter Kautmann, *Discovering the Mind*, 3 vols. (New York, 1980–84).
2. Schenker's fondness for quoting Goethe is an indication of this. Of 116 non-musical quotations occurring in Schenker's published writings just between 1904 and 1924, 57 (approximately 49%) are from Goethe.
3. Schenker said that "Nature refused the princely poet Goethe entrance to music." *Der Tonwille* 5 (1923), p. 46. Unless otherwise indicated, all translations given in this study are mine.
4. For example, Harald Kaufmann, "Fortschritt und Reaktion in der Lehre Heinrich Schenkers," *Neue Zeitschrift für Musik* 126 (1965), pp. 7–8; Thomas Clifton, "An Application of Goethe's Concept of Steigerung to the Morphology of Diminution," *Journal of Music Theory* 14/1 (1970), pp. 165–89; Eugene Narmour, *Beyond Schenkerism: The Need for Alternatives in Musical Analysis* (Chicago, 1977), pp. 31–32; Jamie Croy Kassler, "Heinrich Schenker's Epistemology and Philosophy of Music: An Essay on the Relations Between Evolutionary Theory and Music Theory," in *The Wider Domain of Evolutionary Thought*, ed. David Oldroyd and Ian Langham (Dordrecht, 1983), pp. 221–60.

I

If the modern scholar in the humanities does not readily connect Goethe with the world of science, it is because science all but forgot him after his death. This is understandable, for Goethe's view of science was anti-mathematical and anti-Newtonian (he wrote scathing polemics against Newton in his *Theory of Color*); obviously, such beliefs looked simply ridiculous to most nineteenth-century scientists, who witnessed almost daily astonishing practical advances made possible by the progress of Newtonian science. Goethe's scientific studies quickly took on the air of historical curiosities – amateurish dabblings in science by a genius in another field.

But the scope and intensity of Goethe's investigations into nature went far beyond the limits of amateurism. For Goethe, science was not a hobby, it was a life-long vocation. His first serious scientific studies, which he began during his university days in the late 1760s, centered around botany; in 1790 he composed his first major scientific work, *The Metamorphosis of Plants*, which was not published until 1802. During the 1790s, he studied zoology – especially osteology – became interested in geology, mineralogy, and meteorology, and published papers in all of these fields. In the first decade of the nineteenth century, he turned his attention more and more to the phenomena of light and color; this interest culminated in his most famous scientific treatise, the *Theory of Color* of 1810. Goethe valued this last work so highly that he said to Eckermann in 1829: "I attach no importance at all to anything I have achieved as a poet. . .But I take some pride in the fact that in my century I am the only one who knows the truth in the difficult science of color theory."[5] Goethe clearly placed great importance on his scientific studies.

Out of his investigations into nature, Goethe developed a comprehensive scientific world view that he called "morphology."[6] The name derives from his belief that the study of natural forms and of the processes of their formation constitutes the primary duty of the scientist. The key to Goethe's morphology is his notion of the "type" or *Urphänomen*. He used these terms to designate a conceptual model underlying all the physical manifestations of a class of creatures, objects, or phenomena. The word "type" is employed when the class under consideration consists of living organisms; the word *Urphänomen* when the class consists either of inorganic objects or phenomena. Example 1 is a visual representation of the relations between the type and all its physical manifestations.[7]

5. Johann Peter Eckermann, *Gespräche mit Goethe* (Wiesbaden, 1955), p. 307.
6. The following sketch of Goethe's morphological theories is by no means a comprehensive overview of the subject. It explains only those notions that are most useful in establishing a connection with Schenker's thought; the explanations are drawn from Goethe's own writings. The reader who wishes to look into the vast secondary literature that has developed on Goethe's scientific studies might begin with the bibliography in Christoph Gögelein, *Zu Goethes Begriff von Wissenschaft* (Munich, 1972), which leads one directly to the most important sources in the field.
7. This representation is borrowed from Adolf Meyer-Abich, *Die Vollendung der Morphologie Goethes durch Alexander von Humboldt* (Göttingen, 1970), p. 35.

Example 1

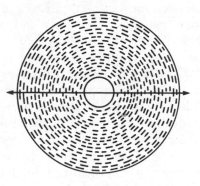

The large outer circle encloses all the members of a single taxonomic group. For example, if the figure represents all the members of the class of flowering plants, then the small dots within the circle represent all the physically existing forms of flowering plants. The small circle in the center represents the type, which contains all of the essential characteristics common to all of the physically existing forms, but none of the accidental characteristics that differentiate one physical form from another. The arrow indicates that the closer the physical forms are to the type, the more they resemble it; the farther away they are, the less they resemble it.

It is clear that the type cannot have physical existence: there is no real plant that fulfills the preconditions for being the type. And yet Goethe insisted that the type could be perceived, and that its presence could be detected in each of the physically existing forms.[8] He claimed to have discovered the type of the plant world (the *Urpflanze*), the type of the vertebrate animals (the *Urtier*), and the *Urphänomen* of geological formations (the *Urgestein*). Eventually, he came to understand the appearance of color as the *Urphänomen* in the realm of light and darkness. But this insistence on the perceptibility and the presence of the *Urphänomen* in all things poses two important questions: How is the *Urphänomen* perceived? and, How does the *Urphänomen* manifest itself in the physical world?

The *Urphänomen* cannot be perceived through the customary use of the senses. Goethe thought of perception as a partnership between the physical senses and the inner, spiritual senses. For him, merely observing an object and letting it go when it leaves the field of vision is not truly perceiving it. Only when "we can bring it forth again in the mind," he

8. In a famous conversation with Schiller, Goethe tried to explain his notion of the prototypical plant, and he even sketched a symbolic design of it. After some time, Schiller shook his head and remarked, "That is not an experience, that is an idea." This irritated Goethe, who replied sarcastically, "How lucky I am to have ideas without knowing it, and even to see them with my own eyes!" AA XVI, pp. 867–68. Goethe's works are cited according to two standard editions: Johann Wolfgang Goethe, *Gedenkenausgabe der Werke, Briefe, und Gespräche* (Zurich, 1949–), referred to as AA; and *Goethes Werke*, issued by order of the Grand Duchess Sophie of Saxony (Weimar, 1887–1918), referred to as WA. In the case of AA, the Roman numeral indicates the volume number; in the case of WA, the Roman numeral indicates the series, and the Arabic numeral indicates the volume.

said, "may we say that we perceive it in a true and higher sense."[9] He called this elevated form of perception *Anschauung*, and he described it as follows: one first seeks "constancy and consistency" in phenomena, and one derives "empirical rules" that explain this consistency. One then applies those rules to further observation and experimentation, and tempers or revises them according to their degree of correspondence with later experiments, until all circumstantial conditions have been accounted for.[10] All of this painstaking observation prepares the intuition for a spontaneous and sudden flash of insight called the *aperçu*, the apperception of the law underlying the varied appearances of similar phenomena. Attaining an *aperçu* was of fundamental importance to Goethe in understanding nature. "Everything in science touches on that which we call an *aperçu*, on a perception of that which really lies at the root of appearances."[11] Scientific knowledge was attained through a special sort of perception that proceeded in two phases: the germination phase, consisting of sustained contemplation of an object or an event – *Anschauung*; and the fruition phase, consisting of a flash of intuitive insight – the *aperçu*.

To address the second question – How does the *Urphänomen* manifest itself in the physical world? – we must consider four principles that Goethe saw as controlling the appearances of physical forms: holism, polarity, intensification, and metamorphosis.

Holism, which Goethe probably inherited from the organicism that was common in idealist nature studies at the close of the eighteenth century, is the principle describing the relations between the parts and the whole in organic life. In an organism, the parts must remain relatively independent, while at the same time subordinating themselves to the whole. Between parts and whole there exists an equilibrium that prevents the whole from dissolving into completely unrelated parts, and the parts from losing their identities in the whole. Goethe called this equilibrium "the harmony of the organic whole,"[12] and he made it clear that he did not envision this balance as a state of stasis achieved after opposing forces have evened out. Rather, he viewed it as a vibrant, dynamic equilibrium, a continual shifting and realigning of opposing forces. He called this interplay of opposites polarity.

For Goethe, everything perceptible exhibited the interaction of polar forces which, like the poles of a magnet, both repel and attract.[13] But clearly, an eternal interplay of the same forces could give rise to nothing except endless repetition of the same appearances. In order for nature to create new forms, another force is needed in addition to polarity. Goethe called this force intensification (*Steigerung*); it causes all things to strive upward toward higher levels of organization. The creation of new forms

9. WA II, 11, p. 164.
10. WA II, 11, pp. 39–40.
11. AA XVI, p. 418.
12. AA XVII, p. 287.
13. "To separate the unified, to unite the separated, is the life of nature. This is the eternal systole and diastole, the eternal syncrisis and diacrisis, the inhaling and exhaling of the world in which we live, breathe, and exist." AA XVI, p. 199.

through the interaction of polarity and intensification could be described in this way:

What enters the world of appearance must divide in order to appear at all. What has been separated seeks itself again, and it can find itself again and unite. This can occur in a lower sense, in which it only blends or meets with its opposite; in this case its appearance becomes worthless, or at least inconsequential. The unification can also occur in a higher sense, however, in which what has been separated first intensifies, and through the combination of the intensified sides brings forth a third, new, unexpected entity.[14]

Polarity and intensification give rise to all manifestations of growth, development, evolution, and epigenesis in the phenomenal world. They lead to the highest possible degree of differentiation among the parts of an organism consistent with the holistic principle that subordinates the parts to the whole. The initial repulsion of the opposites is intensified by the striving for higher levels of organization. When the attractive aspect of polarity seeks to reunite the separated poles, the intensified states combine into something new and unexpected.

A simple example of the interaction of polarity and intensification in Goethe's theory comes from the inorganic realm, where interrelations are not nearly so complex and multiform as in organisms. The phenomenon of color, like all perceptible phenomena, springs from a unified source: light. The interaction between light and objects causes color – an *Urphänomen* – which naturally contains a fundamental polarity, the two poles of which are blue and yellow. If these two poles seek each other out by attraction, the combination of their characteristics produces green, which Goethe considers a most restful and serene color, befitting the restful equilibrium between the two poles. By several physical means, however, including chemical reactions and increasing the opacity of a semi-opaque medium, the basic poles can be intensified, and they immediately take on a reddish tint. If the intensified blue and yellow are then brought together, the result is a new, unexpected color that again seems unmixed – what Goethe calls pure red (*Purpur*). Pure red is the highest and most intense appearance in the realm of color, and thus it has an ennobling effect on the spirit.[15]

This example is the simplest possible. Each of the polar opposites intensifies only once, and there is only a single unification of intensified poles. A similar, but much more complicated and extended process occurs in living organisms: the original poles intensify, and join into a new unity, which in turn manifests another level of polarity, whose poles again intensify and unite into a new phenomenon, and so on. Goethe called this continued generation of new forms metamorphosis. The transformative power of metamorphosis changes the leaf, for instance, into the flower, or the egg into the chick.[16] Of course, metamorphosis cannot violate the holistic relations between the parts and the whole, so

14. AA XVI, p. 864.
15. AA XVI, pp. 186–90 and 211–13.
16. WA I, 22, p. 674.

the drive to create new formations is held in check by the intrinsic unifying power of the organic whole.[17] And ultimately, metamorphosis is also limited by external environmental conditions. The same plant, for example, will grow differently if deprived of water and nutrients than it would under normal conditions.

For present purposes, then, the three principal components of Goethe's morphology can be summarized as follows: First, the type or the *Urphänomen* stands at the center of Goethe's science. Second, his epistemology relies on the two mental operations of *Anschauung* and *aperçu*. And third, his ontology incorporates the principles of holism, polarity, intensification, and metamorphosis.

II

Recognizing some general similarities between Goethe's thought and Schenker's is not difficult, as has been said; but demonstrating a special link between Goethe's morphology and Schenker's musical theories is a different matter. Of those who have noted similarities, only Jamie Croy Kassler has made a serious effort to identify specific passages from Schenker's writings that point directly to Goethe's influence.[18] In addition to the passages cited by Kassler, however, Schenker's published works yield up a great deal of evidence for the contention that Schenker did share at least two, and probably all three, of the principal components of Goethe's morphology.

To begin with, there is certainly enough evidence to show that Schenker accepted Goethe's notion of the type or *Urphänomen*. In the second issue of *Der Tonwille,* Schenker quotes a poem by Goethe entitled "Typus":[19]

> Es ist nichts in der Haut,
> Was nicht im Knochen ist.
> Vor schlechtem Gebilde Jedem graut,
> Das ein Augenschmerz ihm ist.
>
> Was freut denn Jeden? Blühen zu sehn,
> Das von innen schon gut gestaltet.
> Aussen mag's in Glätte, mag in Farben gehn.
> Es ist ihm schon voran gewaltet.

> There is nothing on the skin
> that is not in the bones.
> Everyone is repelled by a misshapen figure,
> for it hurts the eyes.
>
> What pleases everyone, then? To see flowering
> that is already well formed from within.
> Externally, it may be smooth or dappled.
> That has been destined from the start.

17. Goethe called this unifying power the specification force (*Spezificationstrieb*). AA XVIII, p. 177.
18. Kassler, "Schenker's Epistemology," pp. 235, 236, and 240.
19. WA I, 3, p. 119; quoted in *Der Tonwille* 2 (1922), p. 5.

The poem describes the *Urtier*, the model of vertebrate animal life, which Goethe envisioned as a skeletal structure; but the intent is metaphorical, and Goethe placed it under the rubric *Kunst* in the collected edition of his works.[20] The implication is that the artwork, like an animal, is based on an inner model which governs its external, individual characteristics. This Schenker clearly had in mind, for he introduced the poem with a comparison between the *Urlinie* and the human skeleton. It is no coincidence that the notion of the completely organic artwork finally comes to fruition in the very same issue of *Der Tonwille* in which this poem appears; and Schenker develops the anatomical analogy further in his treatment, in the same issue, of Mozart's A minor Piano Sonata, K. 310, where he compares the work's "mysterious relationships" to "the ultimately inaccessible secrets" of the human circulatory system, and envisions organic forces "streaming through every vein" of the work.[21]

Terminological similarities also lead one to suspect a connection between Goethe's *Urphänomen* and Schenker's thought. The following passage from *Kontrapunkt* I, for example, discusses a brief excerpt from Variation 2 of Handel's Chaconne in G major, shown in Example 2a.[22]

We understand the second eighth-note c of the bass as first of all in the service of the expected V, as the neighboring note of the coming fundamental D; but besides this, our imagination independently supplies, before c, components (either B or d) of the major triad on G that is being left: [Example 2b]. Consequently, however – and precisely this is the result inaccessible to superficial perception – even the second eighth note, the passing tone approached by leap, embodies nothing but the original form (*Urtypus*) of the passing tone itself! One sees, then, how one and the same basic phenomenon (*Urphänomen*) manifests itself in so many forms, yet without completely losing its identity in any of them! However much a given variant may conceal the basic form (*Urtypus*), it is still the latter alone that occasions and fructifies the new manifestation. But to reveal the basic form (*Urtypus*) together with its variants, and [thereby] to uncover only prolongations of a fundamental law even where apparent contradictions hold sway – this alone is the task of counterpoint![23]

Example 2. Handel, Chaconne in G major, Variation 2

(a)   (b)

20. Franz Koch, *Goethes Gedankenform* (Berlin, 1962), pp. 79–80.
21. See William Pastille, "Heinrich Schenker, Anti-Organicist," *19th-Century Music* 8/1 (1984), p. 34.
22. Examples 2a and 2b appear as Examples 357 and 358 in Schenker, *Kontrapunkt* I.
23. See Schenker, *Kontrapunkt* I, pp. 314–15. The translation is from *Counterpoint* I, p. 241. Here and in the subsequent quotation Schenker's original wording has been added in parentheses where appropriate.

The similarity with Goethe's terminology in this passage is obvious. But more important is the similarity of conception: Schenker is referring to an underlying type found in the abstract world of strict counterpoint, and this type lies at the heart of all its slightly different "physical" appearances in the real world of free composition.

More examples of Schenker's belief in the underlying type can be found throughout *Kontrapunkt*. For instance, after discussing the strict contrapuntal formula for the dissonant suspension, Schenker goes on to derive fifteen pages of variations on this formula that occur in free composition. At the conclusion of this tour de force he writes, "The dissonant syncope of strict counterpoint represents the basic form (*Urform*) of all possible forms of dissonance in free composition which occur on the strong beat, as well as many other derivative phenomena."[24] Again a term used by Goethe is present (*Urform*); but the crucial element is the notion of a conceptual model, of a musical type underlying an entire class of dissonances found in free composition.

If there is sufficient evidence to show that Schenker accepted Goethe's notion of the *Urphänomen*, there is even more compelling evidence to show that he accepted the basic principles of Goethe's epistemology. In this connection, Kassler cites the following well-known quotation from Goethe's *Theory of Color* that appears near the beginning of *Free Composition*:

A most curious demand is often made, but not fulfilled even by those who make it. One is supposed to report empirical experiences without any kind of theoretical framework, and leave it to the reader or to the student to construct a framework as he pleases. But merely gazing at an object cannot benefit us. Every act of beholding shades into considering, considering into speculating, speculating into connecting; and so one can say that we theorize with every attentive look at the world. To undertake this, to do it with awareness, self-knowledge, freedom, and, to use a daring word, with irony – this sort of ingenuity is necessary if the abstraction we fear is to be harmless, and if the empirical result we expect is to be truly productive and useful.[25]

This passage is a fairly clear explanation of Goethe's notion of *Anschauung*, even though the word *theorizieren* is used instead of *anschauen*. The painstaking attention to detail, the step-by-step connections among events and observations, are indeed present in this description. It is hardly likely, as Kassler rightly points out, that Schenker would have made this passage the epigraph to his magnum opus unless he put great store by it, and unless he agreed with the description of the process that Goethe expressed.

But Schenker did not come to this acceptance of Goethe's *Anschauung* only in his later years. Already in the *Harmonielehre* of 1906, Schenker characterized in Goethean overtones the diligent attention to detail required of the circumspect observer: "In music, it is important, very im-

24. See *Kontrapunkt* I, p. 374. The translation is from *Counterpoint* I, p. 289.
25. AA XVI, p. 11; quoted in Schenker, *Der freie Satz* (1935 edn), p. 13, and *ibid*. (1956 edn), p. 25. The translation given here differs somewhat from that of Ernst Oster in *Free Composition*, p. 3.

portant, to attend to each occurrence – even the smallest – and to hear every single detail – even the tiniest – together with its proper cause."[26] And in his *Erläuterungsausgabe* of Beethoven's Op. 110, Schenker traced the word *theorizieren* back to its Greek ancestor *theorein*, which he translated as *anschauen*.[27]

What especially connects Schenker's notion of theorizing with Goethe's *Anschauung*, however, is that both result in a spiritual, rather than a sensual, moment of clarifying perception. Kassler cites the following passage from *Das Meisterwerk* II as evidence of Schenker's belief in a spiritual "vision":

Religion, philosophy, and science all press toward the shortest formula. A similar instinct led me to comprehend that the musical work too arises solely out of the core of the *Ursatz*. . .I saw through to the *Urlinie*, I did not figure it out![28]

This passage plainly echoes the identifying characteristics of Goethe's epistemology, especially the final sentence, which reads in the original: "Ich habe die Urlinie erschaut, nicht errechnet!" *Errechnen* means "to work out," as one calculates a sum or a formula. To contrast with this word, Schenker uses an uncommon verb – *erschauen* – composed of the prefix *er-*, which indicates the strenuous completion of the task denoted by the verb stem, and of *schauen*, which means "to behold." In his very choice of words, therefore, Schenker is describing a sort of spiritual "vision"; he is claiming that he attained sight of the *Urlinie* through an effort of intuitive observation – how uniquely the word *erschauen* captures both the hard work involved in *Anschauung* and the flash of insight that is its ultimate result! – not through a logical, almost mechanical decoding of the foreground.

But one does not need to go all the way back to the *Urlinie* to see that Schenker's approach to music corresponds to Goethe's *Anschauung*. In our discussion of Schenker's acceptance of the *Urphänomen* as part of his musical world view, his concern for identifying underlying formulas or rules for the diverse appearances of free composition has already become apparent. And we have seen that Goethe prescribed a multi-staged process to identify such underlying rules in nature, involving first empirical rules of thumb, then more inclusive rules that exclude many of the accidental characteristics of the empirical rules. Finally, during the contemplation of the relations between these higher rules, the *aperçu* of the type or *Urphänomen* occurs. In music, however, matters are somewhat easier, because there is a ready-made laboratory for studying musical motions in the abstract: the discipline of strict counterpoint. In strict counterpoint, many of the complicating accidental events of free composition – such as extremely complex rhythms and ornaments, for example – are eliminated, and the student studies the relations among tones in the abstract. Schenker's initial insight into musical structure was that the

26. Schenker, *Harmonielehre*, p. 103.
27. Schenker, *Erläuterungsausgabe, Op. 110* (1914 edn), p. 25; *ibid.* (1972 edn), p. 11.
28. Schenker, *Das Meisterwerk* II, p. 41.

laws of strict counterpoint constitute the underlying models for the appearances of free composition. In Goethean terms, the study of strict counterpoint allows the musician to skip the step of formulating empirical rules of thumb; he can proceed directly to the acquisition of higher rules. The laws of strict counterpoint are the higher rules of music, the abstract formulas that inform the foreground.

In fact, we have already seen Schenker using strict contrapuntal rules as the models for free composition in the previous example from *Kontrapunkt* I. But further examples abound, because it was customary for Schenker to read the sense of free composition according to strict contrapuntal models. For instance, Example 3 shows Schenker's reading of the

Example 3. Bach, *Well-Tempered Clavier*, Book I, Prelude XIII

opening measures from the Prelude in F♯ major in Book I of the *Well-Tempered Clavier.*[29] Schenker explains the passage in this way:

[In measure 2,] I recognize the tone c♯² as the seventh of scale-degree VI in the sense of a passing motion from chord to chord, from scale degree to scale degree – in this case, from VI to II – and not as a suspension, which would have to suggest a sixth-chord on scale-degree IV. . .then I explain the motion of the upper voice in measure 2 as an ornamentation of the seventh, which expands only slightly on the construction allowed in strict counterpoint [Example 4].

29. Example 3 combines Schenker's Figures 1 and 2a from his essay "Die Kunst zu Hören," *Der Tonwille* 3 (1922), p. 22.

Example 4

c.f. 7   (8)

I go on to point out that the fifth progression in the bass falling from the root of scale-degree VI to the root of scale-degree II is matched both in the [upper-voice] ornamentation and in the middle voice by accompanying intervals consonant in themselves, which in turn create the G♯ triad at the upbeat by means of the accidental concurrence of all the passing motions, but without giving the effect of scale-degree II at this point. Remaining in measure 2, I interpret the second sixteenth a♯ as a consonant filler, providing a fifth under the seventh ($\frac{7}{5}$), and the third sixteenth b¹ – which initiates the motion in parallel sixths – as a neighboring tone between the two c♯²s. And finally, moving on to the third measure, I recognize f♯¹ in the middle voice as a seventh over scale-degree II acting as a passing tone [Example 5], and not as a suspension [Example 6].

Example 5. Seventh as passing tone

II⁷ – V⁷

Example 6. Seventh as suspension

VII⁷ ⁶
(V)

Here, however, in opposition to measure 2, the falling of the bass below the root of scale-degree II already brings forth a change of scale degree to V on the upbeat, at the coincidence of c♯ and e♮, because of the altered situation of the middle voice.[30]

It is immediately apparent in this passage that Schenker's approach involves both painstaking attention to details of harmony and voice leading and intuitive recognition of strict contrapuntal models underlying the free composition of the foreground. Here are the musical counterparts of Goethe's *Anschauung* and *aperçu*.

A combination of direct and indirect evidence, then, leads to the conclusion that Schenker did indeed recognize and employ Goethe's episte-

30. *Der Tonwille* 3 (1922), pp. 22–23. Schenker's Figure 3 appears as Example 4; his Figures 4a and 4b are given in Examples 5 and 6.

mological principles in his own work. Furthermore, it would not be going too far beyond the evidence to suggest that the entire course of Schenker's theoretical career was guided by Goethe's epistemological principles, and especially by the systematic exclusion of accidental dissimilarities characteristic of *Anschauung*. Already in *Harmonielehre*, Schenker had decided that the underlying types of free compositional techniques were to be found in the abstract world of strict counterpoint.[31] In the two volumes of *Kontrapunkt*, Schenker began to identify these types, and in his analyses from that period, he described musical content by revealing the strict contrapuntal types behind sections of whole compositions. At some point he must have observed that the strict contrapuntal types behind the surfaces of many pieces were themselves organized according to an underlying model; it was then that he began to perceive the *Urphänomen* of an entire class of musical pieces – the masterworks. It is no coincidence, then, that Schenker calls *Free Composition* a "grammar of tones" (*Ton-Sprachlehre*).[32] What is grammar but a morphological concordance of linguistic forms? And Schenker's last work is nothing less than a true morphology of the masterwork, in the same sense that Goethe's *Theory of Color* is a morphology of color.

So far, we have seen that Schenker accepted Goethe's notion of the type and the principles of Goethe's epistemology; only the relation between Schenker's ontology and Goethe's remains to be considered. Unfortunately, there is very little evidence in Schenker's published writings to support a connection between Goethe's morphological ontology and Schenker's musical ontology. Only the following passage from *Das Meisterwerk* III, which Kassler quotes to support the contention that Schenker assimilated Goethe's idea of organic growth, hints at an ontological connection with Goethe. Starting with the *Ursatz*, Schenker says,

> I then pursue the exfoliation (*Aufblätterung*) of the original horizontal line into extensions – that is, into derivations, diminutions in the form of linear progressions, couplings, neighboring motions, and so on – as they grow, continually stretching out (*dehnend*) into new voice-leading levels and assembling into different forms, until they attain their final unfolding in the foreground as the highest intensification (*Steigerung*).[33]

At first glance, this passage might seem a bit too general to point conclusively to Goethe, because the notion of organic growth presented here could have derived from a common stock of organicist ideas widespread in German idealist philosophy. Schenker's and Goethe's organic beliefs could have come from quite unrelated sources. Yet one hears fairly distinct echoes of Goethe's voice here. The word *Aufblätterung*, while not one of Goethe's special terms, sets a botanical tone reminiscent of Goethe's plant studies; the word *dehnend* intensifies the impression that Goethe's spirit is present, for he regarded plant growth as successive

---

31. *Harmonielehre*, pp. 198–233.
32. *Der freie Satz* (1935 edn), p. 28 and *ibid.* (1956 edn), p. 37; a different translation in *Free Composition*, p. 9.
33. *Das Meisterwerk* III, pp. 20–21.

periods of *Ausdehnung* and *Zusammenziehen* (expansion and contraction);[34] and finally, the appearance of the word *Steigerung* impels one to consider this passage inspired, at least, by Goethe's work. This is, of course, hardly the kind of solid evidence one would like to have. But even in the absence of such evidence, it is reasonable to believe that Schenker's ontology accords with Goethe's. After all, the starting point of the ontological process – the *Urphänomen* – is the same for both Goethe and Schenker, and the latter's adoption of the former's epistemological principles implies at the very least a strong correspondence between the ontological commitments that would make such a common epistemology possible.

In fact, it is not at all difficult to construct an interpretation of Schenker's ontology that follows the lines of Goethe's four ontological principles. First, the principle of organic holism is just as much part of Schenker's world view as it is part of Goethe's, since both took this principle from the larger pool of organic thought.[35] Second, the principle of polarity is immediately evident in the *Ursatz*, where the two opposing forces are horizontalization and verticalization – that is, melody and harmony, or, in Schenker's terms, linear progression and scale degree. Third, the principle of intensification causes the *Ursatz* to strive toward more complex levels of organization. The action of intensification can be seen, for instance, in the creation of a linear progression such as that shown in Example 7.

Example 7

A vertical simultaneity begins to stretch apart; the two opposing forces intensify, that is to say, the horizontal force seeks the greatest possible extension between the pitches, whereas the vertical force seeks to strengthen its control over the distended simultaneity. Then the intensified forces try to recombine, and a new contrapuntal formation arises, in which interpolated passing tones extend the horizontal and new contrapuntal harmonies enrich the vertical. Fourth, and finally, the interaction of musical polarity and intensification gives rise to the several transformation levels – or, in Goethean terms, metamorphoses – of the *Ursatz*, which ultimately culminate in the foreground.

III

Knowing about the influence of Goethe's morphology on Schenker

34. AA XVII, p. 42.
35. Ruth Solie discusses Schenker's understanding of organic holism in her article "The Living Work: Organicism and Musical Analysis," *19th-Century Music* 4/2 (1980), pp. 147–56.

may be of interest to the intellectual historian; but it can also help the inquisitive theorist to understand better some puzzling aspects of Schenker's thought. For example, knowing the epistemological principles shared by Goethe and Schenker helps to explain why Schenker's graphs sometimes place a strain on one's hearing abilities. The reason is that the graphs do not record the perceptions of normal hearing – not even of the most acute normal hearing. On the contrary, they record the perceptions of an elevated sense of hearing, one trained by *Anschauung* (or should one say, in this case, *Anhörung*?) to recognize underlying models, and, ultimately, the *Urphänomen*. The graphic techniques invented by Schenker are therefore not simply tools for representing one's impressions of tonal activity, but devices for revealing the models of tonal activity existing in the ontological "history" of the completed artwork. For this reason, Schenker could not have accepted as valid graphic interpretations that simply record the impressions of listeners unpracticed in hearing the underlying models of tonal motion. Hence his insistence that those who had not learned to hear music in terms of the principles he had discovered had never heard music at all.[36]

On a related matter, an understanding of the ontological principles shared by Goethe and Schenker helps to explain why, in some of Schenker's graphs, very prominent foreground deviations from the underlying models may not be detrimental to the integrity of the work – indeed, may even constitute the particular distinguishing characteristics of the work. In the graph of the Hassler piece shown in Example 8,[37] Schenker singles out the foreground deviations, noting especially that b^1 is composed out in measures 1–4 where a^1 would have been the appropriate pitch in the long-range arpeggiation $f\#^1$–a^1–d^2–$f\#^2$; that the fifth-progression in measures 9 and 10 leading from e^2 down to an imagined a^1 is obscured by the substitution of $c\#^2$ for a^1 at the end of the progression; and that the piece fails to close on $\hat{1}$, but instead turns up to $\hat{3}$.[38] But these deviations do not disturb Schenker, who offered this piece as one of the earliest examples of a masterwork. Such deviations are possible because of the ontological principles governing metamorphosis; a special and particular combination of these forces has resulted in a peculiar and striking individual variation in the foreground; but so long as the foreground permits the recognition of the underlying models and the *Urphänomen*, the piece still belongs to the class unified by the *Urphänomen*. In Example 1, Hassler's piece would be represented by one of the dots closer to the edge of the outer circle than to the edge of the inner circle.

On the other hand, pieces whose foregrounds do not permit the recognition of the underlying models, or whose middleground models

36. *Das Meisterwerk* II, p. 11.
37. Example 8 is taken from *Free Composition*, Figure 116. (Used by permission of Schirmer Books, a division of Macmillan, Inc.)
38. *Free Composition*, pp. 95–96.

Example 8. Hassler, *Lustgarten* (1601), No. 24
(from *Free Composition*, Figure 116)

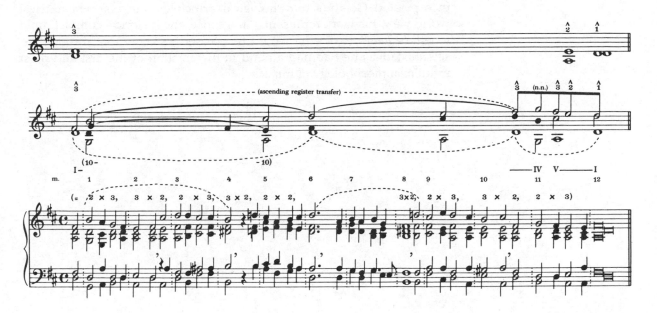

do not permit the recognition of the *Urphänomen* (i.e., the *Ursatz*) do not belong to this class. It is this distinction that leads to Schenker's harsh judgments about many composers who, he believes, cannot compose with the "vision" of the *Ursatz* in mind. The force of this criticism can be seen most clearly in the two principal examples of Schenker's "negative analysis" – the discussion of a short passage from Stravinsky's Piano Concerto[39] and the long essay on a set of variations by Reger.[40]

If further investigation of the connections between Goethe's morphology and Schenker's theories could continue to shed more light on the perplexing aspects of Schenker's writings, the practical theorist might find even more helpful insights in the work of the intellectual historian.

A final observation points to the historical appropriateness of Schenker's inheritance from Goethe. After the success of his *Theory of Color*, Goethe decided that music too could benefit from his scientific approach, and he undertook a morphological study of musical phenomena, which he called his *Tonlehre*.[41] Since he did not consider himself an accomplished musician, Goethe relied on Karl Friedrich Zelter for technical expertise.

39. *Das Meisterwerk* II, pp. 37–39.
40. Schenker, "Ein Gegenbeispiel – Max Reger, Op. 81: Variationen und Fuge über ein Thema von Joh. Seb. Bach für Klavier," *Das Meisterwerk* II, pp. 171–92.
41. A brief description of Goethe's musical ideas, together with a compilation of all the texts related to the projected *Tonlehre*, may be found in Ernst Jürgen-Dryer, *Versuch, eine Morphologie der Musik zu begründen* (Bonn, 1976).

It would not be too unfair to say that Zelter's assistance undoubtedly contributed to the ultimate failure of Goethe's project. But because Schenker incorporated Goethe's morphological principles into his own musical world view, his work represents, in a sense, the historical completion of Goethe's *Tonlehre*. Goethe would be pleased to know that through his scientific ideas he had had a hand in the creation of the first and most influential morphology of music.

Schenkerian theory and the analysis of Renaissance music

David Stern

Heinrich Schenker's monumental theories of musical structure and voice leading have influenced not only the study of the eighteenth- and nineteenth-century repertoire, but also the study of early and modern music. While the value of Schenker's approach for the analysis of music from Bach to Brahms is becoming increasingly recognized, the application of his theories to music of other periods remains somewhat more controversial. In this paper, I shall attempt to show that although there are profound differences between Renaissance and later tonal music, Schenker's theories may nevertheless contribute significantly to the study of structure, voice leading, and motivic organization in Renaissance music.

I would like to begin by discussing some of Schenker's own views on music history. In addition to showing an incomparable understanding of eighteenth- and nineteenth-century masterworks, Schenker's writings demonstrate extensive knowledge of music history from ancient Greece to Stravinsky. Although Schenker never wrote a history of music, he actually devoted considerable attention to historical matters. Over twenty pages of his *Harmonielehre* are devoted to historical discussion.[1] In an essay from *Der Tonwille* entitled "Geschichte der Tonkunst," Schenker stated a series of questions that a "true" history of composition would have to answer. Some of these are:

After the law of consonance. . .had found fulfillment in the vertical direction, which artists were the first to attain an agreement between the vertical and horizontal triad and break the path to a horizontal (melodic) composing-out verified through the vertical direction? How were such composings-out of the triad connected?[2]

In his foreword to *Kontrapunkt*, Schenker made the important observation that

all musical technique is to be explained by two basic ingredients: voice leading and the progression of scale degrees. Of the two, *voice leading* is the earlier and more original element.[3]

Subsequent writings also contain historical references. Various sections of Schenker's final treatise, *Der freie Satz*, contain passages dealing with

---

1. See Schenker, *Harmony*, pp. 85ff., 94–96, 134–41, 163–73, and elsewhere.
2. Schenker, "Geschichte der Tonkunst," *Der Tonwille* 2 (1922), pp. 3–4 (my translation).
3. Schenker, *Kontrapunkt* I, p. xxiii. The translation is from *Counterpoint* I, p. xxv.

historical background.[4] Thus, Schenker not only made many references to music history in his writings, but also showed a strong interest in placing his theories into historical context. Furthermore, while he was largely unsympathetic to early and modern music, the quotations given above show that Schenker nevertheless made observations and posed questions of great interest for the historical study of voice leading and tonal organization.

Although there is at present a growing interest in the analysis of early music, no single analytical approach has become generally accepted, and conflicting opinions on the nature of musical structure in the fifteenth and sixteenth centuries remain. The debate has largely focused on the extent to which the concepts and terminology of tonal theory may or may not be used for analyzing Renaissance music. While theories of tonal music have often been used for this purpose, some writers believe that music should be analyzed primarily in terms of the theory of its own time, and that tonal theory is irrelevant as well as anachronistic to Renaissance music. Analytical work based on Renaissance theory has already yielded valuable results; for example, work by Bernhard Meier, Leeman Perkins, and Leo Treitler has shown that modal theory had far-reaching relevance to polyphonic composition from Dufay to Lassus.[5] Although this historical approach to analysis is indispensable, there is a limit to how much we can reconstruct the musical thought of any period from its treatises; if later analytical methods can contribute anything meaningful to the analysis of Renaissance compositions, they should not be excluded.[6]

One of the most difficult issues facing the analyst of Renaissance music is how to understand fifteenth- and sixteenth-century harmony; some writers have felt that tonal harmony was already present in Dufay, while others have maintained that harmony was intervallic up until ca. 1600, and triadic thereafter.[7] Accordingly, the use of Schenkerian analysis in examining Renaissance music has been criticized on the grounds that it applies triadic principles to music which is not triadic.[8] However, in an important article entitled "Harmonic Theory in Musical Treatises of the Late Fifteenth and Early Sixteenth Centuries," Benito Rivera has shown that there was greater theoretical recognition of triadic sonorities by the time of Josquin than has been generally acknowledged. For example, in

4. See Schenker, *Free Composition*, §§ 4–5, 51, 180, 199, 251, 276, 301, 324, and elsewhere.
5. See Bernhard Meier, *Die Tonarten der klassischen Vokalpolyphonie* (Utrecht, 1974); Leeman Perkins, "Mode and Structure in the Masses of Josquin," *Journal of the American Musicological Society* 26/2 (1973), pp. 189–239; and Leo Treitler, "Tone System in the Secular Works of Guillaume Dufay," *Journal of the American Musicological Society* 18/2 (1965), pp. 131–69.
6. For a thoughtful discussion of the problems of applying later theoretical concepts to the analysis of early music see Daniel Leech-Wilkinson, "Machaut's *Rose, Lis* and the Problem of Early Music Analysis," *Music Analysis* 3/1 (1984), pp. 9–28; see especially pp. 9–12.
7. For example, Heinrich Besseler has argued for functional tonality in Dufay's music in *Bourdon und Fauxbourdon* (Leipzig, 1950). Carl Dahlhaus takes the viewpoint that harmony was intervallic in the Renaissance, and chordal from the seventeenth century on. See Dahlhaus, *Untersuchungen über der harmonischen Tonalität* (Kassel, 1968).
8. See Perkins, "Mode and Structure," especially p. 193.

1496, Gaffurius established the concept of a fifth or sixth divided by a third as being a unified harmonic entity.[9] This concept is also found in Zarlino, who adds:

> When three parts are related to one another by the intervals mentioned [i.e., by a fifth and a third], or the sixth in place of the fifth, any other parts added must form unisons or octaves with one of the original three.[10]

Thus, for Zarlino, notes added to ⁵⁄₃ and ⁶⁄₃ sonorities are not merely considered a further piling up of intervals, but are understood as doubling one of the original three notes.

Rivera points out that such triadically oriented theories were by no means universal in the Renaissance.[11] It is true that fifteenth- and sixteenth-century harmony was taught primarily in terms of intervals, and that only a small number of theorists reduced the possible interval combinations to basic ⁵⁄₃ and ⁶⁄₃ harmonies. Nevertheless, to describe Renaissance harmony merely as the combination of consonant intervals tells us less about its specific nature than Zarlino's discussion of basic ⁵⁄₃ and ⁶⁄₃ harmonies with octave doublings. Furthermore, although it is true that the succession of vertical sonorities in late fifteenth- and sixteenth-century music is largely determined by the interaction of melodies rather than by harmonic progressions, vertical factors also play an important role in determining the melodies; the need to create or stay within ⁵⁄₃ or ⁶⁄₃ sonorities often gives rise to melodic leaps. This may be illustrated by the tenor part from the end of the Christe of Josquin's *Missa Pange Lingua* (see Example 1).[12]

Example 1. Josquin, *Missa Pange Lingua*, Christe, measures 50–52

This is just one out of countless possible examples which could be cited to show that vertical sonorities were not simply by-products of melodic motion, but also exerted an influence on composition. Furthermore, we have seen that although harmony was primarily taught as the combination of consonances, the particular combinations used were by no means foreign to those used in later triadic music. Thus, the division between Renaissance intervallic harmony and tonal triadic harmony does not exclude the possibility of far-reaching relationships between them.

9. Benito V. Rivera, "Harmonic Theory in Musical Treatises of the Late Fifteenth and Early Sixteenth Centuries," *Music Theory Spectrum* 1 (1979), pp. 80–95 (see especially p. 93).
10. Gioseffo Zarlino, *Le Istitutioni harmoniche* (Venice, 1558), Book III, Chapter 59, trans. Guy A. Marco and Claude V. Palisca in Gioseffo Zarlino, *The Art of Counterpoint* (New Haven, 1968; reprint edn, New York, 1976), p. 190.
11. Rivera, "Harmonic Theory," p. 95.
12. Josquin des Prez, *Werken*, ed. A. Smijers (Amsterdam, 1925–), *Missen*, Vol. 4, No. 18; and *Das Chorwerk*, ed. Friedrich Blume (Wolfenbüttel, 1929), No. 1.

Ultimately, the most accurate account of the development of harmony will not draw absolute barriers, but will show both the connections and differences between early and later harmonic practice. Some of these will now be briefly discussed.

There are many readily apparent differences between Renaissance harmony and harmonic practice of the eighteenth and nineteenth centuries; three of these are outlined here. First, although important elements of the major–minor system originated prior to 1600, it is obvious that the entire vocabulary of the major–minor system was by no means established by that time. For example, $^6_4$ chords and seventh chords could not yet be freely introduced, but could only arise through suspensions, passing tones, or neighbor notes. Second, the hallmark of medieval harmony – the $^8_5$ sonority without the third above the bass – was still considered complete around 1500; however, in 1558 Zarlino wrote that it was a fault to omit the third when writing for more than three voices, an indication that the $^8_5$ sonority was giving way to the fuller $^5_3$ sonority in the course of the sixteenth century.[13] Third, the concept of chord inversion is not found in Renaissance treatises, but emerges around the beginning of the seventeenth century.[14]

This last point raises the question of the relevance of the concept of chord inversion to Renaissance music, and it is here that a Schenkerian understanding of harmony becomes particularly helpful, both from a musical and a historical viewpoint. Schenker was far more successful than any other theorist in distinguishing between chords of harmonic and contrapuntal origin. As a result, chords that would be explained by conventional harmonic theory as inversions are often more convincingly shown by Schenker to derive from contrapuntal voice-leading procedures. Returning to Example 1, it is readily seen that the $^6_3$ sonority does not arise through the process of chord inversion; rather, it arises from the tenor's neighbor-note motion, a–bb–a.

A second use of $^6_3$ sonorities in fifteenth- and sixteenth-century music is for passing motion between points of greater stability, which are defined by perfect intervals or $^5_3$ (or $^8_3$) sonorities; a simple example of this is found in Josquin's motet, *Huc me sydereo* (see Example 2).[15] Here, the

Example 2. Josquin, *Huc me sydereo*, measures 104–106

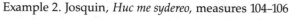

13. Zarlino, *The Art of Counterpoint*, p. 188.
14. See Joel Lester, "Root Position and Inverted Triads in Theory Around 1600," *Journal of the American Musicological Society* 27/1 (1974), pp. 110–19, and Benito V. Rivera, "The Seventeenth-Century Theory of Triadic Generation and Invertibility and its Application in Contemporaneous Rules of Composition," *Music Theory Spectrum* 6 (1984), pp. 63–78.
15. Josquin des Prez, *Werken: Motetten*, Vol. 2, No. 32.

motion from D to A is carried out by stepwise descending $\frac{6}{3}$ sonorities on
C and B♭. Elsewhere, $\frac{6}{3}$ harmonies are used to break up parallel fifths –
using the 5–6 technique – as in the excerpt from the Credo of William
Byrd's *Mass for Five Voices* shown in Example 3.[16] This is not to say that

Example 3. Byrd, *Mass for Five Voices*, Credo, measures 90–94

chords in Renaissance music never behave in the same way that genuine
inversions in later tonal music do. That is an issue beyond the scope
of this paper. For present purposes, it suffices to restate that most $\frac{6}{3}$
sonorities in Renaissance music can be explained as arising from contrapuntal factors. All of the types of voice leading shown in the above
examples (or forms closely related to them) continued to be in use in the
major–minor system; for example, many Baroque ground basses have
essentially the same harmonization as seen in Example 2.

In addition to the voice-leading forms discussed above, other important
connections between Renaissance and later practice are the practice of
basing music on the diatonic scale, the principle of octave equivalency,
the avoidance of parallel perfect intervals, and the subordination of dissonance to consonance. Four further connections may be mentioned
here. First, the concept of the bass as the foundation of harmony is present in the treatises of Glarean and Zarlino – it did not originate with
the advent of basso continuo, but emerges already in Renaissance
theory.[17] Second, in both Renaissance and later tonal music, the bass
tends to move more by disjunct motion, at a slower rate than the more
ornate, rapid, and stepwise upper voices.[18] A third connection is the use
of the fifth as an organizing interval; the melodic fifth-species are basic
components of modal theory, and the fifth is a basic harmonic con-

16. *The Byrd Edition*, ed. Philip Brett (London, 1973–), Vol. 4, p. 91.
17. Heinrich Glarean, *Dodecachordon* (Basel, 1547), Book III, Chapter 13, and Gioseffo
    Zarlino, *Le Istitutioni harmoniche*, Book III, Chapter 58. It is quite clear that Glarean and
    Zarlino understood this concept to apply to the music of all the composers whose works
    were used as examples in their treatises; thus, it would extend at least as far back as
    Josquin.
18. Zarlino discusses these characteristics of bass and upper-voice motion in the Ren-
    aissance in *Le Istitutioni harmoniche*, Book III, Chapter 58; Schenker discusses them in
    regard to the major–minor system in *Free Composition*, §20. Carl Schachter pointed out
    the relationship between these two citations in a seminar, "The Theories of Heinrich
    Schenker," given at the Graduate School of the City University of New York in 1980.

sonance, as it is in later tonal music. Thus, whether one accepts or rejects the presence of the tonic–dominant relationship in Renaissance music, it must be recognized that the interval of the fifth is one of the basic structural elements of the music and that it contributes to the sense of tonal center that is usually present in fifteenth- and sixteenth-century works.[19] Finally, Schenker has shown that strict counterpoint, which derives from Renaissance counterpoint, underlies the voice leading of music written in the major–minor system.

Our study of voice leading and harmony before and after 1600 thus points out some ways in which a Schenkerian understanding of harmony may be useful for studying Renaissance musical vocabulary, and for tracing both the differences and connections between Renaissance and later harmony. Since Schenker's theory provides an understanding of how various types of voice leading and harmonies arise from contrapuntal procedures, it is closer in spirit and substance to Renaissance harmony, which is so contrapuntally oriented, than Riemannian theory, which explains chords in terms of tonal functions, with little acknowledgment of the contrapuntal origin of many harmonies. Historical discussions of harmony influenced by Riemannian theory have sometimes tended to create a sharp division between harmony before and after 1600, and have not shown many of the valid connections between Renaissance and later harmonic practice, such as those outlined above. One could carry the present historical sketch further by expanding the preceding discussion of how $\frac{6}{3}$ harmonies were used in the fifteenth and sixteenth centuries, and could then trace the introduction and development of new types of voice leading over the subsequent centuries.

We turn now to a consideration of some ways in which Schenkerian theory may contribute to the study of motivic organization in Renaissance music. Schenker himself recognized the presence of what he called the "link technique" in Renaissance polyphony.[20] This technique, found frequently in music of the major–minor era, establishes a close link between two sections by using an idea from the close of a section at the beginning of the following one. A particularly beautiful example is found in the Agnus Dei of William Byrd's *Mass for Five Voices*; the bass melody at the cadence of measures 41–42 becomes the main motive for the remainder of the movement.[21]

19. The V–I designation is used for cadences in Renaissance music in Gustave Reese, *Music in the Renaissance*, rev. edn (New York, 1959); in Howard Mayer Brown, *Music in the Renaissance* (Englewood Cliffs, N.J., 1976); and in numerous other writings on Renaissance music (including most Renaissance studies using Schenkerian analytical method). This has been challenged by Ernst Apfel in "Der klangliche Satz und der freie Diskantsatz im 15. Jahrhundert," *Archiv für Musikwissenschaft* 12/4 (1955), pp. 297–313 (see especially pp. 305–6). Richard Crocker takes a position similar to Apfel's in "Discant, Counterpoint, and Harmony," *Journal of the American Musicological Society* 15/1 (1962), pp. 1–21 (see especially pp. 13–14).
20. *Knüpftechnik*. See *Kontrapunkt* I, p. 3.
21. *The Byrd Edition*, Vol. 4, p. 119.

Example 4. Josquin, *Ave Maria. . .virgo serena*

(a) measures 1–4

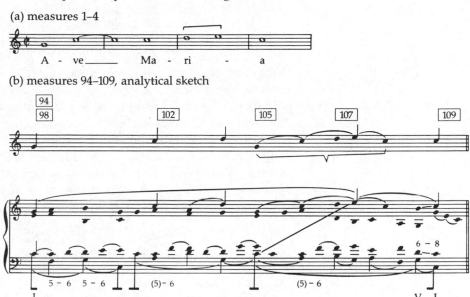

A - ve＿ Ma - ri - a

(b) measures 94–109, analytical sketch

Another specifically Schenkerian motivic concept is that of hidden repetition.[22] In his essay entitled "Motivic Integration in Josquin's Motets," Irving Godt convincingly shows that the famous opening melody of Josquin's *Ave Maria. . .virgo serena* recurs in various transformations throughout the motet.[23] One such transformation, not mentioned in Godt's study, occurs in measures 94–109 (compare Example 4a with the upper staff of Example 4b). In Example 4b, the bracket below the top staff shows a smaller version of the opening idea nested within the larger one. (This passage is not only noteworthy for its display of motivic ingenuity, but also for the canon between the superius and tenor and its clear sense of harmonic progression; altogether, it amounts to a compositional tour de force.) It is probable that the techniques of hidden repetition and motivic enlargement were used less in the Renaissance than in the major–minor era, although there has not been enough work done in this area to permit any firm conclusions at present. Nevertheless, the likelihood that they were at times consciously worked into Renaissance compositions is by no means far-fetched; put in Renaissance terms, these hidden repetitions could arise from the varied diminution of a specific melodic idea.

The next issue to be considered here concerns the understanding of large-scale structure in Renaissance composition. In his treatise of 1555, Nicola Vicentino wrote the following words concerning musical structure:

22. See Charles Burkhart's important study, "Schenker's 'Motivic Parallelisms,'" *Journal of Music Theory* 22/2 (1978), pp. 145–75.
23. Josquin des Prez, *Werken: Motetten*, Vol. 1, No. 1; see Irving Godt, "Motivic Integration in Josquin's Motets," *Journal of Music Theory* 21/2 (1977), pp. 264–94.

The foundation of this structure is to choose a tone, or mode, that will suit the argument of the words, or another musical theme, as the case may be, and on that good foundation he will measure well with his judgment and he will draw the lines of the fourths and of the fifths of this tone and of their limits, which will be the columns that will keep the structure of the composition standing.[24]

Vicentino expresses with exemplary clarity the concept that the modal species form a structural framework which serves as the basis for melodic diminutions and elaborations. While Vicentino's modal framework is not the same as Schenker's *Ursatz* or fundamental structure, the idea that music consists of the elaboration of an underlying structure is common to both theorists. An example of a structure which adheres to Vicentino's principles is the lovely Kyrie from Josquin's *Missa de Beata Virgine* (see Example 5).[25] Example 5a shows the cantus firmus for the first Kyrie of that mass; Examples 5b–5d provide analyses of Josquin's setting.

Example 5. Josquin, *Missa de Beata Virgine*, Kyrie I

(a) cantus firmus: Kyrie from Mass IX (beginning)

(b) analytical sketch

(c) analytical sketch

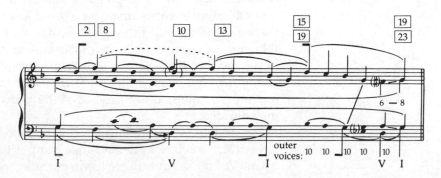

24. The passage, from Vicentino's *L'antica musica ridotta alla moderna prattica*, is translated in Karol Berger, "Tonality and Atonality in the Prologue to Orlando di Lasso's *Prophetiae Sibyllarum*: Some Methodological Problems in the Analysis of Sixteenth-Century Music," *The Musical Quarterly* 66/4 (1980), pp. 484–504 (see p. 489).
25. Josquin des Prez, *Werken: Missen*, Vol. 3, No. 16; and *Das Chorwerk*, No. 42.

Example 5 (*cont.*)

(d) Kyrie I

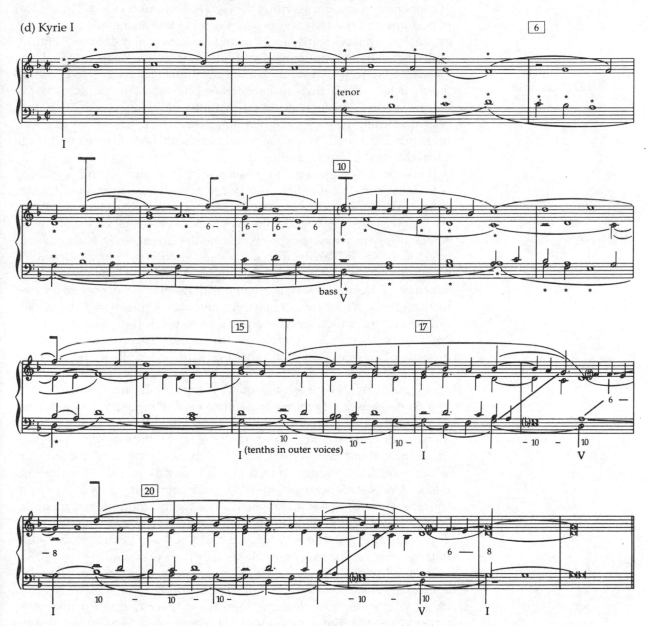

The chant is in the first mode on D; Josquin's setting transposes the mode to a G final, with a B♭ signature. In Example 5d, the cantus firmus notes are indicated by asterisks.[26] The chant initially outlines the mode 1

26. The chant appears in *The Liber Usualis* (Tournai, 1963), p. 40. The incipit is clearly quoted in the imitative entries; furthermore, the alto seems to continue quoting the first chant phrase somewhat more freely. Josquin thus may have used the entire first phrase of chant in the Kyrie I.

fifth species in both ascending and descending direction; thus, from the very opening of Josquin's setting, the G–D fifth is emphasized. The choice of beginning the imitative entries on G and D was also made in order to establish the mode clearly. The alto and bass enter in measures 7 and 10 with strict imitation, outlining the fifth D–A, instead of using a "tonal" or "modal" answer, which would answer the initial fifth from G to D with a fourth, D to G. While this causes a brief emphasis on D in measures 10–13, the prevailing G mode is never thrown into ambiguity or doubt. In the section's closing passage (first heard in measures 15–19 and repeated in measures 19ff.), each voice begins and ends on G or D, thus outlining either the modal fourth- or fifth-species.

The structure of this section as shown in Examples 5b and 5c shows both interesting similarities and differences when compared to the Schenkerian fundamental structure with an upper voice descending from the fifth scale degree. I would like to propose an explanation for the most common way in which structures resembling Schenkerian fundamental structures arise in Renaissance music, and then point out a crucial difference in regard to the approach to the final cadence. The upper-voice structure of many Renaissance compositions may be explained in the following way. An important aspect of musical composition is the use of register; in order to achieve a satisfactory result, it has to be used with special care. Thus, in Example 5d, the initial upper-voice motion in measures 1–5 from g^1 to d^2 and back down to f^1 would sound unsatisfactory if the superius never rose back to the register established by the opening ascent. Of course, in Josquin's composition, the opening ascent to d^2 in measure 2 is followed by a return to d^2 in measure 7, a motion to its upper third, f^2, in measures 8, 10, and 13, and then a return to d^2 in measure 15. Thus, d^2, the upper tone of the mode 1 fifth-species, is prominent throughout the section; it functions as a registral focal point which is repeatedly returned to, and it is from this note that the descent into the final cadence begins. While such upper-voice descents to a cadence were not universal in Renaissance composition, they were quite common; composers undoubtedly felt their strongly conclusive quality. This is surely the reason why Josquin composed this descent at the close of the section; it does not originate directly from the chant.[27]

Thus, when a composition maintains a specific register throughout by continually returning to a note a third or fifth above the mode's final and closes with a stepwise descent from that note to the modal final, the upper-voice structure shows important features that were to be used in compositions written in the major–minor era. The structure is especially similar to Schenker's fundamental structure when the bass moves to the

27. The similar descent at the end of the second Kyrie also does not originate from the chant; rather, it results from Josquin's desire to create a strong cadence. Gaffurius wrote that "since a descent from high to low causes a greater sense of repose, four notes in a low series of tones have been chosen as modal finals." See Franchinus Gaffurius, *Practica Musicae* (Milan, 1496), Book I, Chapter 8; trans. Clement Miller (Rome, 1968), p. 50.

final note by the leap of a descending fifth, or, as in the present example, by that of an ascending fourth; it is probable that the fundamental structures characteristic of the major–minor system grew out of these earlier types. Although the final cadence in Example 5d is not fully triadic (since it ends on the open $\frac{8}{5}$ harmony), the upper fifth of the mode's final is nonetheless strongly present at the cadence and helps to establish the G tonality in a manner analogous to the I–V–I cadence of later tonal music, a cadence which, after all, developed directly from cadences such as this one. (The G sonority, in $\frac{8}{5}$ or $\frac{8}{3}$ form, is not simply contrapuntal here, but serves as a genuine harmonic basis for the Kyrie.)

We have seen that Example 5 possesses a strong relationship to the Schenkerian fundamental structure in that the upper voice maintains a specific register and then forms a cadential descent of a fifth over a bass motion prefiguring the later V–I cadence. We now turn to the important difference between this type of structure and the structures found in later music. Although the upper voice in Example 5 descends a fifth, and uses only stepwise motion, it does not form a direct linear progression of a fifth as it typically would in later pieces whose fundamental melodic line descends from the fifth scale degree. The most striking difference between the descent in Josquin's Kyrie and later structural descents is the absence of the second scale degree as a structural tone in the former.[28] Here, after the arrival on the third scale degree, b♭[1] in measure 17, there is a rapid motion to g[1], and then to the seventh scale degree, f(♯)[1], which appears within the larger structure at a location analogous to that occupied by the second scale-step in later tonal music. Schenker uses the term "substitution" in upper-voice descents where the leading tone appears in place of the second scale degree; in such cases, the second scale degree is considered to be implicitly present in the background.[29] This is justified by the fact that in the works of the great composers of the major–minor era, the stepwise descent of the upper voice was sufficiently established as a norm for the second scale degree to be inferred even when not literally present. During the Renaissance, on the other hand, there was no such established norm for the upper voice, so that the concept of substitution does not apply here.

The absence of the second scale degree in the upper-voice descent of Josquin's Kyrie stems from a general difference between the composition of cadences during the Renaissance and the major–minor period. Throughout the greater part of the fifteenth and sixteenth centuries, the direct descent of a second to the cadence note typically appeared in the tenor, and the upper voice typically ascended a second to the cadential goal, forming a 6–8 cadence with the tenor. Accordingly, when composers wished to write a descending upper-voice motion to a cadence on the

28. The passing tone a[1] in measure 22 does not function as a structural 2; it is not harmonically supported, is not one of the main components of the cadence, and has only local significance.
29. *Free Composition*, p. 51.

mode's final, they usually shaped this voice to move first to the step below the cadence note and then to the cadence note itself. This is why the direct upper-voice descent of a second to the cadence tone was relatively rare throughout much of the Renaissance, and, although examples do exist, particularly in secular music, they are the exception rather than the rule.[30] A comparison between Examples 6a and 6b shows that two basic ideas, the descending fifth from d^2 to g^1 and the traditional superius cadence formula, have been integrated into the upper-voice structure of Josquin's composition. (The upper-voice motion to the seventh scale degree permits the lower voice to support it at the lower tenth up to the penultimate harmony; the parallel tenths in the outer voices of measures 15–18 and measures 19–22 are labeled in Examples 5c and 5d.) Example 6c shows how it was still possible for the second scale degree to appear in upper-voice descents of Renaissance compositions; such structures are closer to Schenker's fundamental structures than that of Josquin's Kyrie shown in Example 5b. However, as long as the descent of a second to the

Example 6. Josquin, *Missa de Beata Virgine*, Kyrie I

(a) analytical sketch

(b) the basic structural components of the superius

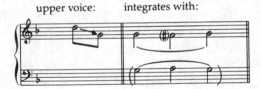

(c) the fundamental structure with $\hat{2}$ in the superius, as found in Renaissance compositions

30. In 3–1 cadences, the upper voice proceeds to the cadence tone by a descending second-step. However, the 3–1 cadence was normally used for weaker internal cadences; in main cadences, the 6–8 progression was usually used in the superius and tenor rather than the 3–1 progression (both in the music of Josquin's era and in much of the music of later Renaissance composers). To find out exactly when the direct $\hat{2}$–$\hat{1}$ upper voice descent began to be used extensively is a subject for further study.

cadence note remained fundamental to the tenor voice, it was necessarily less fundamental to the upper voice than it was to become in later music.

When a Renaissance composition closed with an upper-voice descent to the final of the mode, then, the descent was typically integrated with the 6–8 cadence formula, as shown in Example 6.[31] We have seen that this caused the upper voice to approach the cadence note through an ascending step from the seventh scale degree, rather than through a descending step from the second scale degree. By the early Baroque period the direct upper-voice descent from the second to the first scale degree was quite common. This is related to the fact that the tenor's role in articulating cadences had greatly declined with the emergence of the basso continuo. For example, in a song for solo voice and continuo, only the outer voices would be written, and the upper voice was free to descend to the cadence tone by step, instead of having to counterpoint a descending second-step in the tenor.

This historical change in the composing of upper voices may be illustrated by comparing Examples 7a and 7b.[32] Example 7a shows the final cadence of Heinrich Isaac's famous *Innsbruck, ich muss dich lassen*. Here, the superius forms a 6–8 cadence with the tenor, and moves to its final note by an ascending second-step. A modified version of Isaac's tune

Example 7
(a) Isaac, *Innsbruck, ich muss dich lassen*, measures 20–23

(b) Bach, *St. Matthew Passion*, Chorale: "Ich bin's, ich sollte büssen," measures 11–12

31. Such descents usually spanned the interval of a third or fifth; however, in the Phrygian mode, other intervals were sometimes spanned. For sixth descents in the Phrygian mode, see Saul Novack's analysis of Josquin's *Missa Pange Lingua* in "Fusion of Design and Tonal Order in Mass and Motet: Josquin Desprez and Heinrich Isaac," in *The Music Forum*, Vol. 2 (New York, 1970), pp. 187–263 (see especially pp. 232–33). Of course, structural upper-voice descents through intervals other than the third, fifth, or octave were rare or obsolete in the major–minor era.
32. Heinrich Isaac, *Innsbruck, ich muss dich lassen*, in *An Anthology of Early Renaissance Music*, ed. Noah Greenberg and Paul Maynard (New York, 1975), pp. 183–84. See Saul Novack's analysis in "Fusion of Design and Tonal Order," pp. 235–37. For Schenker's analysis of "Ich bin's, ich sollte büssen," see his *Five Graphic Music Analyses*, pp. 32–33.

appears in the soprano voice of the chorale "Ich bin's, ich sollte büssen" from Bach's St. Matthew Passion. The closing cadence of this chorale is shown in Example 7b; here, the final soprano note is approached directly by the second scale degree.

The final analytical issue to be discussed here concerns Schenker's understanding of parallel perfect intervals. Schenker has shown that parallel octaves and fifths may be permitted if they do not occur between essential harmony tones; in such cases, there is an underlying "correct" counterpoint in which the fifths do not appear.[33] An example of such permissible fifths appears in the first Kyrie from Josquin's *Missa de Beata Virgine*. The parallel fifths between the upper voices of measure 18 are labelled in Example 8a. The first fifth is formed by a passing tone, a^1, above a suspension, d^1, and the second fifth by two harmonic tones. The underlying counterpoint is shown in Example 8b, in which the parallel fifths do not occur at all. The fifths in measure 18 thus do not offend the ear, and are perfectly acceptable. We need not view them as an error marring one of Josquin's greatest works.

Example 8. Josquin, *Missa de Beata Virgine*, Kyrie I

(a) the parallel fifths in measure 18

(b) the underlying correct counterpoint

In this article, I have tried to show that Schenkerian theory may be productively used for historical study, and that it has far more potential for historical research than has been generally recognized. It is true that Schenkerian theory does not solve all problems involved in the analysis of early music, and that knowledge of Medieval and Renaissance music theory is essential for this task. It is also true that Schenker's theories cannot be used without modification when applied to the analysis of early

---

33. Schenker himself used an example from Josquin's music to illustrate allowable parallel fifths. See *Free Composition*, Figure 54/12; this example is discussed in my article, "A Quotation from Josquin in Schenker's *Free Composition*," *Theory and Practice* 7/2 (1982), pp. 33–40.

music, and that the analyst must be aware of the possibility that structures in early music may be different from the tonal structures outlined by Schenker. Nevertheless, Schenker's graphic technique is a uniquely clear means for communicating ideas on musical structure, and for showing the tonal path taken in a composition. It is also capable of showing structures that are not the same as the fundamental structures of the major–minor era. Furthermore, the musical languages of the Renaissance and of the major–minor era are sufficiently related to permit a thoughtful application of Schenkerian theory in order to illuminate aspects of Renaissance composition. Indeed, considering the exceptionally advanced nature of Schenker's theories, it would be most surprising if they were not able to contribute to the historical study of voice leading and musical structure.

Foreground, middleground, and background: their significance in the history of tonality

Saul Novack

One criticism of Heinrich Schenker's theories is that he chose to apply his formulated analytical procedures to the "masterworks" from Bach and Handel to Brahms. All other music, before and after, as well as including most significantly Richard Wagner, failed to meet his criteria, and therefore was relegated to a lower level of artistic achievement.

Central to Schenker's theoretical exposition, as expressed in *Free Composition*, is the concept of hierarchical structural levels, i.e., background, middleground, and foreground. In this brief essay I shall consider the significance of this monumental concept of levels in regard to the study of the history of tonality, tracing the role of these hierarchical levels from the emergence of tonality in polyphonic composition through tonality's historical course. This examination may help us to understand why Schenker chose to limit himself to a circumscribed period and to a relatively small number of composers. This broad overview and brief exposition is not, however, intended as a definitive answer to the historical problems surrounding Schenkerian studies. While the reader will find lacunae and generalizations, it is my hope that this essay will provide some insight into basic evolving changes in concepts of composition within the history of tonality, and that it will suggest paths for further study.[1]

Several remarkable characteristics of tonal order spring forth following the birth of polyphony: first, the supremacy of the octave and the fifth as simultaneities; second, the horizontalizations of these intervals through the motion of the upper voice against the sustained tone of the liturgical melody. While these two factors do not occur in the earliest stages, they are convincingly present in a number of examples from the twelfth century. Further, some examples from the School of Compostela reveal the once "consonant" fourth yielding frequently to the third which, in turn, becomes the principal passing tone in the outlining of the fifth.[2] The

---

1. The first systematic overview of the development of triadic tonality during the Middle Ages and the Renaissance was undertaken by Felix Salzer in his imaginative study *Sinn und Wesen der abendländischen Mehrstimmigkeit* (Vienna, 1935). This innovative work, springing from Schenkerian principles of voice leading, paved the way for future studies.

2. For greater detail, see my analysis of the setting of *Benedicamus Domino*: Saul Novack, "The Analysis of Pre-Baroque Music," in *Aspects of Schenkerian Theory*, ed. David Beach (New Haven, 1983), p. 120. Regarding the fourth, it is to be noted that theory lags behind

treatment of each tone, in succession, sets up a series of miniature prolongations. Linear connections between these units are dependent upon
fortuitous relationships between the tones of the polyphonized liturgical
chant. A hierarchical level beyond the foreground is hardly more than a
clarification of foreground activity. This wholly foreground process is
elaborated and expanded in the organa of the School of Notre Dame.[3]
The generative force of the sustained liturgical tones causes the units
of prolongation to be much longer. As many as three voices – duplum,
triplum, and quadruplum – share in the prolongations through voice
exchange and the mutual filling-in of the octave and fifth. A further remarkable facet of the new concept of prolongation is the role of the lowest
voice. Occasionally the "upper" voices, in the durational values of the
rhythmic modes, dip down below the level of the cantus to capture for the
moment the role of supporting lowest voice, thus allowing two successive
units to be prolonged as a unified chord at such times when the successively different tones of the cantus would have prevented a single prolongation. The foreground, even as successive units, cannot be understood in such cases without a basic hierarchical level.[4]

These small dimensions are succeeded by other genres of the thirteenth
and fourteenth centuries wherein the spatial units are defined through
emerging principles of motion and direction. Such units were identified
and delineated through two media: poetry and dance. Even in the mono-
phonic chanson of the trouvère the principle of repetition creates a sense
of spatial identity by means of poetic organization. For example, the
rondeau with its recurrent refrain ultimately leads in frequent usage to
the *ouvert* and *clos* (similar to first and second endings) of the virelai and
ballade and their Italian counterparts. Dance compositions are even more
forceful in the shaping of space because of the physical dance-created
patterns, normally balanced in duple groupings. Such recurrent rhythmic
patterns cause the spatial identities to be filled in with design motives.

Polyphonic compositions using the poetic forms reveal further develop-
ments of structural unity. Both French and Italian fourteenth-century examples show motions that tend to outline a descending fundamental line
in the top voice which, together with lowest voice activity, clearly identify
tonality through direction toward definite terminal points, embracing as
well the already established penultimate leading tone. The shaping of the
foreground is quite clear, but is at times difficult to separate from the
newly emerged fundamental line, which is very close to the foreground.
While this line may occur internally, and more than once, it appears most
frequently at the conclusion of the final unit. The development of various

practice, for it was not until the late fifteenth century that theorists, e.g., Tinctoris, began
to recognize a fourth as a dissonance.
3. See Salzer, "Tonality in Medieval Polyphony," in *The Music Forum*, Vol. 1 (New York,
1967), pp. 35–98, with particular attention to p. 45. While Graphs 2a, 2b, and 2c theoretically represent different levels, they are so close to one another as to constitute the
feasibility of clear representation in only one graph.
4. See *ibid.*, for examples by Perotinus: Example 13 shows voice exchange; Examples 9 and
10 show the exchange of outer voices.

techniques to intensify tonal prolongations includes, but is not restricted to, the most obvious usage of the varied leading-tone chord at cadences. At such cadences, however, it is important to note the descent of the uppermost voice to the leading tone as an *inner* voice, a practice continued and refined throughout the history of triadic tonality. Occasionally, in the *ouvert–clos* setting, the principle of interruption appears for the first time, resulting in a clear inner form.[5] Poetic order tends to create strongly unified outer form: the varied endings of a repeated section may be emphasized by a corresponding leading-tone chord (or even a true dominant) and tonic chord; a similar emphasis may be found at the endings of the A and B sections of a trecento madrigal. In such compositions the coincidence of design space and structural space is most important. Foreground techniques have become more refined and controlled, and the outer-design form created by the force of poetic order is joined by tonal order, as described above. The tonal divisions frequently are accompanied by structural divisions which rely primarily on the motion of the lowest voice, less often assisted by an upper fundamental line. The latter, as we have noted, tends to descend most often at the end of the composition, and thus does not have a connection to outer form.

The Renaissance ushers in a clarity of tonal order that is characterized by a number of features. Chief among them is the emergence of the frequent use of harmonic motions which go beyond the use of dominant–tonic at cadences. The transparent triadic motions found in Dunstable, Dufay, and their contemporaries are fortified by prolongations of the dominant with their own spatial identities. Descending lines in the superius outline the octave, fifth, or third, such motions often being repeated within the work.[6] These repeated motions occasionally lead to genuine middlegrounds which shed light on the organization of the tonal structure. Any background has no relevance to the spatial disposition. Design repetition develops rapidly in the latter part of the fifteenth century, especially in the case of its first master, Jacob Obrecht. This is particularly evident in his numerous settings of the Mass, which thus contribute to the creation of spaces delineating boundaries for tonal prolongations. It is interesting to note that some sections in the Mass – the Kyrie, Osanna, and Agnus Dei, all having very brief texts – are in effect among the first examples of absolute music, devoid of textual causality. Connections form-

5. For an example of the motion into the leading tone as an inner voice see Salzer, *Structural Hearing* (New York, 1952; reprint edns, 1962, 1982). In Example 532, *Plus Dure*, a virelai by Machaut, has this motion at both the close of Part A and the *clos* ending of Part B, as shown in the reductions on pp. 332 and 333 of Vol. 2. This example is also a very early illustration of the principle of interruption. The final reduction, a background, achieved without any significant middleground, explains the clear outer form.
6. For examples, see Dunstable, *O Rosa Bella*, in *Historical Anthology of Music*, ed. Archibald T. Davison and Willi Apel (Cambridge, Mass., 1950), Vol. 1, No. 61, pp. 65–66, and Dufay, *Alma Redemptoris Mater* (the superius paraphrase version of the Antiphon setting), *ibid.*, Vol. 1, No. 65, pp. 70–71. In the latter example the falling line in the superius fills in the octave, c^2–c^1, descending stepwise, e.g., measures 7–22, 25–43, 45–60, etc. Each descent involves harmonic support, including V–I.

ing a unified whole, particularly in the case of the three-fold Kyrie, are achieved primarily through the force of the lowest voice. The middle-ground, though quite incomplete, reveals the overall unity.[7]

Repetition and motivic elements of larger durational span begin to appear. There are distinct prolongations which reflect organization and subdivision of text into musical units with occasional motivic profiles. Thus the inner life of the foreground has become more significant in the large-scale Mass and motet. In spite of the force and effect of the frequently controlling cantus firmus, the composer either took advantage of it for tonal prolongations through groupings and divisions of the melody, or contradicted it through the polyphony. The latter is the case in Josquin's *Missa L'Homme Armé Super Voces Musicales*, in which the chanson tune as cantus firmus is projected successively in each movement on a different tone while the polyphonic setting remains D Dorian-Aeolian throughout. The prolongations are strengthened by expanding harmonic factors, including the use of successive fifths.[8] Middleground progressions encompass larger foreground dimensions, and at times several middleground levels are necessary to explain the events. The falling fundamental line appears on the foreground level for internal units, thus creating inner forms, but not with predictability or consistency. The falling fundamental lines of the outer forms are almost always still crowded into the concluding measures. Then, too, modal considerations frequently result in suggestions of background that do not outline the structural line of the triad, or any part thereof. They are not always harmonically supported, nor do they necessarily terminate on the first degree, especially when conditioned by the plagal form of the mode. The background, limited as it is, sheds light on some facets of the polyphonic treatment of modes.[9]

Following the period of Josquin and his contemporaries, the sixteenth century produced a diversity of genres and practices. Generalized observations can be made, but they have many exceptions and variations. Design techniques become more complex, especially as cultivated by composers such as Gombert, who concentrated on unrestrained successive "points of imitation." This caused the design procedure to dominate, weakening the boundaries of inner form through textual and imitative overlappings, and resulting in far less effective tonal prolongations.[10] The

---

7. In Novack, "Fusion of Design and Tonal Order in Mass and Motet: Josquin Desprez and Heinrich Isaac," in *The Music Forum*, Vol. 2 (New York, 1970), see the discussion on pp. 219–20. Example 12 illustrates the connective force of the lowest voice in achieving structural continuity between sections of inner units of Josquin's *Missa Pange Lingua*.
8. For a number of examples of harmonic usage, see Novack, "Tonal Tendencies in Josquin's Use of Harmony," in *Josquin des Prez, Proceedings of the International Josquin Festival-Conference,* ed. Edward E. Lowinsky in collaboration with Bonnie J. Blackburn (London, 1976), pp. 317–33.
9. See the study of the motet, *Miserere mei, Deus,* in Novack, "The Fusion of Design and Tonal Order," pp. 251ff. The descending line of Pars III, especially as realized in the final reduction, helps to explain the plagal form of the setting of the motet in the Phrygian mode.
10. A readily available example by Gombert is the motet, *Super Flumina,* in *Historical Anthology of Music,* Vol. 1, No. 114, pp. 118–20.

later masters of Mass and motet, especially Palestrina, Lasso, and Byrd, curbed such excesses *and* sought greater balance in the use of multilinear repetition and tonal organization. In their settings, foreground units are more connected, and middlegrounds reveal harmonic connections of foreground prolongations. Harmonic frameworks for entire compositions do occur. A careful study of foreground and middleground of this period exposes the widespread misunderstanding of the so-called contrapuntal art of the sixteenth century – above all, the style of Palestrina.[11]

The later madrigal is a heightened dramatic vehicle within which structure unfolds on an adventurous path, following sensitive response to the meaning of the text. Musical–textual phrase repetitions, also conditioned by word meaning, are more extensive, varied in contrasting registers and pitch. Foreground becomes more fascinating through the use of motivic intervals tied to the word. Middleground, frequently related to the organization of the text, assumes greater significance. All these tendencies are brought to a high point in Monteverdi.[12] The descending structural tones of the background's top voice are frequently postponed to the end, the tension mounting in some cases with a lengthy prolongation of the penultimate dominant – a truly dramatic realization. The clarity of bass motion, harmonically directed and rhythmically emphasized, further intensifies the inner divisions – not at all surprising in the light of contemporaneous cultivation of ground basses such as the passamezzo and romanesca. The early seventeenth century thus begins to reveal the roles of tonality in its relation to thematic design, and in the creation of both inner and outer form.

Of the various genres that developed and flourished in the seventeenth century, we shall first consider the dance suite (especially the suite for keyboard). In each of the individual movements the design is usually divided into two parts, each terminating with a cadence, and each part repeated. In the earlier stages the details of abundant ornamentation and affect tend to obscure foreground voice leading. Middleground offers few clues to the significant outline of the tonal structure. Background does not have convincing meaning; it does not have sufficient coincidence with design divisions. The development is uneven, but ultimately acquires motivic–thematic character and structural clarity. The suite gradually becomes a collection of dances with complete realization of two-part form

11. See Novack, "Tonality and the Style of Palestrina," in *Music and Civilization: Essays in Honor of Paul H. Lang*, ed. Edmond Strainchamps and Maria Rika Maniates in collaboration with Christopher Hatch (New York, 1984), pp. 428–43. For additional analyses see Felix Salzer and Carl Schachter, *Counterpoint in Composition* (New York, 1969). The examples are found in Chapter 10, "Voice-leading Techniques in Historical Perspective." The entire chapter is a valuable contribution.

12. For a detailed study of a madrigal see Salzer, "Heinrich Schenker and Historical Research: Monteverdi's Madrigal *Oimè, se tanto amate*" in *Aspects of Schenkerian Theory*, pp. 135–52. Examples 8 and 10 are of special interest in regard to the extended penultimate dominant and the final descent. Salzer demonstrates a striking feature of this work: the important interval of the third as the embracing motive springing from the expressive opening word, "oimè," is seen as an integrative force on both foreground *and* middleground levels. Schenker's principle of diminution prevails!

in which design and structure are entirely integrated. By the time of J. S. Bach, the background's fundamental line and harmonic order fully reflect the two-part form. In the suites of Bach, the shapes of the critical divisions of the dances, as well as the subdivisions, are defined by motivically derived voice leading, as seen in the foreground. These divisions, most notably at the beginning of the B section, are highlighted most often by the *Kopfmotiv* of the mono-rhythmic design – a feature which has significant relevance to the ultimate development of the sonata-allegro procedure. There are other occasionally observed foreground events which in expanded forms are seen in middleground levels of the later sonata-allegro.

In the late Baroque the various and quite different procedures create unique possibilities for organic unities as are revealed by middleground and foreground. Also, the fundamental line of the background is spaced quite differently in the various genres. In some of the preludes of the *Well-Tempered Clavier*, especially in Book I, the middleground reveals the new and important role of the obligatory register and the registral shifts of the fundamental tones in creating inner form.[13] The nature and role of the post-structural coda is also identified in new and significant ways. In the unaccompanied string suites and sonatas of J. S. Bach, for example, the foreground is characterized by the intensive use of the technique of unfolding, a stylistic feature of much of Bach's instrumental and vocal music.

Bach's chorale settings are, as a whole, a fascinating reflection of the old and the new. While much attention has been given to them for the valuable study of voice-leading techniques and foreground procedures, the melodies are frequently problematic. Many of them have a long history, stemming from modal sources other than major or minor; there are frequent deviations from the structural norms implicit in triadic tonality. Bach's varied treatment of such melodies attempts to draw them into the major–minor structural orbit without necessarily contradicting their melodic "modal" character. In some cases the mode is preserved in the polyphonic totality. Some of the chorales, as interpreted by Schenker and others, do lead to middlegrounds and backgrounds.[14] In the majority of cases, however, the tonal structures of individual phrases or groups of phrases, while convincing, are in effect successive rather than governed by an overall background. This is especially true of a descending fundamental line in a melody that reflects a governing triad. Here, too, the ultimate descent frequently occurs in the last phrase. This kind of fundamental line, therefore, does not reflect an outer form in any way. On the other hand, the middleground provides insight into the nature of some of

13. See Schenker's analysis of the Prelude No. 1 in C major in his *Five Graphic Music Analyses*, pp. 36–37.
14. See *ibid.*, pp. 32–33, for Schenker's analysis of the complete chorale, "Ich bin's, ich sollte büssen." The melody lends itself to a fundamental line and harmonic support. The chorale is only twelve measures in length, and divided into two parts, equal in length, with the second part a variant of the first. The sixteenth-century melody is clear-cut Ionian.

the successive units of the foreground and their interrelationships. It is in the chorale preludes and chorale cantata settings that Bach was able to transcend the restrictions of the *cantus prius factus*, capturing structural unity through compositional inventiveness.

Appreciation of the greatness of Bach's fugues suffers from the attention given to the categories of procedures, since traditional analysis is limited to design and surface description. Schenker and others have demonstrated the importance and relevance of all the hierarchical levels that not only expose the reality of structural form, but also indicate the conditions that are unique to any particular fugue – the events arising out of the shape and character of the fugue subject itself.[15] We thus have reached a stage in the history of the structure of triadic tonality in which the relationship of the various levels to each other is so intimate that a full comprehension of *all* the hierarchical levels – background, middleground(s), and foreground – is required for an understanding of compositional processes.

The sonata-allegro procedure – so-called sonata form – is the most extended and fascinating example of organic tonal structure. Much attention has been given to it in Schenkerian analysis, and understandably so. Each of the divisions – exposition, development, recapitulation – has characteristic features that are reflected in foreground and middleground levels. In the largest sense, the background is closely tied to these divisions, most often projecting in one of several ways the principle of interruption as a structural form-creating procedure. Both foreground and middleground reveal envelopes or enclosures of complete unities that frequently mirror the background. In the exposition, the initial theme, or first thematic group, is frequently organized in a closed harmonic progression fused with a complete fundamental line for this unit of inner form. The second thematic group often has within itself a contained area characterized by a complete harmonic prolongation with its own subsidiary line, as 3 2 1 or 5 4 3 2 1 motion within the dominant or, less frequently, the mediant. Such subsidiary envelopes – examples of structural diminution – are particularly characteristic of Haydn, Mozart, and a good deal of Beethoven.

The development section becomes a fascinating area for large-scale prolongation, and its representation in middleground and foreground abounds in motivic diminutions. The importance of the study of the foreground character of the development section must be emphasized. It is much too easy to deal with this large-scale prolongation, e.g., of either the dominant or a motion from the mediant to the dominant, in a perfunctory way. The relationship of the design – both thematic and motivic

15. See the study by Schachter of the B♭ major Fugue from Book I of the *Well-Tempered Clavier*, in *The Music Forum*, Vol. 3 (New York, 1973), pp. 237–69. This important study reveals how the myriad details of design that characterize fugue composition only come to life through their intertwining relationship with foreground voice leading and, ultimately, with the middleground. The spatial entities of exposition, episodes, middle entries, and the like take on vital meaning through their fusion with tonal structure.

– to the paths of motion should be a major concern of analysis. Beethoven especially demonstrates the coordination of design changes at critical points in the tonal motion. The changes in thematic material, texture, mode, motive, and even orchestral color are not matters of chance unrelated to structural morphology. Middleground reductions do not necessarily reveal the details of such changes, yet they are significant guides to large-scale features of prolongation. The dynamic character of the development is perceived primarily in foreground events. The sometimes frequent and rapid "modulations" that are reflected in the foreground as transient prolongations must be evaluated contextually. It is the middleground that provides the understanding of the basic motion and direction. It thereby becomes an important object of study in observing the rapid expansion of tonality from the time of Haydn and Mozart well into the succeeding century.

The background is not to be taken for granted. In the sonata-allegro the principle of interruption explains the large-scale relationships of the three sections. The positioning of the tones of the fundamental line in the recapitulation is extremely important, reflecting, in comparison with the exposition, the necessary alterations of tonal space. The recapitulation, in its struggle between parallelism and alteration, becomes more fascinating than the exposition.[16] The middleground and foreground provide the explanation for the spacing of the fundamental line and its harmonic framework.

It is no wonder that Schenker chose so many compositions from the Classic era. The complete envelopes of structural unities, that is, the perfection of inner form, is demonstrated amply in his analyses of complete movements, especially those from works by Beethoven. Beyond the so-called Classic era, the composer most singled out by Schenker for examples on all levels is Chopin. There are several analyses of complete pieces in *Free Composition*. The larger share of these are etudes and mazurkas, for reasons that may be self-evident. The etudes, while mono-motivic (as are most of the preludes of Bach), are internally well-ordered, frequently with symmetrical phrases and repetitions. Fused with corresponding harmonic progressions, these spaces become identifiable, thus creating inner form, the units of which often reveal features of prolongation that can be represented on the middleground level. In the broader framework, the etudes are usually divided into three large "parts," almost totally dependent upon structural events. The mazurkas have a different character. Multi-sectional, with no set pattern of division, these fifty-eight works offer a multitude of examples of structural order. In *Free Composition* Schenker draws on many examples from no fewer than seventeen mazurkas, providing graphs for six complete pieces. The divisions of design into complete internal units, frequently with enclosed structures – especially in the opening recurrent refrain section – illustrate

---

16. See Roger Kamien, "Aspects of the Recapitulation in Beethoven," in *The Music Forum*, Vol. 4 (New York, 1976), pp. 195–235.

complete small-scale Classical structures, often with interruption and/or repetition within the inner forms. The prolongations within each of the enclosed units are varied foreground examples of developed techniques of chromaticism viewed against their own diatonic inner-form structure. Design units as middle sections are subordinate to the refrain sections, understood only through the middleground levels which, in turn, illuminate the diminutions seen in the foreground. Such diminutions in some cases even spring from the background. Thus unusual examples of mixture and chromaticism permeate the levels of middleground and foreground against a Classically oriented concept of spatial divisions. The background and middlegrounds reflect the coordination and fusion with the design divisions.

In §266 of *Free Composition* Schenker calls attention to the general decline of diminution concurrent with the genius for diminution exhibited by Schubert, Mendelssohn, Chopin, and finally, Brahms – "with his own special mode of diminution." Schenker criticizes Wagner as one who turned away from diminution to make expressiveness his guiding principle of music. We should realize that dramatic unities may provide boundaries or enclosures which *may* serve to identify musical unities, just as the aria in earlier music is a textual, emotional, and musical unit. In Wagner, especially after *Lohengrin*, the musical unities often tend to be very long. We are not aided by purely musical contents, such as repetitions and/or groupings of design factors, in finding the possible bases for structural units. There are some, to be sure, and analysis provides revealing facets of small-scale organic structure. For the most part, however, design elements do not assist in furnishing the clues to voice leading beyond the immediate surface level of the music. To a considerable extent the motivic life which generates the voice leading provides a fascinating foreground as an outgrowth of expressiveness. Inner form, with its own contained *Ursatz*, does not appear systematically. The middleground levels are there, primarily as explication of the chromatic process. There may be backgrounds, but for the most part they are not related to spatial identities. It is possible that the problems posed in identifying spatial units, with their own subdivisions into inner forms, and inner forms within these inner forms, constitute an important reason for Schenker's rejection of Wagner. Yet the reduction of highly chromatic surfaces do lead in Wagner (and in others) to foreground exposition. The reduction to the next hierarchical level also has an important purpose: the search for a diatonic "background" as explication for the contrapuntal-harmonic chromaticism. But in so many cases this method, valuable as it may be, may not constitute a true process for realizing ultimate levels that are *structural* in function and meaning.

The study of the hierarchical levels is essential to the understanding of the historical development of structural form and structural style. For this purpose, the collective interrelationships must be examined especially in regard to two factors: first, diminution, the importance of which cannot be overestimated; second, the diatonic–chromatic expansion leading ultimately to the attenuation of triadic tonality. The study of the background as conceived by Schenker must go beyond the recognition of the *Ursatz*. The spatial positions of the degrees in the fundamental line, as well as the fundamental bass motion, are intimately related to the form of the composition. The middleground in itself provides the clues to the interrelationships of the inner forms, one to another, as well as to the outer form. The number of middleground levels required to move to the foreground has relevance to diminution, and also explains the transformation of diatonicism to chromaticism, the details of which are revealed in the foreground. The foreground is, indeed, the important level of detail in regard to the individual units which Schenker calls "transference of forms of the fundamental structure," as well as to the various techniques which help shape the hidden repetitions. It is important to grasp the manner whereby these techniques, described in detail by Schenker, arise out of motive and theme, conditioning the directions and diminutions that in extension are explainable through middleground study. The style of the foreground is in part conditioned by the medium of performance. In *Free Composition*, Schenker states that "organic coherence. . .underlies the art of orchestration and the treatment of instruments in chamber music. In the masterworks, orchestral colors are not mixed according to whim and applied at random; they are subject to the laws of the whole."[17] Thus, the shaping of foreground prolongations, possibly reflected in the middleground, leans heavily on the medium, e.g., piano sonata, string quartet, symphony, etc. Relatively recent studies have demonstrated the effect of poetry on the structure of nineteenth-century lieder. Historical study reveals the intimate relationship of medium to foreground and the changing shapes that evolve. Particularly critical is the gradual emergence of idiomatically instrumental writing in contrast to the *voces aequales* style of the sixteenth century.

I have tried to outline in a general sense some of the changes in the nature and significance of the structural levels in the history of triadic tonality. In conclusion, I wish to emphasize some salient points.

In the early stages of polyphony, foreground alone usually explains the events. When another level is projected, it serves primarily as clarification. Interest is centered on the level closest to the music. The attainment of a true lowest voice with linear shape and direction is to be seen as a primary achievement.

Identity of units also begins to take place, especially through the forces of poetry and dance. Falling top-voice lines mirror in small dimensions the conditions that ultimately ripen into fundamental lines. From the late Medieval era through the Renaissance units of inner form are diversely identified. The design factors and word factors that create these identities

17. Schenker, *Free Composition*, pp. 7–8.

are increasingly identified by tonal prolongations that now draw as well upon the newly-emerged fifth relationship in the lowest voice – the new harmonic force, the dominant. Our interest is focused on these intensifications which can be seen as foreground events, with another hierarchical level, not far removed, that occasionally illuminates early forms of diminution conditioned by the limited range of the uppermost voice.

Quasi backgrounds reflecting Schenkerian concepts of stepwise descent in the upper voice, supported by a governing tonal unity in the lowest voice, appear in the Renaissance. But there are difficulties, especially in sacred music – governed as it is by the force of the text – both in Mass and motet. These backgrounds do not usually have spatial relevance to the succession of musical–textual units. The successive compositional procedures make it difficult to find an "outer form" which a true background would express.

During the Baroque era the cultivation of design factors and the refinement of their relationships to both inner and outer structural forms mature in Bach and Handel. Now the background is intimately related to inner form.

The changes leading to the Classic era result in the refinement of space and inner and outer form:

1. Backgrounds, with their fusion of fundamental line and bass arpeggiation in the articulation of the tonic–dominant–tonic phenomenon, are spaced in the steps of their motion to correspond to the motivic and thematic divisions of the design – achieving a perfect balance of design division and structural division.

2. The high art of diminution, integrating the hierarchical levels into an organic coherence of extended form, is achieved in a variety of ways intimately related to outer form. The principle of interruption frequently plays a vital role in the shaping of the background's illumination of the structure of outer form.

3. The balance of inner form and outer form compels the analytical process to concentrate attention on all levels, each one serving its purpose in the delineation of what can be called the "Classical ideal."

It is apparent that this Classical ideal goes beyond Beethoven, embracing as well so much of the music of Schubert, Chopin, Mendelssohn, Schumann, and Brahms, among others. Thus, I feel that we must revise our concept of the nineteenth century. Romanticism as the term identifying this period is not applicable to the structural Classicism of these composers. Simultaneously, there are other creative threads and aesthetic goals that are proper to the concept of Romanticism. Perhaps we should not *strive* to find in truly Romantic music backgrounds that accord consistently with Schenker's principles. In agreement with Schenkerian theory, interest would be concentrated primarily on foreground events, with middleground clarification. One would expect that the increasing complexities of chromaticism characterizing the fin-de-siècle styles would require several levels of middleground to explain tonal expansion. This multi-level middleground activity is sometimes difficult to uncover and is frequently not convincing. Furthermore, it does not usually lead to a background that has spatial and outer-form significance. At best, and rewardingly, it can reveal the beauty of diminution.

We must recognize that Schenker presented us with a formidable view of the phenomenon of music through the notion of levels. The concepts of a hierarchical order which can be explained only through the reductive process is in itself a monumental contribution by Schenker. All art music, from the beginnings of polyphony to the present day, has varying forms of hierarchical levels, the nature and character of which in each case must be generated from the matrix governing the compositional concept.

The history of triadic tonality, from the beginnings of polyphony until more recent times, may be represented in the form of an arch which, beginning in the foreground events of the twelfth century, represents a gradual ascent to a stage whereby interest is focused on middleground as well, though a significant background may not as yet exist. The next stage embraces a definitive background level, the characteristics of which are first seen in foreground events. This background, in its refinement, reveals a fusion of structural form and design form, this balance permeating all levels, now articulated by the organic force of diminution. The apex of this arch occurs in the Classic era as described above – a period of continuous development from Haydn to Brahms. Somewhere during this period the arch begins to descend, reflecting the lessening of these forces because of other conditions in the nineteenth century. At this time we see two streams flowing simultaneously, occasionally converging and mixing. This concurrent "Romantic style" directs attention to the levels more immediate to the surface of the music. While hierarchical levels still exist, as they must, the balance is gone. The background is less focused on the character of the *Ursatz*, as it is expounded by Schenker. There are many exceptions, of course, as have been demonstrated in a number of analyses, but they do not represent the main currents.

Finally, we should recall the remarks made by Schenker on the importance of orchestration and the use of instruments. In calling attention to the intimate relationships of such factors to structural order, we stress that thematic–motivic and other design factors are closely related to structural events as well. They condition these events which, in turn, are molded by structural necessities. Design and structure have worked together intimately to create spatial identities in various ways in the history of triadic tonality, creating thereby the organic coherence of inner forms and outer form. The formative interrelationships of design and structure are observable on foreground, middleground, and background levels. No true history of triadic tonality can afford to ignore their basic interdependency, the nature of which is revealed through the hierarchical structural levels.

Introduction

The studies presented in this section all include Schenkerian analyses of musical works. In each essay, however, analysis is placed in a larger framework, and a specific theoretical issue is addressed. Thus David Loeb examines the special problems associated with the analysis of dual-key movements; Larry Laskowski considers the issue of form and its relationship to voice leading; and Roger Kamien, in tracing the use of the Neapolitan sixth chord in several works of Mozart, shows how Schenkerian analytic techniques can contribute to the study of style. Concentrating on a single work of Mozart, Eric Wen points to the subtleties expressed through enharmonic transformation on several structural levels. Patrick McCreless's essay on chromatic tonicization demonstrates the analytic strength of Schenker's approach to chromaticism. Charles Burkhart illustrates the relation between text and unusual musical structure as seen in two Schumann songs, and Carl Schachter discusses the important question of analytic alternatives.

The first years of this decade have seen a considerable increase in Schenkerian analytical studies.[1] Many more such studies have appeared recently, and again these include some that were presented as papers at the 1985 Schenker Symposium and were subsequently published or scheduled for publication elsewhere. This is the case with David Beach's study of the Adagio and Arioso of Beethoven's Sonata, Op. 110,[2] Allen Cadwallader's essay on several late piano works of Brahms,[3] and Harald Krebs's paper on some tonally deviating Schubert lieder.[4] Unfortunately, Edward Laufer's valuable and stimulating presentation, "Interpolations and Parenthetical Passages," has not appeared in published form, nor was it possible to include it in this volume. No attempt will be made here to catalogue the many additional analytic studies that continue to appear regularly on the programs of conferences and symposia and find their way into print; it will suffice to mention the prominence given to Schenkerian analytic papers in two recent meetings – the 1986 Cambridge University Music Analysis Conference,[5] and the tenth annual meeting of the Society for Music Theory held in Rochester, New York, in 1987.[6]

The great rewards gained from a Schenkerian analytic study are matched by the musical and intellectual demands made on its readers, and these demands are often increased by the presence of specifically Schenkerian terms and symbols. A preparatory step for less experienced readers might be to consult one of the several extant glossaries. A pioneering glossary of the elements of musical notation, symbols, and abbreviations often found in graphic analyses was published by William J. Mitchell and Felix Salzer in the first volume of their series *The Music Forum*; it is accompanied by an analysis (of the theme of Mendelssohn's *Variations Sérieuses*) that illustrates the elements they define.[7] Several later publications also include glossaries of terms, giving English equivalents for Schenker's German terminology: Felix Salzer's reissue of Schenker's *Five Graphic Music Analyses*,[8] Larry Laskowski's annotated index to the musical works analyzed by Schenker,[9] and Ernst Oster's translation of *Free Composition*.[10] These lists of terms are supplemented by the prefatory material in these books; the editors' introductions to Schenker's *Harmony* and *Counterpoint* provide valuable information as well. In the past, readers turning to standard musical dictionaries found almost no entries on Schenkerian terminology; this changed with the appearance of *The New Grove Dictionary* in 1980. Outstanding among the articles that deal with Schenkerian theory is Ian Bent's "Analysis." It has recently been revised and issued separately in a book that includes a glossary of analytical terms by William Drabkin (revised and expanded versions of his *New Grove* entries).[11] The books and articles written to explain Schenker's theories have been fully catalogued in David Beach's series of bibliographic articles.[12] For specific areas, the references given in the articles of the present volume will lead the reader to important supplementary material.

Notes

(Selected bibliographic information on Schenkerian analytical studies)

1. See David Beach, "The Current State of Schenkerian Research," *Acta Musicologica* 57/2 (1985), p. 276; see also the listing, "Analytical Applications," on pp. 302–3, and the discussion, "Analytical Studies," on pp. 283–88. Cf. Beach, "A Schenker Bibliography," *Journal of Music Theory* 13/1 (1969), pp. 2–37, reprinted in *Readings in Schenker Analysis*, ed. Maury Yeston (New Haven, 1977), pp. 275–311; and "A Schenker Bibliography: 1969–1979," *Journal of Music Theory* 23/2 (1979), pp. 275–86.
2. A revision of Beach's paper is included in his article, "Motivic Repetition in Beethoven's Piano Sonata Op. 110, Part II: The Trio of the Second Movement and the Adagio and Arioso," *Intégral* 2 (1988), pp. 75–97. The first of his series of articles on Op. 110 appeared in the same journal's inaugural issue: "Beethoven's Piano Sonata Op. 110, Part I: The First Movement," *Intégral* 1 (1987), pp. 1–29.
3. Allen Cadwallader, "Foreground Motivic Ambiguity: Its Clarification at Middleground Levels in Selected Late Piano Pieces of Johannes Brahms," *Music Analysis* 7/1 (1988), pp. 59–91.
4. Harald Krebs, "The Background Level in Some Tonally Deviating Works of Franz Schubert," *In Theory Only* 8/8 (1985), pp. 5–18.
5. See Richmond Browne, "The 1986 Cambridge University Music Analysis Conference," *Journal of Music Theory* 31/1 (1987), pp. 165–71.

6. A special plenary session on the state of research in music theory was held at the meeting, as part of the Society's commemoration of its tenth anniversary. The first paper of the session was a report on Schenkerian theory by David Beach. The pamphlet distributed at the meeting, "The State of Research in Music Theory: A Collection of Selective Bibliographies," ed. Marie Rolf, will be published in revised form in *Music Theory Spectrum* 11/1 (1989).

7. "A Glossary of the Elements of Graphic Analysis," *The Music Forum*, Vol. 1 (New York, 1967), pp. 260–68.

8. Schenker, *Five Graphic Music Analyses*, pp. 23–26.

9. Larry Laskowski, *Heinrich Schenker: An Annotated Index to his Analyses of Musical Works* (New York, 1978), pp. xlviii–xlix.

10. Schenker, *Free Composition*, pp. 163–64. See also the supplementary volume of examples, p. viii, for a list of abbreviations used in the graphs.

11. Ian Bent, *Analysis* (London and New York, 1987).

12. In "The Current State of Schenkerian Research," pp. 275–76, Beach speaks of a decline in purely explanatory publications; such a focus was more characteristic of American writings of the 1930s and 40s. Several articles from that period have been reprinted under the title *Schenkerian Theory in America: The Early Introductory Articles* in *Theory and Practice* 10/1–2 (1985). Current British publications, however, show a concern for the explanation of broad issues, such as the nature of analysis itself. Many include discussions and explanations of Schenker's theories; see the bibliography appended to Jonathan Dunsby's article in the next section of the present book.

Dual-key movements

David Loeb

All of us strive to perceive compositions or movements as single unified tonal structures extending over an entire work, with details understood in the perspective of these structures. If a movement begins or ends in a key other than the main tonality, we view such passages simply as appendages to structures which still operate over nearly entire pieces. However when pieces begin and end in different keys such that neither key is understood as subsidiary to the other, then we must abandon our usual approach and seek a different kind of overall structure. The most frequent instances of such dual-key movements are recitatives, which we tend to dismiss as transitional. Very little analysis has been done of recitatives, other transitional movements, or dual-key movements which are not transitional. This last type is very rare, but the unique nature and special relationships of such movements teach us much about tonal organization within larger entities.

This study examines two examples by J. S. Bach: the recitative "Und siehe da" with the arioso "Mein Herz, indem die ganze Welt" from the St. John Passion, and the second movement of the Brandenburg Concerto No. 6. Just two examples are assuredly insufficient for making generalizations, but they will allow us to speculate on what an examination of a larger number of pieces might prove.

Let us first consider the recitative and arioso separately. The recitative by itself would be understood in E minor. The descriptive downward rush in the bass represents the first tonic chord; it is followed by a Bb_3^6 (very dramatic even for a recitative), which is soon understood within IV (as the progression $bII^6-V_2^4-I^6$). This emphasizes the IV within the larger progression $I-IV^6-V_{4-3}^{6-5}-I$ in E minor, constituting the entire recitative after the opening V^6. There is no need to question this until one examines the arioso.

Even a hasty examination of the arioso reveals that we cannot consider it an independent entity. Although we initially interpret the G major chord of the first two measures as a tonic, that impression is gradually contradicted, despite the continuation of the pedal point. Viewing the next two measures as a typical use of IV within a tonic pedal point is questionable since the chord is C minor rather than C major. One begins to consider the possibility of V–I in C minor, especially at the end of measure 4 and the beginning of measure 5, where Bach seems to prepare another motion to C minor. However, the end of the pedal point provides neither this resolution nor a return to G major; instead we are surprised by a motion to D minor. The D minor chord moves to the final C major chord by a 5–6 motion, but even the presence of B♮ (rather than the diatonic B♭ of D minor) does not immediately clarify the harmonic status of the C major chord. Certainly it is not perceived as a tonic; the tentative earlier sense of C minor was effectively erased by the cadence to D minor. After a D minor cadence the most likely function for a C major chord would be V of F major, and this dominant possibility is of course confirmed by the first few notes of the following aria in F minor.

In view of the rather tenuous tonic status of the opening G and the even more tenuous dominant status of the final C chord, is it convincing to summarize the harmonic activity of this arioso as a typical transitional recitative? The change of tempo and texture with the arrival of D minor suggests that the piece will continue somewhat longer; one certainly does not expect it to end on the next downbeat. The sense of ending is further weakened by the ascending leap to G in the voice part, a most expressive way to set the question posed by the text. All of this is very different from the typical recitative, in which final cadences are perfectly clear in themselves, regardless of connections to what follows.

All these difficulties can be surmounted by considering the recitative and arioso together as a single transition from the preceding aria in D major to the succeeding aria in F minor. This reading is shown in detail and reduction in Examples 1a and 1b, in which the transition process is treated as an embellishment of an ascending series of 5–6 suspensions.

Example 1. Bach, St. John Passion, Recitative, "Und siehe da," and
　　　　　Arioso, "Mein Herz, indem die ganze Welt," with surrounding arias

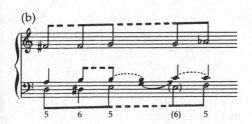

The preceding aria has a melodic structure of a descending third from F#. This tone is linked to the first F# in the recitative melody, which in turn coincides with the B in the inner voice providing the sixth of the first 5–6 motion. The bass D# is a chromatic passing tone tonicizing the following E minor chord. If the recitative is considered independently, the applied dominant has little importance, but as part of the larger sequence it attains greater emphasis.

From the E minor chord that extends over the remainder of the recitative, the 5–6 series should move to a C major $\frac{6}{3}$. This chord appears instead in root position, at the end of the arioso, and its resolution to F minor at the beginning of the following aria completes the soprano ascent to Ab and the bass ascent to F. Can the reading of a 5–6 series be justified if it takes the entire arioso to reach the C major chord, only to have it arrive in the wrong position?

I believe this reading can be justified; the explanation rests on the relationship of the arioso to the suspension series. The 5–6 series has five essential vertical sonorities, whose distribution is shown by the double bars in Example 1a. The first and last sonorities belong to the arias and the middle three to the recitative and arioso. The recitative takes up two of these middle sonorities; their V–I relationship in E minor provides the recitative's harmonic content and overall contrapuntal framework. The arioso therefore expresses only one sonority, the C major $\frac{6}{3}$. Harmonically this chord could certainly be prolonged as a single movement in C major; such would have been the prosaic choice, but this would have greatly lessened the transitional feeling of the movement. By inserting the G major chord and giving it some extent of tonic sense, Bach de-emphasizes C as a tonal center, and does so further by the brief motion to D minor. Thus the final C major chord is emphasized by a variety of factors: its position at the end, the connection with the return of the high G in the voice part, and its relationship to the following aria. All of these factors ensure our perception of its importance without giving it a tonic sense. The root position is a necessary consequence of its location at the end of the movement; while Bach provides us with many instances of movements ending on chords with a clear dominant function, I have yet to find one not in root position. Finally, I suggest that the arioso deserves its title only because of instrumental treatment and textures; the harmonic practice is far closer to the recitative tradition.

Let us now turn to the Adagio ma non tanto from the Brandenburg Concerto No. 6. Although this is an instrumental work, one cannot categorically rule out the possibility of a transitional function for this movement. Bach had precedents: Buxtehude's *Suonate a due*, Opp. 1 and 2 (published in Hamburg in 1696), of which several pieces contain transitional movements, in particular both Largo movements of Op. 2, No. 2. If Bach had not encountered these works before going to Lübeck, he almost certainly saw or heard them there.

Two empirical aspects suggest a transitional function is unlikely. First, the placement of the slow movement between two outer movements in the same key removes any harmonic necessity for a transition. Second, the use of fugal treatment tends to be associated with harmonic relationships dependent on tonal stability. Since the movement satisfies many of the requirements of a fugue we should begin by examining it in fugal terms.

The subject has ten entrances which can be grouped into three large sections. The first section includes four entrances alternating between the violas, with a harmonic order of tonic–dominant–dominant–tonic. Thus each viola plays both subject and answer, and the section as a whole is perceived as an exposition in E♭ major. Each entrance has the same accompanying bass line with slight changes in figuration. It should be noted that Bach chose a real answer in spite of the fact that a tonal answer is expected and could easily have begun in measure 4, whereas the real answer requires a delay until measure 5 in order to establish the dominant. One likely reason for this choice lies in the design of the subject. Example 2a is a graph of the subject emphasizing polyphonic construction in which the descent 5–4–3 is mirrored by a corresponding ascent 1–2–3. This relationship disappears in a tonal answer.

Example 2a. Bach, Brandenburg Concerto No. 6, second movement: the subject

The second section comprises four more statements of the subject, again alternating between the violas. As one expects, there is some divergence from the key areas of the exposition; the entrances are in C minor, F minor, E♭ major, and A♭ major. Our first impulse is to regard the C minor entrance as a typical motion toward the relative minor, but the E♭ on which that entrance should end (as 3 in C minor) is replaced by an E♮, the third of the dominant chord that prepares the next entrance in F minor. The following E♭ entrance might be thought of as a return to the tonic, but it does not seem to be heard as such. The tonal answer, which Bach avoided in the exposition, is used for the first time here. The entrance therefore begins on A♭ instead of B♭; this A♭ occurs in the context of the codetta following the F minor entrance, and consequently the tonicization of E♭ is limited to a brief moment at the end of the entrance. If conventional practice of motion to the relative key and back to the tonic is not followed here, then how should one understand this section?

One must first note that instead of grouping entrances in fours one can also consider them in pairs: E♭ major / B♭ major, B♭ major / E♭ major, C minor / F minor, and E♭ major / A♭ major. A codetta follows the second entrance of each pair, strengthening the key of that entrance. At first the ear does not perceive this pairing; the succession I–V–V–I can hardly be heard as anything other than a group of entrances within the tonic, followed by a codetta in the tonic, concluding the exposition. From this point the pairs take on greater significance. The C minor entrance is actually the answer to the succeeding F minor subject (as confirmed by its ending on V of F minor), and the next E♭ entrance is similarly an answer (that status being clarified by the use of the tonal answer) to the succeeding A♭ subject. Thus the second section of the fugue is harmonically defined by the key areas of F minor and A♭ major, which are of course relative keys.

This second section is followed by an episode – the only one in the movement (unless one insists on regarding the codettas as episodes). Certainly this is the only episode that performs the traditional function of moving from one key area to another. The motivic basis of the episode is the opening motive of the subject. This motive is stated in the bass line, which moves from A♭ major to G minor via F minor and C minor. One should note that Bach varies the tonal functions within the repetition; the last note of the motive, which is the leading tone of the next tonicized chord in the first statement, is the tonic itself in the second and third statements. In this way the sequence first moves down a third, and thereafter down in fourths. The last motive of the sequence becomes the beginning of the next entrance of the subject, although one cannot know this until one hears the second phrase of the subject (Bach uses this eliding procedure in other fugues, e.g., in the C minor Fugue from Book I of the *Well-Tempered Clavier*). This entrance is in G minor, and with it the last section of the fugue begins. Harmonically we have no immediate reason to attach any importance to the key area of G minor, and it is only through insistence that Bach forces us to regard it as something more than one more subsidiary key area within E♭ major. Bach prepares G minor dramatically by an episode which, in addition to being the only one in the movement, has a cello part that for the first time in the movement refrains from ornamenting the continuo line, thus drawing our attention to that voice. The entrance in G minor might be understood as an answer; indeed it begins as a tonal answer. But Bach follows it with a real entrance in the same G minor. Thus these entrances form another pair, again followed by a codetta which tonicizes G minor even more strongly. The codetta concludes with a contraction eliding the chord of resolution with a coda that remains in G minor. The final four measures move to the V of G minor, as if to suggest that the next movement might continue in that key.

All of this emphasis of G minor is necessary to counteract our expectation of a return to E♭ major, and to convince us that G minor really is the tonic key for the latter part of the movement, structurally equal to the opening key of E♭ major. If that becomes our perception of the harmonic structure of the movement, then the second section becomes a transition from E♭ major to G minor. For that reason F minor becomes a passing key area and might be given more weight than A♭ major.

We should now examine the graph of the entire movement, given in Example 2b. (The measure numbers given in the graph locate the ten entrances of the subject; the numbers in parentheses locate other elements of the fugal design, i.e., episode and coda). There is little need to discuss the bass line of the graph, since we have already considered harmonic factors and relationships.

Example 2b. Bach, Brandenburg Concerto No. 6, second movement

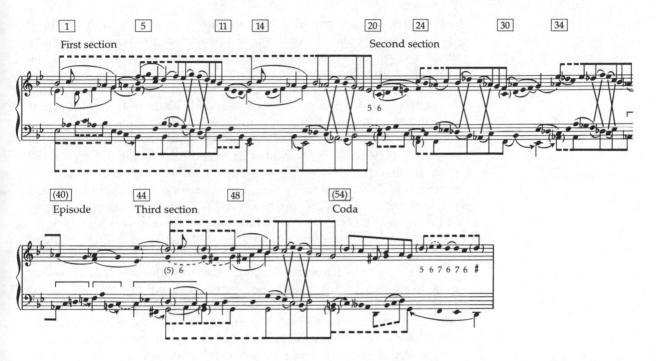

Certainly the most significant point revealed by examination of the melodic line is the relationship of the fugue subject and codetta to the structural descents. As can be seen in the graph, the descent from $\hat{5}$ in the subject never continues beyond $\hat{3}$, but after the second entrance of each pair Bach immediately returns to $\hat{5}$ and then descends to $\hat{1}$ within the codetta. This not only reinforces the harmonic significance of the statements of the codetta, but shows that they are indispensable for melodic reasons. It is of further interest to note that the five codetta statements tonicize the five principal tones of the subject in the order of their initial appearance.

I should mention several other interesting points. After the second entrance of the exposition, the descent from F to B♭ within B♭ major is typical of the dominant mid-point in binary structures, and helps to convey the sense of the exposition as a complete structure within E♭ major – a necessity, since there is no significant return to E♭ later. In three instances the melodic structure of the subject does not conform to the graph given in Example 2a. These are the C minor entrance and the two statements of the tonal answer; according to reasons already given one should not expect the same structure. The coda begins with a restatement of the structural descent in G minor, and in the final four measures ends with a suspension series quite unlike the rest of the movement. This series is present in several analogous endings on dominant chords (e.g., the Sonatas in A minor and C major for unaccompanied violin, the Sonata in G major for violin and harpsichord, and the Harpsichord Concerto in F minor).

The foregoing analysis does not attempt to explain why Bach chose such an irregular plan. I would suggest two reasons which are not mutually exclusive. First, let us consider again the location of structural descents and supporting progressions within the codetta statements. For the movement to have ended in Eb major, it would have been necessary to end with the subject and codetta again in Eb, which seems repetitive and unconvincing in comparison to the actual piece. A coda following this last statement of the subject could not have ended on Bb; confusion between V of Eb and I of Bb would have resulted. Second, the plan chosen has interesting harmonic connections with the outer movements. In the first movement, the last strongly tonicized key before the final tonic is Eb major, giving a possible connection to the beginning of the fugue. The last movement has a *da capo* form in which the middle section is mainly in G minor, starting on V of that key, possibly intended as an echo of the last chord of the fugue.

To these reasons I would add another more subjective one. It seems quite likely that Bach was intrigued by the unusual possibilities arising from uncommon types of relationships between movements. Some works have already been cited; to them I would add numerous instances of dual-key movements in cantatas, and also places in the B minor Mass in which movements end with passages serving as transition to the following movements. One particularly unusual case comes from the Sonata in F minor for violin and harpsichord, in which the harmonic aspect of the ending of the third movement does not seem to make much sense with respect to the following movement. The third movement is in C minor, but ends with a bass ascent to Ab major. The last movement begins in F minor with a fugue subject ascending from C to Ab, giving us a transition in which the bass line at the end of the third movement prepares the subject of the following fugue (see Example 3).

Example 3. Bach, Sonata in F minor for violin and harpsichord, third movement
(with opening of the fourth movement)

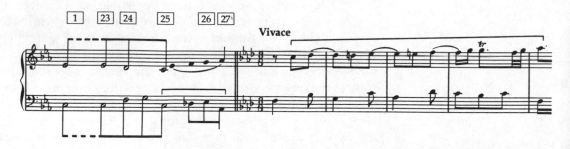

As stated at the outset, the number of examples examined thus far is insufficient to permit generalizing with confidence. I would say that as a rule one must look at other movements of the piece in any instance of a dual-key movement. I would also say that the main practical obstacle to understanding such movements is our usually correct assumption that everything which happens in a movement can be, and indeed must be related to one central key within a logical hierarchy. In dual-key movements one is often confronted with a tonal "no-man's land" between two clearly defined tonalities; this seems especially true in the Sixth Brandenburg Concerto. The problem is particularly difficult in longer movements.

I will conclude by observing that examples from the Classic or Romantic repertoire are very few in comparison to those found in the Baroque literature. Perhaps one can say that for Baroque composers the idea of a movement as an absolutely self-contained, discrete tonal entity was not entirely fixed, and that what we regard as movements in some works are rather sections of a larger entity. For now this is only a working hypothesis.

J. S. Bach's "binary" dance movements: form and voice leading

Larry Laskowski

Schenker's main contribution to music theory undoubtedly lies in his conception of tonal structure. His ideas about voice leading, however, have important implications for other aspects of music theory such as rhythm and form, for historical and stylistic studies, and for performance, composition, and pedagogy. One can hardly fault Schenker for failing to work through these implications completely, for, seen in historical context, his ideas about tonal structure represent a remarkable breakthrough which understandably required a lifetime of work and study. He did seem to realize the need for extensive revisions of traditional views of these areas in the light of his discoveries. For example, Schenker calls for new approaches to the teaching of music, though he does little more than suggest the general outlines of these revisions.[1] His ideas on performance can be found in many analyses and editions of individual works. Rhythm and form are discussed briefly in separate sections of *Free Composition*.[2] In part because of the circumstances which complicated the completion and publication of *Free Composition*, we should not take these discussions as full expositions of Schenker's thought, even though they did turn out to be his final published words on these subjects. (Schenker did intend to publish a separate volume on form after *Free Composition*, but the work never saw the light of day.) Now that Schenker's ideas have gained considerable understanding and acceptance it is important that we ourselves try to understand the implications of Schenker's view of tonal structure on other aspects of the field. Form and its relationship to voice leading is the subject of this study.

All too often, it seems, we view music in two distinct ways. We see it in terms of tonal structure, i.e., voice leading, and we see it in traditional formal terms. Sometimes it is easy to relate and reconcile the two views. For example, we can say that the development section of a certain sonata-form movement in a minor key is defined by a motion from $\overset{\hat{3}}{_{\text{III}}}$ to $\overset{\hat{2}}{_{\text{V}}}$, or that a second-theme area accomplishes a $\hat{3}$–$\hat{2}$–$\hat{1}$ structural descent in a second key. At other times, though, the two views remain separate, seeming to have little to do with each other, and sometimes, indeed, contradicting one another. We may suspect that the traditional formal view is in a way old-

1. For example, see Schenker, *Free Composition*, pp. xxii–xxiii.
2. *Free Composition*, pp. 118–45.

fashioned, and does not adequately deal with the organic relationships among the piece's formal sections, but, on the other hand, we may also, if we are honest with ourselves, admit that tonal structure alone often does not adequately account for some very striking formal features.

The analyst might have an easier time with sonata form, for a number of reasons:

First, the traditional formal sonata-form prescription was for a time so overly defined, so inflexible, that even to non-Schenkerians it had become incompatible with a large proportion of the works which it purported to describe. Revisions were introduced that made the formal prescription more flexible, less tied to themes, more closely linked to tonal events, and hence somewhat more compatible with Schenkerian principles.

Second, from the large number of Schenkerian studies of pieces in sonata form has evolved a relatively small number of voice-leading models, that is, ways in which background and earliest middleground structure can be seen in relation to the traditional formal design. Of course much work remains to be done in this area, and the many exceptional works in sonata form will continue to revise our thinking in the area. However, the basic groundwork has been laid, mostly by Schenker and Oster in *Free Composition*.[3]

Third, the large scale on which most sonata-form movements are composed seems to make experimentation with remote layers of structure more unlikely. If the piece is to hold together, the large-scale connections must be composed in a relatively clear way, and are often dramatically highlighted by stylistic factors as well. This is not to say that sonata-form movements are not challenging to the analyst, but only to suggest that in most cases certain large-scale connections can almost be taken for granted.

Traditional ternary form often expresses a voice-leading structure that has three relatively independent sections. The outer sections, and sometimes the middle section as well, often contain their own structural descents. Though again there is considerable room for variation, experimentation, and irregularities, the general tendencies remain.

Traditional binary form, however, is a broad category which can relate to tonal structure in any number of ways. I do not refer here to what Schenker calls two-part form in *Free Composition*. Schenker's discussion of form in *Free Composition* is fascinating but sketchy and, perhaps, somewhat problematic. Rather, I refer to the traditional binary form as typically found, for instance, in dance movements of the Baroque suite. I shall briefly discuss two such movements, the Menuet and the Sarabande, from the E major French Suite of J. S. Bach, first in terms of voice leading, and then in terms of the relationship between tonal and formal structures.

The Menuet (see Example 1), while it is short and seemingly rather simple, is not without its analytical challenges. The opening eight measures arpeggiate upward in the upper voice from $g\sharp^1$ to $g\sharp^2$, then move to

---

3. *Free Composition*, pp. 133–41.

the dominant with f#² on top, followed by a cadence in the dominant with a quick upper-voice descent from f#² to b¹. It is interesting to note that the upper voice's first move up from g#¹ is through a¹ to b¹; this motion represents a motive which is important throughout the E major French Suite. (See, for example, the very beginning of the Allemande.)

Example 1. Bach, French Suite in E major, Menuet

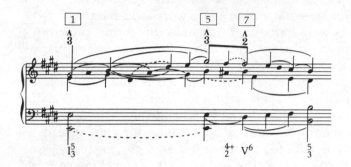

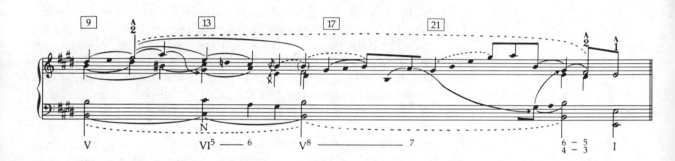

The second half of the Menuet begins on V with f#² on top. Over the course of this section, the upper voice falls an octave from f#² to f#¹ over a prolonged dominant. In the first eight measures (measures 9–16), the upper voice falls to b¹ as the bass completes a neighbor-note motion to and from VI. In the last eight measures the upper voice completes the octave descent f#²–f#¹ over the dominant by moving from b¹ to f#¹, followed, of course, by the final tonic. This descent begins with a motion from b¹ to a¹, which is a straightforward 8–7 over V. The right hand's quotation, in measures 17–18, of the Menuet's opening is a good example of reinterpretation of tonal material. The opening of the movement, felt mostly as a structural downbeat, with the first g#¹ stronger than the b¹ of measure 2, returns here with the feeling of an upbeat, with g#¹ leading to a stronger b¹. But even the opening, with its ascent up to g#² and silent left hand in measure 1, suggests a crescendo from a weaker first measure to a stronger fifth measure. This upbeat quality, built into the opening phrase, is what is brought to the fore in a new way in measures 17–18.

Measure 21 initiates a rising third-progression, G#–A–B, which is expressed as g#^{1}–g#^{2}–a^2–b^1. This third-progression is an upbeat to measure 23, where g# in the bass continues the upper-voice middleground descent from the a^1 of measure 20. This strong g# in the bass frees the upper voice to complete its motivically significant foreground ascent from g#^{2} through a^2 to b^1 (register displaced) by allowing the a^2, harmonized as the seventh of V, to move to b^1 in the right hand. The bass g# is then quickly transferred to the upper register, where it falls to f#^{1}, completing the octave descent f#^{2}–f#^{1}. This descent is followed by the final tonic, e^1. The unusual parenthetical ascending third G#–A–B in measures 21–23 is thus integrated into a descending motion from f#^{2} to f#^{1}. Its motivic significance is clear, as is its relationship to the rising motion from g#^{1}, heard at the opening and at measure 17. It also paves the way for the Bourrée (which follows in most editions), for the Bourrée begins with a similar arpeggiation up g#^{1}–b^1–e^2–g#^{2}, followed by a strong a^2. In the Bourrée the a^2 is in fact a neighbor note that resolves quickly back to g#^{2}. In the Menuet the a^2 of measure 22 is part of a passing motion to b^1, but Bach emphasizes the resemblance of the two passages by using b^1 instead of b^2 at measure 23 of the Menuet. Thus both passages have a^2 as the top of the phrase.

The Sarabande of this suite exhibits unusual structural features. The movement opens with a statement of the familiar G#–A–B motive in the upper voice (measures 1–5; see Example 2). As in the closing measures of the Menuet, the middle note, A, of this motive, is harmonized as the seventh of V^7, the resolution of which is transferred to the bass. The inner-voice substitution of d#^{1} for e^1 in measure 5 is extraordinarily beautiful, and avoids the vertical fifth b^1–e^1 in the right hand. The approach to this fifth would have been less than ideal; in addition, there would be the potential danger of parallels with the subsequent fifth f#^{1}–c#^{2} on the next downbeat. The inner-voice motion d#^{1}–e^1 helps to preserve the Sarabande's typical second-beat stress in a measure in which the harmony moves in quarter notes; it also relates to the bass's motion d#–e in measure 3.

Example 2. Bach, French Suite in E major, Sarabande

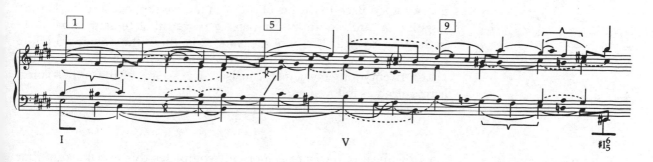

(*example continues on following page*)

Example 2 (*cont.*)

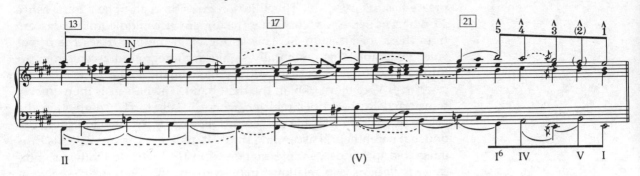

After completing the motion g#^{1}–a^1–b^1, the upper voice continues up
to c#^{2}, and then more quickly to e^2, forming a tonic arpeggiation g#^{1}–b^1–e^2
reminiscent of the Allemande and Menuet openings. The bass mean-
while moves to a#, causing the upper voice's e^2 to fall to d#^{2} over the
dominant. The subsequent 3̂–2̂–1̂ descent in the key of the dominant
brings the first part of the movement to a close.

The first part of the second half continues the ascent with accelerated
versions of the first half's upper voice. The motivic association of measures 11–12 with measures 1–2 suggests the structural connection shown in
the graph. The bass E# in measure 12 is a chromatic passing tone from the
movement's opening e to the F# in measure 13. The upper voice achieves
b^2 in measure 12, completing two nested statements of the G#–B motive:
a small one in measures 11–12, and a large one spanning measures 1–12
(this is shown in Example 3).

The $\frac{\hat{4}}{\text{II}}$ of measure 13, then, is connected to the opening $\hat{\overset{3}{1}}$. The intervening dominant is not a structural dominant, despite its placement at the
double bar, but rather a connecting chord between the opening tonic and
the altered tonic of measure 12.

Measures 13–16 represent a 3̂–2̂–1̂ descent in F# minor. Measures 17–20
move to a dominant chord, which represents a 5–6 motion c#^{2}–d#^{2} over
the stronger II chord of measures 13–16. The motive g#–a–b, this time with
a#, while contradicted by the voice leading, is certainly suggested in the
bass of measures 18–19. A desire to imitate this motive in measures 20–21
may have led Bach to the beautiful d♮ in the bass of measure 21. This d♮
disguises a tonic chord and initiates a powerful statement of g#^{2}–a^2–b^2
in the upper voice. The b^2 of measure 22 is, then, the opening 5̂ of the
fundamental line. The initial ascent, which spans twenty-two of the
piece's twenty-four measures, consists of g#^{1}–a^2–b^2 in the upper voice,
harmonized as follows:

$$\begin{matrix} \hat{3} & \hat{4} & \hat{5} \\ \text{I} & - \text{II}^{5\text{-}6} & - \text{I}^6 \end{matrix}$$

The downbeat of measure 22 not only completes this initial ascent, but
also begins another G#–A–B motion in the bass, which counterpoints the
fundamental line.

These two movements are especially interesting in that they exhibit striking similarities in design, and equally striking differences in voice-leading structure. A look at Example 3 shows that both movements are twenty-four measures long with a double bar and a cadence on the dominant after eight measures. Both movements are in triple time and can be divided into four-measure units. Thus in terms of traditional form the two movements are quite similar. But an examination of the voice leading reveals important differences. The fundamental line of the Menuet is distributed evenly over the movement, and the most obvious surface division, the double bar, plays a role in articulating the descent. In the Sarabande, a long initial ascent delays the appearance of the first tone of the fundamental line, and the dominant at the double bar is not part of the fundamental structure.

Example 3. Bach, French Suite in E major, Menuet and Sarabande

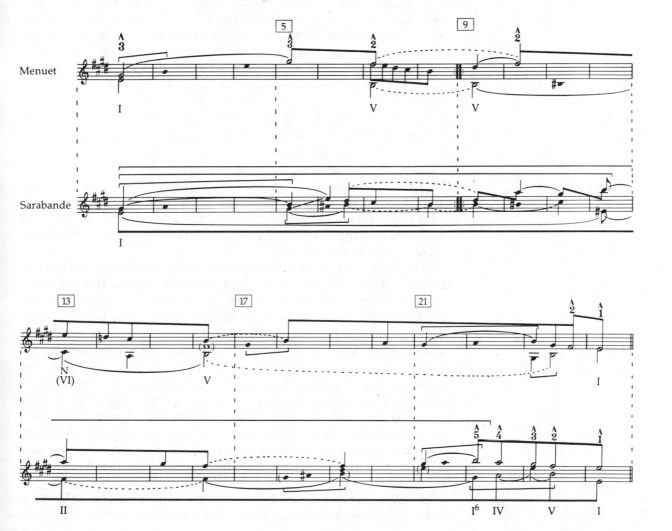

Schenker indicated that form is, at least in part, determined by voice leading, in particular by background and remote middleground levels. If this is so, it is hard to imagine how we can conclude that our two movements have the same form, despite their surface resemblance in formal terms. On the other hand, it does not seem appropriate to conclude that their resemblance is inconsequential, and that the movements are composed in entirely different forms. To develop formal categories based solely on remote levels of voice leading would dismiss many events (such as the double bar in the Sarabande) which clearly have formal significance even though they may not penetrate to the deepest levels of structure.

The dilemma stems, perhaps, from a one-dimensional concept of form itself. Schenker was able to show that traditional concepts of harmony were inadequate in that they considered only the surface of the music. In order to understand the meaning of a given chord in a piece, we must understand its place not only in the foreground, but also in the entire complex of structural levels. Only in understanding what one might call the "heritage" of a tonal event, its origins in the dimension of growth from remote to superficial structural levels, can a more complete understanding be achieved.

The same is true in considering the form of a piece, but Schenker's emphasis on the background in *Free Composition* might lead one to conclude that, for Schenker, form is determined simply and only by the deepest levels. But his dogmatic emphasis on background structure is in many cases not to be taken quite literally. It is not that the deepest levels of structure tell us everything in and of themselves, but rather that recognition of the existence of background structure reveals a crucial added dimension: the growth from background to foreground which forms the complex of structural levels, all of which, if accurately untangled, are part of the musical experience of the piece, and all of which must be taken into account in discussing the form.

After all, because every piece is based on a fundamental structure, on that level all pieces must be in one-part form. Schenker himself suggested that even in the background, the potential for division into parts is present in the bass arpeggiation, while the need to continue forward is present at all times in the fundamental line. Both of these forces are present in all structural levels, and it is the shifting balance between them, as the piece grows from background to foreground, which creates form. One might view these opposing tendencies in human terms: Each tone tries to assert itself as much as possible, to extend its sphere of influence, so to speak. But ultimately every tone also gives way to the larger forces which govern the entire piece – the fundamental structure and indeed tonality itself. The individual will must submit to a higher authority or risk a breakdown of the overall system which is, after all, the source of all individual power.

One important consequence of these ideas is the resultant difficulty in devising strict formal classifications. Form becomes an almost entirely individual attribute of each piece. Surface formal features can arise at different stages and for different reasons as both form and tonal structure evolve during the growth from background to foreground. We should not try to use Schenker's concept of voice leading to develop new criteria for pigeon-holing pieces into formal categories. Rather, we should realize that implicit in Schenker's thought is a concept of heritage, or spatial depth, which, while it enriches our appreciation and understanding of formal events, also prevents us from providing a simple answer to the question "In what form is this piece composed?" We can no longer categorically reply: "This piece is in two-part form." There is thus a breakdown of neat formal categories and this might perhaps be troubling. However, the bridge between traditional formal considerations and voice leading that this viewpoint provides is, one hopes, adequate compensation.

Returning to our Bach suite movements, we can say, for instance, about the E major Menuet, that superficial division into two parts is a natural reflection of the tendency of $\overset{\hat{2}}{V}$ to divide a continuous fundamental structure from $\hat{3}$ into two halves. The Sarabande is much more complicated, but we should not deny that superficially, at least, the movement is also in two parts. We might add, though, that this surface division is not a reflection of a segmentation of the fundamental structure, but is accomplished at a considerably later level. The different functions of the double bar in these two movements can be expressed in performance. The feeling of continuous upward growth through the double bar of the Sarabande is quite different from the more conventional division of the Menuet. Part of the musical experience of the Sarabande is the feeling of striving upward toward $\hat{5}$ (b^2) during most of the movement. The articulation at the double bar and the cadence on II can be felt as temporary rests in the reaching upward – a process which is strongly tied to motivic forces. Considerable tension exists among structural levels here: the surface division into two halves is opposed by the underlying initial ascent that bridges over this division.

Surely the traditional designation "binary" is meaningful, but we cannot expect voice leading to relate to the binary division in any preconceived way. There are, of course, certain binary voice-leading schemes which are much more common than others. The scheme of the E major Menuet is common, while that of the Sarabande is quite unusual. But the contrast between these movements is representative of the range of possibilities and should make us think twice about any classification of forms based solely on voice-leading structure.

It is interesting to speculate for a moment about the stylistic features of Baroque dance movements which allow for such flexibility in relating voice leading to form. Schenker points out near the end of *Free Composition* that the contrapuntal nature of the diminutions in such pieces can often make both form and voice leading difficult to understand.[4] Also, the continuousness, the flexibility of larger metrical groupings, and the

4. *Free Composition*, p. 145.

lack of regular periodic phrasing, combined with the relative brevity of the pieces make them difficult to analyze.

This flexibility continues to some extent in the binary menuets, scherzi, and variation themes of the Classical period. Schenker's graphs of Haydn's binary variation theme from the slow movement of the String Quartet Op. 76, No. 3, show an initial ascent to $\hat{5}$ which crosses over the double bar as in our Sarabande.[5] (Schenker cites the Haydn theme as an example of what he calls one-part form.[6])

The expansion and transformation of binary form into sonata form is made possible partly by stylistic features: more regular periodic phrase structure, which makes it easier to perceive larger groupings, and the dramatization of large-scale tonal events. Such tendencies open new possibilities for larger and larger structures, but at the same time decrease the flexibility in the relationship between large-scale form and voice leading which the smaller binary form enjoys. Only a limited number of binary voice-leading schemes are suitable for large-scale expansion. It is hard to imagine a sonata-form movement with an initial ascent to a point near the end of the movement, for instance. This is not to say that many irregular and flexible features are not to be found in sonata-form movements, but rather to suggest that in order for large-scale structure to hold together, a significant coincidence of design and large-scale tonal structure is probably required.

Too often the study of traditional forms and the study of voice leading are separated in our teaching. In a class on form, students learn the traditional labels without much discussion of voice leading, and in a class in Schenkerian analysis the focus is mainly on voice leading. This division can lead to considerable confusion for the student, and discomfort for the instructor, especially one who teaches both classes. Formal categories are useful tools as long as we are clear that they represent oversimplifications which tell us much less than the whole story. We need not be embarassed as Schenkerians to teach them as long as we keep them in perspective. Perhaps more important, though, we must, in our teaching of Schenkerian analysis, be sure to go beyond merely untangling the voice leading (difficult as that task may be) and relate the voice leading to other aspects of the piece, including form. Only then will we avoid giving the student the impression that Schenkerian studies represent an isolated area of endeavor, sealed off, so to speak, from other aspects of music, and hence to be discarded when leaving the specifically Schenkerian arena.

We can and should admit that, as Schenkerians, we do not have a taxonomy of form which is better than anyone else's. Nor should we seek one; rather we can try to rid ourselves and our students of the need for a strict formal taxonomy – one that could settle all questions of form simply by categorizing, by whatever criteria. And we can view form along with other aspects of music as the product of musical forces which work a little

---

5. *Free Composition*, Figures 120/6, 119/3, and 39/3.
6. *Free Composition*, p. 131.

differently in each case, and which are subject to subtle shades of meaning and contradictory implications.

Like people, musical works, if we do them justice, are best studied as individuals, not as faceless examples of a species. Individuality penetrates all aspects and dimensions. In accepting both the rewards and limitations of this approach, we stop trying to categorize, we abandon the taxonomist's stance, and we station ourselves firmly with composers and performers who, for centuries, have learned to live with – and to make the most of – the ambiguities, tensions, richness, and beauty that characterize our art.

Aspects of the Neapolitan sixth chord in Mozart's music

Roger Kamien

Since the mid-seventeenth century the Neapolitan sixth chord has been an important chromatic resource.[1] Bukofzer observed that this chord "was established as a cadential idiom in the bel-canto style and can be found in nearly all middle baroque composers."[2] In Baroque and Classical works, the Neapolitan chord appears almost exclusively in the context of the minor mode and is often used for the expression of pathos and tension.[3] Like other chromatic chords it frequently occurs at climactic moments and is emphasized through rhythm, texture, or dynamics.[4]

The present study will focus on the use of the Neapolitan sixth in conjunction with a melodic contrast in the top voice between the natural and lowered second scale degrees ($\natural\hat{2}$ and $\flat\hat{2}$). This contrast is often found at cadences and semicadences in which the dominant chord supports the natural second scale degree in the soprano. A particularly strong contrast results when a musical idea is first presented with a dominant or diatonic II^6 chord and then repeated with a Neapolitan sixth.[5] This often occurs when thematic material in major is transposed to minor later in a movement. The most common instance is the recapitulation of material from the second-theme group in minor-key movements.

A beautiful example occurs in the recapitulation of Mozart's Adagio in B minor, K. 540 (Example 1a). Measures 47–49 are a varied repetition of measures 45–47. The Neapolitan sixth is more emphasized than the diatonic II$^6_5$ chord (see the brackets in Example 1a). The $\flat$II^6 is rhythmi-

1. Two recent comprehensive studies place the Neapolitan sixth chord in historical perspective: Saul Novack, "The Significance of the Phrygian Mode in the History of Tonality," *Miscellanea Musicologica: Adelaide Studies in Musicology* 9 (1977), pp. 82–127; and William Kimmel, "The Phrygian Inflection and the Appearances of Death in Music," *College Music Symposium* 20/2 (1980), pp. 42–76.
2. Manfred F. Bukofzer, *Music in the Baroque Era: From Monteverdi to Bach* (New York, 1947), p. 122.
3. An early example may be found in the final scene of Giacomo Carissimi, *Historia di Jepthe* (ca. 1650). The Neapolitan chord occurs on the affective word "ululate!" (wail) as Jeptha's daughter bewails her imminent death. The excerpt is included in Claude V. Palisca, ed., *Norton Anthology of Western Music*, Vol. 1 (New York, 1980), pp. 436–41.
4. In J. S. Bach's Prelude in E$\flat$ minor (*Well-Tempered Clavier*, Book I), for example, the $\flat$II^6 occurs at a dramatic moment (measure 26) when the left-hand accompaniment suddenly breaks off leaving the melodic line unsupported – recitative-like – for the first time in the piece.
5. See Edward Aldwell and Carl Schachter, *Harmony and Voice Leading*, Vol. 2 (New York, 1979), p. 143; 2nd edn (San Diego, 1989), p. 458. This textbook contains an excellent discussion of the Neapolitan sixth chord (pp. 141–55; 2nd edn, pp. 456–70).

cally highlighted by the first use of triplet-sixteenth rhythm in the Adagio. Here, as in other Mozart works, an "exotic" chord gives rise to a fresh rhythmic pattern. Additional emphasis is given to the Neapolitan by the dramatic skip from b^2 down to c♮^{1} at measures 47–48 and by the ascending arpeggio from c♮^{1} to c♮^{3} of bar 48 that contrasts with the ascending diminished fifth c♯^{2}–g^2 at the beginning of measure 46. It is interesting to compare the two-measure phrase containing the Neapolitan with the corresponding phrase (in major) from the exposition (Example 1b). The emphasis of the Neapolitan chord – through rhythm and register – contrasts with the more neutral treatment of the IV and II^6 chords of measure 18, the parallel position within the phrase in the exposition.

This study will explore some of the ways in which Mozart highlights the contrast between the natural and lowered second scale degrees in the context of a repeated musical idea.[6] We shall see how the ♭II^6 chord is

Example 1. Mozart, Adagio in B minor, K. 540

(a) measures 45–49

(b) measures 17–19

6. Mozart's use of the Neapolitan sixth is briefly discussed in the following publications: Werner Lüthy, *Mozart und die Tonartencharakteristik* (Strasbourg, 1931; reprint edn, Baden-Baden, 1974), pp. 82–83; Wilhelm Fischer, "Zu W. A. Mozarts Tonartenwahl und

emphasized and used as a springboard for harmonic excursions and expanded phrases.[7] Sometimes the contrast between ♮$\hat{2}$ and ♭$\hat{2}$ is used as a basic compositional idea within a movement.[8] Though this contrast is found occasionally in Mozart's early works, it is far more common from *Idomeneo* onward. The increase is probably due to the larger number of minor-key works in Mozart's Vienna years and to a growing preference for minor-mode episodes within major-key movements.[9]

The contrast between the ♮$\hat{2}$ and ♭$\hat{2}$ appears not only in the context of motivic repetitions that are obvious and immediate – as in the preceding example – but also within repetitions that are hidden and of longer range.[10] A remarkable instance may be found in the opening theme of the String Quintet in G minor, K. 516. We shall focus on the first four measures and on measures 20–24. The voice-leading graph of Example 2 shows that the top voice of measures 1–4 descends stepwise from d^2 to a^1. By ending the phrase with a ♮$\hat{2}$ supported by the dominant, Mozart creates a sense of incompleteness.[11] Only toward the end of the theme, in measures 20–24, does the top voice descend stepwise from d^3 to g^2 via the ♭$\hat{2}$ (ab^2) supported by a dynamically emphasized Neapolitan chord (Example 3). This ♭$\hat{2}$ in measure 23 creates a long-range contrast with the ♮$\hat{2}$ in measure 4 (compare Examples 2 and 3).[12] Despite obvious differences of rhythm, texture, and register, there are hidden motivic parallelisms between measures 1–4 and measures 20–24 that strengthen this long-range contrast between the natural and lowered second scale degrees. The top voice in both phrases contains a stepwise descent from

Harmonik," *Mozart-Jahrbuch 1952*, p. 14; Gustav Gärtner, "Der neapolitanische Sextakkord bei Mozart: Einige Beispiele," *Acta Mozartiana* 3/4 (1956), pp. 10–12; and Hellmut Federhofer, "Die Harmonik als dramatischer Ausdrucksfaktor in Mozarts Meisteropern," *Mozart-Jahrbuch 1968–1970*, p. 79.

7. The present study will deal exclusively with Mozart's use of the Neapolitan chord in $^6_3$ position, not with the so-called "Neapolitan $^6_4$." Like other composers, Mozart sometimes uses "a 'Neapolitan $^6_4$' as if it were a cadential $^6_4$ resolving to a V or V^7" and then transforms "the supposed dominant into its enharmonic equivalent, the German $^6_5$." (Aldwell and Schachter, *Harmony and Voice Leading*, Vol. 2, p. 181; 2nd edn, p. 499.) A clear instance is found in measures 233–240 of the concluding Allegretto from the Piano Concerto in C minor, K. 491. Other examples of Mozart's use of the "Neapolitan $^6_4$" are discussed in Roger Kamien, "Subtle Enharmonic Relationships in Mozart's Music," *Journal of Music Theory* 30/2 (1986), pp. 173–77.

8. See the Fantasy in D minor, K. 397, which is brilliantly discussed in Oswald Jonas, *Introduction to the Theory of Heinrich Schenker*, trans. and ed. John Rothgeb (New York, 1982), pp. 5–7.

9. See Fischer, pp. 10–11.

10. For valuable discussions of Heinrich Schenker's approach to concealed motivic relationships see Charles Burkhart, "Schenker's Motivic Parallelisms," *Journal of Music Theory* 22/2 (1978), pp. 145–75; and John Rothgeb, "Thematic Content: A Schenkerian View," in David Beach, ed., *Aspects of Schenkerian Theory* (New Haven, 1983), pp. 39–60.

11. The diagonal line in Example 2 indicates that the bb^1 of the top voice forms a vertical interval with the eb^1 of the bass but is rhythmically displaced by the suspended c^2.

12. Mozart's music offers other examples of repeated musical ideas in which the ♮$\hat{2}$ is supported by V and the ♭$\hat{2}$ by a Neapolitan sixth chord; see the Sonata for Piano and Violin in A major, Presto, measures 200–216; the Rondo in F major, K. 494 (which is the concluding movement of the Piano Sonata in F major, K. 533), measure 55 (V$^4_2$) and measure 63; and the Clarinet Concerto in A major, K. 622, Allegro, measures 214 and 216. For examples in Haydn's works, see the Piano Sonata in C minor, Hob. XVI/20, Moderato, measures 4 and 8; and the String Quartet in Eb major, Op. 76, No. 6, Fantasia (Adagio), measure 32 (V^6) and measure 36.

pitch-class d. In addition, the chromatic melodic descent in the first violin line of measures 1–3, g^2–$f\#^2$–$f\natural^2$–$e\natural^2$–$e\flat^2$–d^2–c^2, appears in the bass of measures 20–23, where it takes longer to unfold (compare Examples 2 and 3).[13] Moreover, the 5–6 progression over the bass g–f# in measures 1–3 reappears in concentrated form in measure 20 (Examples 4a and 4b). Amazingly, the first five triads of measures 1–2 reappear in varied and inverted form as the basic voice-leading progression of measures 20–22 (Examples 5a and 5b).[14]

Example 2. Mozart, String Quintet in G minor, K. 516, Allegro, measures 1–4

Example 3. Mozart, String Quintet in G minor, K. 516, Allegro, measures 20–24

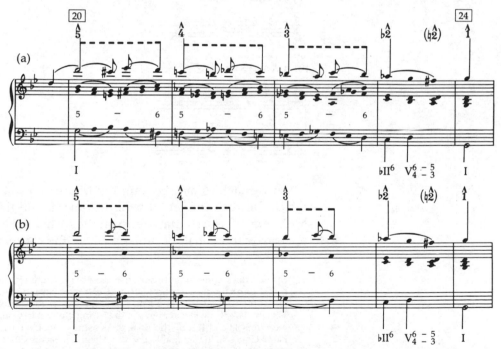

13. A somewhat similar example of the expansion of foreground chromatic detail is found in the Piano Sonata in F major, K. 280, Allegro assai, measures 3–4 and measures 17–22. See Allen Forte, "Generative Chromaticism in Mozart's Music: The Rondo in A Minor, K. 511," *The Musical Quarterly* 66/4 (1980), p. 460.

14. In the coda, measures 235–242, an expanded variant of measures 1–4 contains elements of measures 20–24. Here, the stepwise descent from d^2 in the top voice contains a prominent $\flat\hat{2}$ supported by $\flat II^6$ (measure 241). The chromatic descent g–f#–f♮–e♮–e♭–d now appears in the bass (measures 236–240) with almost the same rhythmic pattern as in measures 1–3, violin 1.

Example 4. Mozart, String Quintet in G minor, K. 516, Allegro

(a) measures 1–3

(b) measure 20

Example 5. Mozart, String Quintet in G minor, K. 516, Allegro

(a) measures 1–2

(b) measures 20–22

Many examples may be found in Mozart's music of repeated ideas in which the $\natural\hat{2}$ is supported by a diatonic II^6 and the $\flat\hat{2}$ by a Neapolitan sixth chord.[15] The contrast between the II^6 and the Neapolitan sixth often appears within a pair of phrases where the consequent phrase is an ex-

---

15. For examples other than those considered here, see the Piano Concerto in E flat major, K. 271, Andantino, measures 101 and 104; *Idomeneo*, the aria "Tutte nel cor vi sento," measures 129 and 132; the Piano Concerto in A major, K. 488, Allegro assai, measures 343 and 347–51; two movements of the String Quintet in G minor, K. 516, the Menuetto, measures 38 and 41, and the Adagio, measures 23–24 and 60–61; two movements of the Piano Concerto in D major, K. 537, the Allegro, measures 180 and 182, and the Allegretto, measures 90 and 94; the Symphony No. 40 in G minor, Allegro assai, measures 251–252 and 267–268; and *Die Zauberflöte*, the aria "Ach, ich fühl's," measures 26 and 32. Two examples from *Don Giovanni* contain a contrast between II^6 and $\flat$II^6, but neither form of $\hat{2}$ is prominent in the top voice: the Introduzione, measures 183 and 188; and the aria "Dalla sua pace," measures 30 and 34. Examples in which the $\flat$II^6 precedes the diatonic II^6 include the String Quartet in D minor, Allegro moderato, measures 97 and 101; *Le Nozze di Figaro*, the duettino "Crudel! perchè finora," measures 23 and 25; and the Symphony No. 40 in G minor, Allegro assai, measures 267–268 and measure 275.

panded repetition of the antecedent.[16] This procedure is found in the
Eb major aria "Mi tradì quell'alma ingrata," composed 30 April 1788 –
six weeks after the B minor Adagio – for the Vienna premiere of *Don
Giovanni*. In this aria, Donna Elvira's conflicting feelings of love and hatred
are vividly expressed. "Mi tradì quell'alma ingrata" is a rondo with two
episodes. The contrast between ♮II⁶ and ♭II⁶ appears in a pair of phrases
in G minor at the end of the second episode (Example 6). The antecedent
phrase, containing the II⁶, is four measures in length (measures 103–106)
and the consequent, containing the Neapolitan chord, lasts eight measures
(measures 107–114). The II⁶ (measure 104) occupies the second measure of
a four-measure metrical unit. In the consequent phrase – a varied repetition of the antecedent – the second measure is expanded to five measures
(measures 108–112). This procedure exemplifies the Schenkerian concept of *Dehnung* (expansion), which occurs when a group of measures
enlarges "one or more measures of a metrical prototype."[17] The metrical
expansion in this passage is supported by parallelisms of melody and
text. Note that the progression eb²–d² in the vocal line in measures
112–113 corresponds to the eb²–d² in measures 104–105 and has the same
text, "[palpitan-]do il cor." The Neapolitan chord (measures 108–109) lasts
almost twice as long as the diatonic II⁶ (measure 104) and is emphasized
by an applied V⁴₂ (measure 108). It is also highlighted by the repeated
melodic pattern in measures 108–109. Elvira's florid run lasts five full
measures, vividly illustrating the palpitating ("palpitando") of her heart.

Example 6. Mozart, *Don Giovanni*, Act II, "Mi tradì quell'alma ingrata,"
measures 103–114

(example continues on following page)

16. Besides those to be considered below, the following examples illustrate this specific
procedure: the Piano Concerto in A major, K. 488, Allegro assai, measure 343 and
measures 347–351; and the String Quintet in G minor, Adagio, measures 23–24 and
60–61. The last example is perceptively discussed in Charles Rosen, *The Classical Style*
(New York, 1971), p. 88.

17. Schenker, *Free Composition*, p. 124. Valuable discussions of Schenker's concept of expansion are contained in William Rothstein, "Rhythm and the Theory of Structural
Levels" (Ph.D. diss., Yale University, 1981), pp. 150–80, and Carl Schachter, "Rhythm
and Linear Analysis: Aspects of Meter," in *The Music Forum*, Vol. 6, Part 1 (New York, 1987),
pp. 40–58. For a recent study dealing with the relevance of eighteenth-century descrip-

Example 6 (*cont.*)

This pair of phrases in G minor (Example 6) is a transposed variant of an earlier section in B♭ major at the end of the first episode (Example 7). In this earlier section – as in the G minor passage – a four-measure phrase is followed by an expanded repetition lasting eight measures (Example 7, measures 64–67 and 68–75). But the II⁶ chord in the second phrase is less highlighted than the corresponding Neapolitan chord in the G minor passage (compare Example 7, measures 68–75 with Example 6, measures 107–114). The diatonic II⁶ is sustained for only one measure – not two – and is *not* emphasized by an applied dominant. Moreover, in this phrase the florid run lasts only two measures, not five. Here the tonic (B♭ major) is already reached in the next-to-last measure of the phrase (measure 74) as opposed to the G minor passage, where the harmonic tension is not resolved until the very last measure of the phrase (measure 114). These musical differences parallel an important change in Elvira's mode of verbal expression. In the B♭ major passage her words are somewhat general and abstract: "provo ancor per lui pietà" ("I still feel pity for him"). In the G minor passage they are more concrete and vivid: "palpitando il cor mi va" ("my heart is still palpitating").

Example 7. Mozart, *Don Giovanni*, Act II, "Mi tradì quell'alma ingrata," measures 64–75

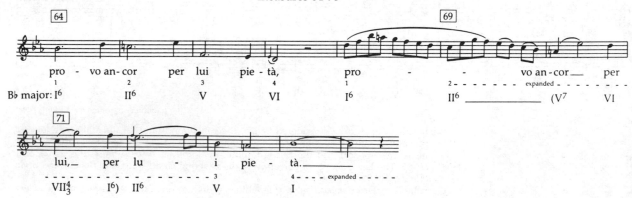

tions of phrase expansion to Haydn's music, see Elaine R. Sisman, "Small and Expanded Forms: Koch's Model and Haydn's Music," *The Musical Quarterly* 48/4 (1982), pp. 444–75.

When the Neapolitan sixth appears within an expanded consequent phrase – as in the preceding example – it is sometimes followed by a series of chords that are of less structural significance. This means that even though the Neapolitan chord is not literally sustained, it maintains its harmonic significance until the cadence at the end of the phrase. The function of such subordinate chords can be understood more precisely through Schenkerian concepts and notation.

To illustrate, we shall consider an example in which the Neapolitan sixth is prolonged by a long series of passing chords, Ilia's aria "Padre, germani, addio!" from *Idomeneo*. Here, as in the preceding example, the heroine is torn by conflicting emotions. Ilia is loyal to her father and homeland, yet she loves Idamante, an enemy of her people. Her inability to resolve this emotional conflict is mirrored by the repeated avoidance of a cadence in the concluding section of the aria (Example 8). The avoidance of a cadence begins in measure 103, where the ending of a six-measure phrase (measures 98–103) is elided by the beginning of another phrase. This six-measure phrase contains a melodic descent from g^2 to $f\sharp^1$ that is repeated in condensed form within measures 103–105 (see the asterisks in Example 8). Notice that the phrase beginning in measure 103 contains a prominent $a\natural^1$ ($\natural\hat{2}$) supported by a diatonic II^6 (measure 105). When this phrase is repeated, starting in measure 106, we expect a return of this tone and its accompanying chord. Instead, we are surprised by a rhythmically emphasized ab^1 ($b\hat{2}$), supported by a Neapolitan sixth (measure 108). Example 9 shows that this Neapolitan chord is prolonged by a series of passing $\substack{6\\3}$ chords which lead up to a G minor $\substack{6\\3}$ chord at the second quarter of measure 111. This is not a true tonic, but a neighboring chord to the Neapolitan in measure 108. The neighboring chord descends to the diatonic II^6 in measure 112. Thus, the Neapolitan chord is contrapuntally prolonged from measure 108 to measure 112, where it becomes a diatonic II^6 that leads to the long-delayed cadence to I in measure 115. All the tension produced by the prolongation of the Neapolitan chord is closely linked to the text. The vocal run in measures 108–112 magnificently expresses the passion of Ilia's "odiare ancor non so" ("I cannot hate him").

Within an extended phrase, the Neapolitan chord is sometimes used as a springboard for a tonal excursion in which the submediant or submediant minor is emphasized. Even though this new tonal area may be strengthened through tonicization, it is usually subordinate to the larger progression bII^6–($\natural$II^6)–V–I. A fascinating instance is found within the second theme of the Finale (Allegro) of the Symphony No. 39 in Eb major, K. 543 (Example 10a).[18] The theme consists of a six-measure antecedent phrase (in Bb major) and a twenty-one measure consequent that begins with a varied repetition of the antecedent (measures 42–47 and 48–68). The $\natural\hat{2}$ in the antecedent, supported by the diatonic II^6 (measure 46), is contrasted with the $b\hat{2}$, supported by the Neapolitan (measure 52). We

18. An extraordinary work in which the Neapolitan sixth chord – without a contrasting diatonic II^6 – is repeatedly used as a springboard for tonal excursions is the Adagio from the Adagio and Fugue for strings in C minor, K. 546.

Example 8. Mozart, *Idomeneo*, Act I, "Padre, germani, addio!," measures 98–115

Example 9. Mozart, *Idomeneo*, Act I, "Padre, germani, addio!," measures 108–115

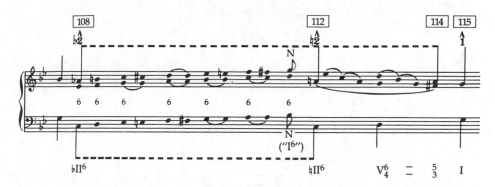

note that the two eighth-note c¹s of measure 46 are augmented into the two half-note b♮¹s (really c♭¹) of measures 52–53. The Neapolitan of measures 52–53 ushers in a tonal excursion in which the $^6_4$ positions of the F♯ major and F♯ minor (really G♭ major and G♭ minor) chords are emphasized by applied dominants (measures 54–61). A graph of this passage is shown in Example 11, in which some tones are respelled to show their true function. We see that the pedal point on d♭ (c♯ in Mozart's notation) in measures 54–61 is part of a chromatic descent in the bass from the e♭¹ of the Neapolitan sixth chord in measure 52 (d♯ in Mozart's notation) to the a♮ of the V$^6_5$ in measure 65. Thus, the excursion touching upon the ♭VI major and minor in measures 54–61 is a tonal parenthesis between the Neapolitan sixth and the V$^6_5$. The forte passage leading into V$^6_5$ chord contains a delightful touch of wit. The melodic figure c²–b♭¹–a¹–c² in the last two measures of the antecedent phrase (measures 46–47) is "omitted" in the parallel measures of the consequent (measures 52–53). The asterisks in Examples 10a and 10b indicate that the violin line of measures 62–65 is an expanded and varied return of the "missing" melodic figure, a humorous form of musical compensation!

Example 10. Mozart, Symphony No. 39, K. 543, Finale (Allegro)

(a) measures 42–53

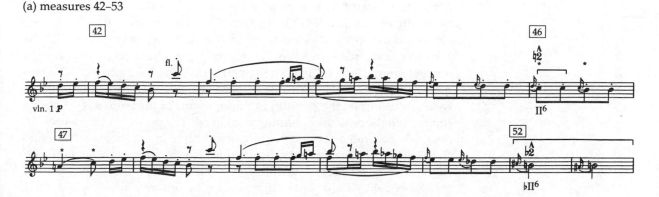

Example 10 (*cont.*)

(b) measures 62–66

Example 11. Mozart, Symphony No. 39, K. 543, Finale (Allegro), measures 42–68

We shall conclude with a discussion of a work in which the contrast between a diatonic II⁶ and a Neapolitan sixth chord is a basic compositional idea. Such contrast occurs several times and with increasing emphasis in the F♯ minor Adagio from the Piano Concerto in A major, K. 488. In the opening theme the contrast is quite subtle because it occurs within the context of a concealed repetition. The theme is composed of two units of unequal length: measures 1–4 and measures 5–12. Despite obvious differences between them, the units are closely related. As the graph of Example 12 shows, both units contain a stepwise melodic descent from c♯² to e♯¹ (see the large brackets in Example 12). The correspondence extends to details of sonority and melodic diminution as well. For example, the passing F♯ minor chord of measure 6 is a delicate sonoric reference to the opening tonic chord. The melody in measures 7–8 is a more decorated variation of the melodic line in measures 2–3 (second sixteenth note). There is a rhythmic and melodic contrast between the g♯² (♮2̂) and II⁶ of measure 3 and the g♮¹ (♭2̂) and Neapolitan sixth chord of measures 9–10. The II⁶ lasts only a half measure and appears in a weak metrical position while the Neapolitan sixth lasts two measures and begins on the downbeat. The melodic pattern $g\sharp^1$–d^2–$f\sharp^1$ in measures 3–4 is magically expanded in range to g^1–d^3–$f\sharp^1$ in measures 10–11.[19]

Example 12. Mozart, Piano Concerto in A major, K. 488, Adagio, measures 1–12

The Neapolitan sixth chord is highlighted even more when the opening theme is restated in measures 53–68. After eleven measures of literal recapitulation, the theme is extended by an unexpected deceptive cadence to VI and a varied repetition of the concluding subphrase containing the Neapolitan harmony. This harmony is emphasized by a dramatic leap from g to d^3 in measures 65–66, a span that is an octave wider than the ascent from g^1 to d^3 in measures 61–62.

The contrast between the diatonic II[6] and the Neapolitan sixth chord is most striking at the beginning of the coda (measure 84). For the first time, this contrast occurs in the context of a motivic repetition that is obvious, not concealed. Measures 89–92 are a varied repetition of measures 85–88, with the Neapolitan of measure 90 taking the place of the II[6] of measure 86. The Neapolitan chord is emphasized by the leap from $g\natural$ to d^3 (measure 90), which is an octave wider than the leap from $g\sharp^1$ to d^3 in measure 86. The Neapolitan is also emphasized by the wind

19. The two parts of the theme are also unified by the neighboring-tone figure $c\sharp$–d–$c\sharp$, which appears on various structural levels: $c\sharp^2$–d^2–$c\sharp^2$ of measure 1, $c\sharp^1$–d^1–$c\sharp^1$ of measures 1–3, middle voice, and $c\sharp^2$ (measure 1) – d^2 (measure 5) – $c\sharp^2$ (measure 6). In its use of a neighboring-tone figure and in other respects, there is a striking similarity between Mozart's theme and measures 1–8 of the third movement (in F♯ minor) of C. P. E. Bach's "Essay" Sonata (*Probestück*) No. 4. See the analysis of these bars in John Rothgeb, "Thematic Content: A Schenkerian View," p. 51.

instruments which join on the restatement of the phrase. The $\flat\hat{2}$ is doubled in two octaves by the clarinets. These coda phrases sound like vague recollections of the opening theme. Measures 85–86 recall measure 3 and measures 89–90 recall measures 8–10.

We have discussed some of the ways in which Mozart exploits the contrast between the $\natural\hat{2}$ supported by the II^6 or the dominant, and the $\flat\hat{2}$ supported by the Neapolitan in the context of a motivic repetition that is either obvious or concealed. Mozart emphasizes the Neapolitan most imaginatively and uses it to create expanded phrases and tonal excursions. Occasionally, as in the Adagio from the Piano Concerto in A major, K. 488, the contrast between the diatonic II^6 and Neapolitan sixth is of great importance for the overall musical form. The procedures we have described are significant elements of Mozart's mature style.

Enharmonic transformation in the first movement of Mozart's Piano Concerto in C minor, K. 491

Eric Wen

While the Concerto in D minor (K. 466) is perhaps the more well known of Mozart's two piano concertos in the minor mode, the Concerto in C minor (K. 491) has always held a place of honor among musicians. Beethoven was particularly entranced by the work, and his own Concerto in C minor, Op. 37, begins with a unison arpeggiation which is clearly modeled after its predecessor. Brahms was another fervent admirer of the work and made no secret of preferring Mozart's Concerto in C minor to Beethoven's. In an illuminating conversation with the Viennese composer Richard Heuberger, he stated:

[Mozart's] C minor Concerto: a masterpiece of art and full of inspired ideas! I always find Beethoven's Concerto in C minor much slighter and weaker than Mozart's. . .it is perhaps more modern but not as significant.[1]

One immediately striking feature of the first movement of K. 491 is the sheer breadth of its exposition. In addition to its length (the exposition is longer than the development and recapitulation combined), it contains a variety of thematic ideas including a restatement of the opening theme in the remote key of E♭ minor. Two of the exposition's most prominent themes, in fact, are not present in the opening orchestral ritornello, a situation which led Tovey to cite K. 491 as "utterly subversive of the doctrine that the function of the opening tutti was to predict what the solo had to say."[2]

The number of themes presented after the exposition arrives in the mediant key of E♭ major has generated much discussion in analytic considerations of K. 491. The two themes "missing" in the orchestral ritornello appear in the key of E♭ and have been called the "two second themes" by several commentators.[3] In his characteristically provocative manner, Glenn Gould remarks:

Having successfully avoided the mood and pleasure of the relative major key (E-flat) throughout the orchestral tutti, the piano now leads us there with a vengeance – and gets hopelessly stalled in that key.[4]

1. Richard Heuberger, *Erinnerungen an Johannes Brahms* (Tutzing, 1971), p. 93 (my translation).
2. Donald Francis Tovey, *Essays in Musical Analysis*, Vol. 3 (London, 1936), p. 43.
3. See, for example, Cuthbert Girdlestone, *Mozart's Piano Concertos* (London, 1948; reprint edns, Norman, 1952; New York, 1964), p. 394.
4. Glenn Gould, *The Glenn Gould Reader*, ed. with an introduction by Tim Page (New York, 1984), pp. 129–30.

The extensive thematic material in E♭ motivates Charles Rosen to speak of K. 491 as having a "'double' solo exposition (making a triple exposition with the first ritornello)."[5] Pointing out that the exposition closes in E♭ twice (in measures 200 and 265), Rosen reasons that the unusual construction of the exposition is due to the irregularity of structure of the opening theme, with "the fragmentation of the larger form corresponding to the inner divisions of the opening statement."[6] As for the return of the opening theme in the minor form of the mediant (E♭ minor) at the end of the exposition, Rosen says:

> If we half expect a development section instead of the second solo exposition, we are also half granted one within it by the far-reaching modulations of the main theme in E flat minor (from measure 220 on). Here the fragmentation of the harmonic movement of the exposition corresponds to the fragmentation of the structure (as well as to the melodic and rhythmic fragmentation of the material). The series of diminished chords in the opening statement of the main theme clearly presage and justify such a large-scale chromatic instability. . .[7]

Rosen's use of fragmentation as an associative principle is questionable. The diminished seventh chords have a distinct tonal function in the opening theme's expression of C minor, and the E♭ minor passage has a place in the structure of the exposition as a whole. The coherence of the movement is therefore not due to the irregularities of the individual parts but the motivic relationships between them. This study will look at the motivic connections which exist between the opening theme and the "two second themes" in E♭ major, and will examine the significance of the opening theme's remarkable reappearance in the key of E♭ minor at the end of the exposition.

The opening theme

The opening theme of K. 491 is notable in several respects. Its unison statement simultaneously suggests both a bass and top voice and is characteristic of sonata movements in minor with a *Sturm und Drang* quality.[8] Usually, however, these unison statements are presented in forte. The piano dynamic marking of the opening theme of K. 491 creates a mood of hushed urgency which is particularly memorable.[9] The chromatic succession of diminished seventh chords which begins at measure 4 is perhaps the most distinctive feature of the theme. The inclusion of such a sequence as part of the theme itself is not only unusual but adds to the theme's forbidding character.

5. Charles Rosen, *The Classical Style* (New York, 1971), p. 248.
6. *Ibid*.
7. *Ibid*., p. 249.
8. Haydn was especially fond of presenting the opening theme of a sonata movement in a unison statement (e.g., in the Symphony No. 44 ("Trauer"), the Symphony No. 95, and in the Piano Sonata Hob.XVI/36 in C♯ minor). Mozart adopted this procedure in several instances (e.g., in the Piano Sonata in C minor, K. 457), as did Beethoven in his Piano Concerto in C minor, modeled after Mozart's in the same key. Brahms's Piano Concerto in D minor, despite the sustained opening tonic pedal, also follows in this tradition.
9. Mozart's Violin Sonata in E minor, K. 304, also begins with a unison statement of the first theme marked piano.

Before we examine the tonal meaning of the chromatic sequence of diminished seventh chords starting at measure 4, we must call attention to the neighbor-note motion Ab–G in the preceding measure. Not only does Ab descend to G in measure 3, but it originates from an implied G over the C minor tonic harmony of the opening two measures. A contrapuntal 5–6 succession over the bass note C is implied and thus the neighbor-note figure G–Ab–G spans the opening three measures.[10]

As shown in the successive analytic graphs of the opening theme (Example 1), the neighbor-note idea which appears at the very outset of

Example 1

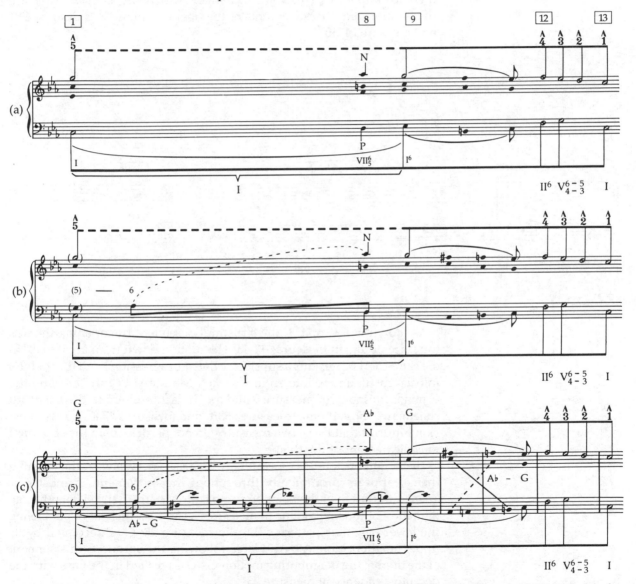

10. This implied motion points up the non-literalness of contrapuntal successions in free composition. See the discussion by Oswald Jonas in his *Introduction to the Theory of Heinrich Schenker*, trans and ed. John Rothgeb (New York, 1982), p. 83.

the movement is expanded over the course of the theme. The ab² in measure 8, appearing in the oboes as a new and distinct upper voice, refers back to the Ab in measure 3, the high point of the opening measures. It descends to g² in measure 9; thus the neighbor-note figure is reiterated in the first nine measures of the top voice. The bass note supporting the ab² in measure 8 also relates back to the opening tonic of the movement; it functions as a passing note between C in measure 1 and Eb in measure 9.

During these first nine measures the voice exchange shown in Example 2b may be inferred, with the eb² in measure 4 representing a displacement (Example 2a). This voice exchange, incidentally, is made explicit in the harmonized tutti statements of the opening theme in measures 63ff. and measures 473ff.

Example 2

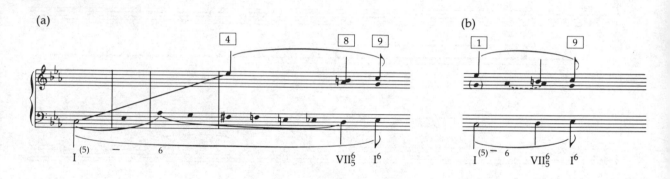

As shown in Example 1, the structural descent of the opening theme's top voice occurs in measures 12–13. The motion down from g² (5̂) to eb² in measures 9–11 represents a subsidiary linear progression from the theme's initial structural tone into an inner voice. Measures 10 and 11 extend the C minor harmony of measure 9 and are, in fact, omitted in the later tutti statements of the theme (measures 63ff. and measures 473ff.). This omission confirms that these two measures do not participate in the structural melodic descent of the theme.

The neighbor-note idea, G–Ab–G, which is so pervasive in the opening theme, appears prominently throughout the movement. A most poignant diminution of the neighbor-note figure occurs in the sixteenth-note figuration of the first violins in measures 30 and 32. Instead of paralleling the lower-neighbor pattern set up in measure 28, G is decorated by its upper neighbor-note Ab. And later, following the second tutti statement of the theme, the neighboring motion G–Ab is recalled in the bass with the deceptive cadence at measure 73.

The neighbor-note figure recurs at the entry of the solo piano in measure 100 (Example 3). The neighboring motion of scale degrees $\hat{5}$ and $\hat{6}$ also forms the basis of the primary melodic motion in the second theme of the exposition (measures 147ff.). Because of this theme's appearance in Eb major, however, the neighbor-note figure is transposed to Bb–C–Bb (Example 4a). The neighbor-note motive of G–Ab–G is preserved, however, in the inner voices (in the viola in measures 153–154 and in the second bassoon in measures 157–163). When this theme is cast in C minor in the recapitulation (measures 410ff.) the original form of the neighbor-note figure, G decorated by its upper neighbor Ab, recurs (Example 4b).

Example 3

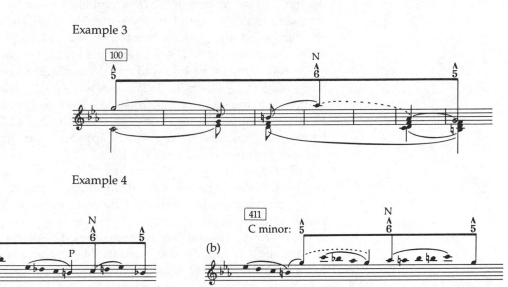

Example 4

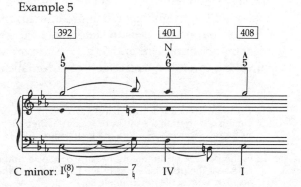

One of the unusual features of the recapitulation is the reversal of the order of the "second" and "third" themes presented in the exposition. Following its appearance in the tonic, the "third" theme of the exposition is cast in the subdominant before continuing on to the "second" theme. This subdominant statement of the "third" theme in the recapitulation (measures 401ff.) allows for yet another appearance of the neighbor-note idea in the large-scale prolongation of G in the top voice (Example 5).

Example 5

We may now return to the unison statement of the opening theme and examine it further. It is apparent that the Ab–G neighbor-note motion in measure 3 continues to F♯ in the following measure. The change of articulation as well as the beginning of the sequential pattern at this point highlights this chromatic motion from Ab down to F♯. This linear progression of a diminished third is another important motivic idea which occurs throughout the movement. Frequently it appears transposed down a fifth as Db–C–B♮. The diminished thirds Db–C–B♮ and Ab–G–F♯ are strongly associated with each other and their connection is made explicit when the opening theme returns in the development section in the key of F minor (measures 302ff.): in the F minor statement of the theme the Ab–G–F♯ of the third and fourth measures is transposed to Db–C–B♮.

The diminished third Db–C–B♮ is initially stated by the flute in measures 18–20. It is immediately followed by a rhythmically varied statement in the first violins in measures 22–23 and measures 25–26. The diminished third reappears in the first violins in measures 74–76 and recurs in the context of Eb major at the end of the exposition (measure 271) in the second violins. It makes its final and most poignant appearance in augmentation in the coda (in the flute, measures 511–516).

Within a tonal context the horizontal interval of a diminished third emphasizes the degree of the scale to which it resolves, surrounding this degree with both upper and lower diatonic half steps. Frequently the two notes of the diminished third are connected by a passing note; this results in the succession of two diatonic semitones. The dominant scale degree is the one most frequently decorated in this fashion and the chromatically inflected $\hat{4}$ immediately preceding it acts temporarily as its leading tone.[11]

In measure 5 of the opening theme, G (scale-degree $\hat{5}$ and the goal of the F♯ in measure 4) is decorated by its upper neighbor Ab. This interpolation of Ab before the resolution of F♯ to G results in yet another appearance of the neighbor-note figure (Example 6a). The interpretation presented in Example 6a is suggested in the unaccompanied unison statement of the opening theme, but when the theme returns in its harmonized form in measures 13ff. and 63ff., the G on the second beat of the measure is heard as a passing note between Ab and F♮, not as a goal tone decorated by an appoggiatura. This interpretation is made unequivocal by the voice exchange of Ab and F with the oboe part (Example 6b). The intimation of the neighbor-note figure in measure 5 nevertheless remains.[12]

In comparing the unison statement of the theme with its harmonized form in measures 13ff. and 63ff., it is apparent that the sequence in measures 4–8 implies a succession of chromatically descending diminished

11. The b6 and ♯4 scale degrees hardly ever occur simultaneously as a vertical interval of a diminished third in the music of Mozart; rather, they appear together in the interval of an augmented sixth. See Eva and Paul Badura-Skoda, *Interpreting Mozart on the Keyboard* (London, 1962), pp. 230–31.
12. In the passage beginning in measure 36 the second beats of the second bassoon part represent the principal notes of the bass line, and the Ab–G–F in measure 38 is in fact heard as represented in Example 6a.

Example 6

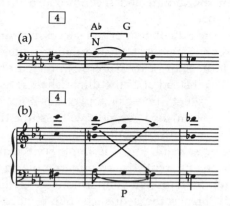

seventh chords. This sequence follows a two-measure pattern with the alternation of root position and second inversion diminished seventh chords. In order to understand the significance of this successive pattern, it is necessary to determine the meaning of the first diminished seventh chord in the larger tonal scheme of C minor.

The diminished seventh chord in measure 4 is built on the raised fourth scale degree and represents a IV^7 chord with a chromatically inflected bass that intensifies the pull towards the dominant. The bass motion of a descending fifth from C to F♯ is suggested over the first four measures; the A♭ in measure 3, while representing a top voice above the bass note C, also serves as the mid-point in the bass arpeggiation down in thirds from C to F♯ (Example 7a). Instead of continuing to the dominant G as expected, however, the F♯ in the bass in measure 4 is followed by F♮. Although G as the bass tone of V is elided in this succession of F♯ to F♮, the ♯IV^7 in measure 4 continues on to dominant harmony. The diminished seventh chord in second inversion in measure 5 has a function similar to that of a dominant seventh chord in third inversion (Example 7b).

Example 7

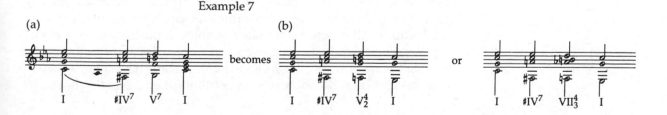

Within the context of C minor one would expect the diminished seventh chord in measure 5 to resolve to a tonic chord in first inversion in the following measure. Another diminished seventh chord appears in measure 6, however, and the tonic chord in first inversion does not arrive until measure 9. Instead of returning to the tonic in measure 6, three chromatically descending diminished seventh chords are interpolated between the diminished seventh chord in measure 5 and its expected resolution.

While the articulation of the successive diminished seventh chords in measures 6–8 parallels the alternating pattern initiated in measures 4–5, the melodic skip in measure 8 is notated enharmonically as the major sixth D–B♮ instead of as the diminished seventh D–C♭. This enharmonic change is "silent," however, and at this point the listener, still hearing the skip as a diminished seventh, will assume that the sequence will either continue as before (Example 8a) or resolve the active interval of the diminished seventh, D–C♭ (Example 8b).[13] Only retrospectively at measure 9 will it be apparent that an enharmonic change has taken place in the preceding measure. The enharmonic respelling of C♭ as B♮ in measure 8 not only breaks the sequence, but is necessary in order to return to C minor; it transforms a root position diminished seventh chord leading to E♭ into a first inversion diminished seventh chord which leads back to C minor. As will be shown later, this enharmonic equivalence of C♭ and B♮ is significant throughout the movement. For the moment it introduces a subtle element of tension into the opening theme.

Example 8

A series of descending diminished seventh chords derives from a pattern of applied dominant seventh chords with elisions of their resolutions (Example 9).[14] A curious fact about successions of diminished seventh chords is revealed by the enharmonic change in measure 8: in this and any similar series of chromatically descending diminished seventh chords the fourth chord will necessarily restate the notes of the first, with one note respelled enharmonically (in this case B♮ as C♭). In measures 5–8 of the opening theme of K. 491, however, the enharmonic respelling, a natural occurrence in a descending series of diminished seventh chords, is

---

13. The enharmonic transformation of a diminished seventh as a major sixth is more frequently exploited in descending skips (e.g., in Mozart's *Eine kleine Nachtmusik*, fourth movement, and in Chopin's Sonata in B♭ minor, in the introduction to the first movement). A particularly breathtaking example where a diminished seventh is reinterpreted as a major sixth in an ascending leap occurs in measure 3 of Variation 25 of Bach's "Goldberg" Variations.
14. See the discussion in Edward Aldwell and Carl Schachter, *Harmony and Voice Leading*, Vol. 2 (New York, 1979), pp. 212–13; 2nd edn (San Diego, 1989), pp. 530–32.

denied. A significant consequence of this is that the diminished seventh chord in measure 8 is exactly equivalent in spelling to that in measure 5. The diminished seventh chord in measure 8 thus becomes an extension in another inversion of the diminished seventh chord in measure 5 (Example 10). Instead of continuing the pattern of diminished seventh chords indefinitely, the change in measure 8 allows for a reorientation back into the context of C minor (highlighted by the entrance of the winds).

Example 9

Example 10

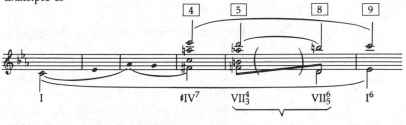

The bass voice in the sequence of diminished seventh chords in measures 5–8 extends the diminished-third motive of measures 3–4 into a chromatic line leading from Ab in measure 3 to D in measure 8. This descending chromatic line becomes another important motive within the movement. Not only is it echoed in the first oboe's line (measures 8ff.), but it appears in inversion in the bass of measures 10–11. The rising chromatic line from Ab appears later in the orchestral introduction in measures 35ff. (oboe), measures 76ff. (bass) and in diminution in measure 82 (flute). It also reappears in measure 146 just before the first of the two themes in Eb.

So far in our discussion of the opening theme there have been three principal motives which are directly related to each other. Since the chromatic line in measures 3–8 continues from the filled-in diminished third in measures 3–4 and the diminished third is itself an extension of the neighbor-note idea in measure 3, both the diminished third and chromatic line can be seen as outgrowths of the same neighbor-note figure.

The evolution of the chromatic line from the simple neighbor-note figure occurs in several places throughout the movement. The deceptive cadence on VI in measure 73 results in the bass succession G–Ab; this initiates a chromatic ascent five bars later. At the appearance of the second theme in the recapitulation (measures 410ff.) the neighbor note Ab is embellished by a chromatic line from Ab up to C (see Example 4b).

The most dramatic expansion of the neighbor-note figure into a chromatic line occurs in the third movement of the concerto. The poignant diminished thirds of the coda (measures 241ff.) derive from the neighbor-note figure Db–C at the end of the main theme in the last movement (measures 13–14), and these diminished thirds lead into a chromatic line going in reverse direction up to F (Example 11).[15]

Example 11

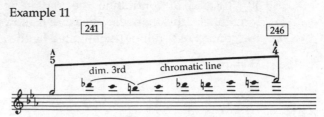

Now that we have established a connection between the three principal motives of the opening of K. 491, we may examine the later tonal events of the movement and show their relationship to the opening theme.

The transitional section of the exposition

At the reappearance of the opening theme in measure 118 the sequence of parallel diminished seventh chords is recomposed. Instead of continuing as at the beginning of the movement, the diminished seventh chord in measure 123, which parallels that of measure 6, resolves to an F minor chord in measure 125 with Ab in the bass. This F minor chord in measure 125 is important in helping to establish the mediant as a new key area. The mediant harmony is tonicized through its own dominant which is preceded by a large-scale voice exchange between the F minor chord in measure 125 and the augmented sixth chord in measure 134 (Example 12). The large-scale bass motion in this section brings in Cb, the enharmonic of B♮, as a chromatic passing note between C and Bb. The Cb supports the augmented sixth chord that leads to the dominant of the "second" theme in the mediant harmony. Also evident is a chromatic motion leading from Ab in the bass (measure 125) through A♮ in the top voice to Bb (measure 135).

Example 12

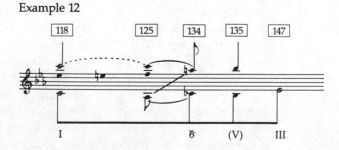

15. The f[3], the culmination of the chromatic line, is extremely important since it articulates the structural $\hat{4}$ in the top voice of the movement. Beethoven was particularly entranced by this passage, and reportedly exclaimed to Cramer upon hearing it: "Cramer, Cramer! we shall never be able to do anything like that!" See *Thayer's Life of Beethoven*, rev. and ed. Elliot Forbes (Princeton, 1967), p. 209.

The E♭ chord in measure 131 (and measure 133), heard between the F minor chord and the augmented sixth chord, supports a passing note B♭ in the top voice. It would be more usual for a root-position chord to form the intermediate step in the bass arpeggiation down a sixth (as in Example 13a). Mozart, however, uses an E♭ chord in first inversion to support the passing note in order to highlight the A♭–G neighbor-note figure once again (Example 13b, bass voice).

Example 13

(a)   (b)

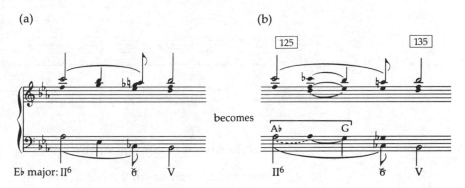

These E♭ chords (measures 131 and 133) are both preceded by a diminished seventh chord with A♭ in the bass, which supports a chromatic passing note C♭ between C and B♭. The right-hand part of the solo piano articulates a leap of a diminished seventh, D–C♭, in measures 130 and 132. This leap is the same as that in measure 8 except for the enharmonic change of B♮ to C♭ in the spelling of the diminished seventh chord. The direct recollection of measure 8 is significant here as the passage now carries forth the motion to E♭ that was thwarted in the descending diminished seventh chord sequence of measures 5–8. The top voice respells the chromatic line C–B♮–B♭ of the flute (measures 121–123, paralleling measures 4–6), as C–C♭–B♭. The C♭ intimated at the beginning of the movement now comes into its own in tonicizing the key area of the mediant.

Example 14 shows the large-scale voice leading of these measures. In addition to the chromatic motion contained within the bass descent from A♭ in measure 125 to B♭ in measure 135, another chromatic line begins at the E♭ in the inner voice of measure 118 and moves to g♭^{2} in measure 134.[16]

16. The chromatic line from E♭ to G♭ shown in Example 14 enharmonically foreshadows the chromatic line from E♭ to F♯ in measure 200, which leads to the beginning of the third (or second "second") theme in measure 201.

Example 14

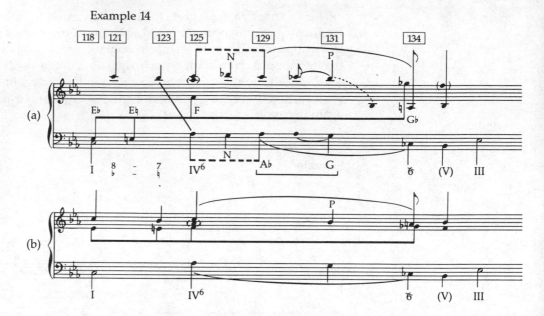

The E♭ minor statement of the opening theme

After the appearance of the two distinct themes in the mediant key in the exposition, the opening theme of the movement returns in measure 220. In order to accommodate its reappearance, E♭ major is altered to its parallel minor. Measures 223–227 correspond to measures 4–8 and consist of a series of five chromatically descending diminished seventh chords. If the unison statement of the opening theme in C minor were literally transposed up a minor third to E♭ minor, the melodic skip in measure 8 would appear as an interval of a major sixth leaping up from F to D. Instead of paralleling measure 8, however, the skip in measure 227 is expressed as a diminished seventh, E♯–D, not as a major sixth. In the unharmonized opening theme, the series of diminished sevenths ended with an implied first-inversion chord; here the spelling would imply a root-position diminished seventh chord if the theme were similarly unharmonized. Instead of returning back to E♭ minor, the diminished seventh resolves to an F♯ major chord in the succeeding measure.

At this point it is important to determine the tonal meaning of F♯ in the context of E♭. The passage in F♯ major in measures 228ff. represents an enharmonic respelling of G♭ major, the mediant harmony of E♭ minor. The diminished seventh skip of E♯–D in measure 227 thus represents an enharmonic respelling of F–E♭♭ which resolves in the following measure to the fifth, G♭–D♭. If one spells measures 224–227 in terms of G♭ rather than F♯ and then transposes them into C minor, the notation of Example 9b results, with the inevitable enharmonic change from B♮ in the first chord to C♭ in the last. The E♭ minor statement of the theme thus follows a course avoided at the opening of the movement, and leads on to its mediant harmony.

While awkward notes such as Fb, Bbb, and Ebb in measures 225–227 are avoided by Mozart's notation of this passage in the key of F# major, the enharmonic respelling is not absolutely essential (i.e., Gb major has the same number of flats as F# major has sharps). Mozart's notation serves a purpose, however, as will be shown later.

The F# (=Gb) chord in first inversion is prolonged for five measures after measure 228 by means of a neighbor note in the bass that supports an applied dominant seventh chord in third inversion. In Mozart's notation of these measures in the context of F# major, A# is decorated by its upper neighbor B♮. In the "true" key of Gb, however, the bass articulates the neighbor-note motion of Bb decorated by Cb. The enharmonic respelling of Cb as B♮, which occurred initially in measure 8, thus recurs here.

Immediately following the prolongation of the Gb harmony, the bass descends from A# (=Bb) through a passing $^6_4$ chord (measure 233) which leads to a diminished seventh chord in measure 234. A linear progression of a descending minor third results in the bass, with G♮ understood as a chromatic inflection of Gb (Example 15). Within the context of Gb major this chromatic inflection is a natural procedure in tonicizing the dominant (Example 16). The diminished seventh chord in measure 234, however, is followed by another; in fact, three further diminished seventh chords follow in chromatic descent. This succession of five diminished seventh chords is one of the most striking passages in the Classical literature. A sense of tonal continuity seems temporarily to be held in abeyance. Only when the descending succession is broken off does one regain a sense of tonal context. The arrival on the Bb chord at the beginning of measure 239 reorients the listener back into the tonal realm of Eb.

Example 15

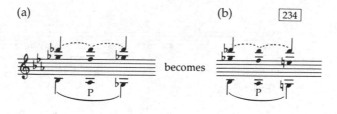

Example 16

While the first diminished seventh chord of the descent (measure 234) can be understood as a chromatic inflection of the prolonged Gb chord, and the last (measure 238) as a leading-tone seventh chord of the Bb chord in measure 239, the three intervening chords have a motivic rather than functional significance. The entire descent articulates a chromatic line from G♯ in measure 233 to D in measure 239. Though in a different tonal context, this chromatic line is enharmonically the same as that in measures 3–8 of the opening theme. Here the left-hand octaves of the solo piano begin the chromatic motive on A♭, the original spelling; this creates the curious simultaneous enharmonic of G♯ and A♭ in measure 233. The skip in register up to the A♭ isolates the motivic restatement from the preceding descent.

Not only are all the prominent motivic ideas of the opening theme brought together in this passage, but the order of their occurrence parallels their initial appearance as well. The chromatic base line from A♭ through D in measures 233–239 succeeds the neighbor-note motion in the bass of the G♭ passage in measures 228–232. The connecting descent through a minor third (notated A♯–G) in measures 232–234 is reminiscent of the diminished-third motive of measures 3–4. Here, as in the opening, the motion continues on to become a chromatic line. (The descending third would in fact be diminished if the G♭ major passage were cast in the parallel minor.) Example 17 isolates the bass line of measures 228ff. and shows how all three motivic ideas follow each other. Within this motivic scheme, the context of G♭ major can be heard up through measure 235 and even measure 236 (see Example 18). The diminished seventh chord in measure 235, which could imply an elision of A♭ in the bass motion G♮–G♭ (recalling the chordal succession of measures 4–5), could have moved to V in G♭ major, while the diminished seventh chord in measure 236 could have resolved directly back to G♭. Despite these continuing intimations of G♭ major, the main significance of these measures remains primarily motivic.

Example 17

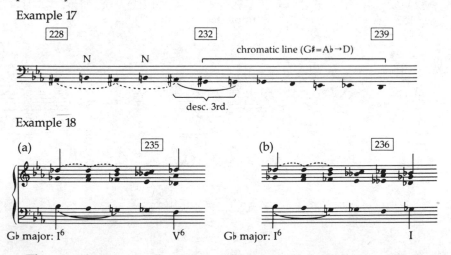

Example 18

Gb major: I⁶ ... V⁶ ... Gb major: I⁶ ... I

The simultaneous enharmonic of F♯ and G♭ in measure 235 is yet another assertion of the conflict between the notational and real meanings of the respellings in this passage. The bass succession in measures 235–236 is essentially a diatonic half step; thus the F♯ that precedes F♮ really represents a G♭. The F♯/G♭ enharmonic, so dramatically exploited within the E♭ minor statement of the opening theme, is also suggested at the beginning of the section. The chromatic inflection of G to G♭ when E♭ major is altered to its parallel minor is an enharmonic echo of the succession G–F♯ in measures 3–4.

The direct enharmonic transformation of F♯ to G♭ is most subtly suggested, however, in measures 10–11 of the opening theme. Example 19 presents a detail of the voice leading in measures 9–11. The C minor chord in measure 9 is prolonged until measure 11 through a subsidiary harmonic progression in which the augmented sixth chord in measure 10 continues untypically to a diminished seventh chord (equivalent in function to a dominant seventh chord in first inversion) which resolves back to the tonic.[17] Because G is elided in the top voice of measure 11, the F♯ over the augmented sixth chord in measure 10 continues directly to F♮, forming part of another statement of the motive of a descending chromatic line, as noted earlier. Example 20 shows a further detail of the voice leading presented in Example 19c. In the motion from the augmented sixth chord of measure 10 to the diminished seventh chord on the second beat of measure 11 there are two chromatic passing notes, A♮ and B♭, supporting the top-voice succession of F♯–F♮. These two intervening steps between the second beats of measures 9 and 10 imply the motion of an applied diminished seventh chord leading to a B♭ chord. The F♯ on the third beat of measure 10 thus temporarily represents a G♭ which, supported by A♮ in the bass, resolves to F, supported by B♭. This most subtly foreshadows the enharmonic notation of F♯ major as G♭ in measures 228ff.

Example 19

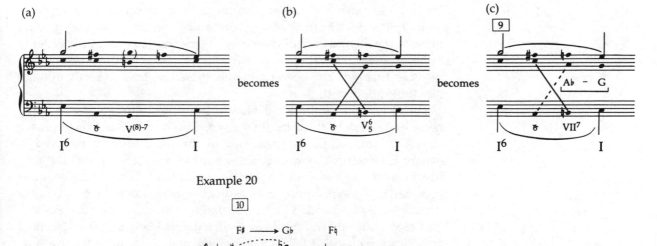

Example 20

17. This corresponds to the interpretation given by Aldwell and Schachter in *Harmony and Voice Leading*, Vol. 2, p. 176; 2nd edn, p. 493.

Example 21 presents the large-scale tonal plan of the passage that begins with the Eb minor statement of the opening theme in measure 220. Though a diminished seventh chord, being a dissonant sonority, cannot be prolonged, there is an association between the diminished seventh chords of measures 223 and 238. In a sense the structural tonal motion is suspended between these points.[18] The measures that follow these diminished seventh chords are also associated with each other by means of the enharmonic relation of B♮ and Cb. In measure 224 Cb continues on to Bb whereas in measure 239 Bb is followed by its chromatic inflection to B♮ before leading on to C.

Example 21

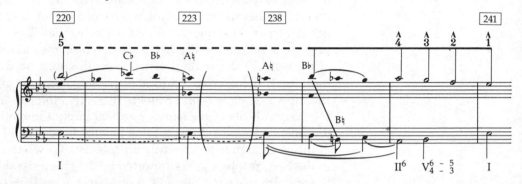

The transitional section in the recapitulation

The F#/Gb enharmonic exploited in the exposition occurs once again in the recapitulation, in the passage connecting the return of the opening theme to the second and third themes. As mentioned earlier, the order of the second and third themes presented in the exposition is reversed in the recapitulation. The opening theme, therefore, leads directly into the third, not the second, theme.

Example 22 shows the tonal motion from the return of the opening theme in C minor to the third theme, also in C minor. Since the thematic material of the recapitulation is cast in the tonic there is no need to tonicize the mediant as in the exposition. Mozart recomposes the passage, however, in a way which retains several important motivic features presented in the exposition. The neighbor-note figure in the bass of measures 369–373 is expanded in the succeeding measures. The diminished-third motive occurs during this expansion and leads to the augmented sixth chord in measure 380. The chromatic motive also appears, this time in the form of parallel tenths between the top and bass voices (measures 373–379). More significantly, the inner-voice motion in measures 362–380

18. A similar large-scale connection between equivalent diminished seventh chords occurs in the third movement of Mozart's Piano Concerto in Eb major, K. 449. Between the diminished seventh chords in measures 253 and 262 a remarkable excursion to Db minor takes place.

implies another chromatic line, an ascent from Eb. This rising chromatic line at first echoes the Eb–Gb ascent of the transitional section of the exposition (measures 118–134; see Example 14), but then continues on to G in measure 381 as Gb is enharmonically transformed into F♯. The entire line from Eb up to G is summed up later in measure 488, immediately after the cadenza.

Example 22

The closing passages of the exposition and recapitulation are linked by an enharmonic association. The V of the exposition's Eb cadence is immediately preceded by a root-position diminished seventh chord with A♮ in the bass (measure 279). In the parallel place at the end of the recapitulation (measure 506), the diminished seventh chord is built on F♯. The notes of both these chords are exactly the same except for the enharmonic spellings of Gb and F♯. Not only are the closing gestures of both passages the same but the F♯/Gb enharmonic is again recalled.[19]

At the outset of this article, we gave evidence of Brahms's particular affinity for K. 491. This concerto is also mentioned by Brahms in a letter he wrote to Clara Schumann encouraging her to play the work.[20] As no

19. For another example, see Eric Wen, "A Disguised Reminiscence in Mozart's G minor Symphony," *Music Analysis* 1/1 (1982), pp. 55–71. Additionally, in the last movement of our concerto, see the poignant articulation of the F♯–Gb enharmonic that appears in the coda (especially in measures 233–234).
20. See Brahms's letter to Clara dated 7 February 1861, written from Hamburg, in Berthold Litzmann, ed., *Clara Schumann–Johannes Brahms: Briefe aus den Jahren 1853–1896*, Vol. 1 (Leipzig, 1927), p. 355.

cadenza by Mozart exists, Brahms wrote one of his own and most likely offered it to Clara for her performances.[21]

It is always fascinating to study cadenzas not written by a concerto's composer. While featuring elements of a composition in an improvisatory style, these cadenzas often reveal insights about one musician's perceptions of another. In the case of Brahms and Mozart it is hardly surprising that there exists an organic connection in the former's cadenza to the latter's C minor Concerto.

In Brahms's cadenza to K. 491 the remote key area of G♭ major is strongly emphasized. Not only is there the reiterated leading-tone motion of F–G♭ in the bass, as seen in measures 33–34, but the tonal motion leading into G♭ major recalls the exposition of K. 491 itself. E♭ major is extended from measures 15 to 25 and is chromatically inflected to E♭ minor (measure 26) before the arrival at G♭ in measure 34. What is particularly noteworthy is that the bass motion F–G♭ of measures 33ff. is emphatically reinterpreted near the end of the cadenza by the enharmonically transformed bass motion F–F♯–G in measures 56–62. The cadential $^6_4$ chord over the bass note G in measure 62 ultimately leads through a $^5_4$ chord in measure 73 to the dominant in measure 75. While perhaps "unstylistic," Brahms's cadenza explores an essential feature of K. 491: the enharmonic relation of F♯ and G♭. In so doing, Brahms reveals a subtle insight into one of Mozart's greatest compositions.

21. See Johannes Brahms, *Complete Transcriptions, Cadenzas and Exercises*, ed. Eusebius Mandyczewski (reprint edn, New York, 1971), pp. 109–11.

Schenker and chromatic tonicization: a reappraisal

Patrick McCreless

The strength and analytical usefulness of Schenker's theories concerning chromaticism and chromatic tonicization have long been recognized. The advantages of his system, as opposed to other nineteenth- and twentieth-century theories that deal with chromaticism, are immediately apparent. His system establishes a background – both in the general sense, and in the specific sense of his concept of the *Ursatz* – in terms of which all chromatic motion can be heard and explained. Rather than hearing tonicizations of chromatic elements merely as distant modulations, somehow "expressive" or "programmatic," but strangely detached and separated from the diatonic underpinnings of a piece, he subsumes all chromatic motion into an ultimate diatonic structure. The analytical power of such a point of view is clear, since the seemingly random and unmotivated modulations described by earlier theorists can now be heard as all directed toward a single goal and controlled by a single principle. Furthermore, Schenker shows that chromatic tonicizations often arise from the expansion of linear motives, thereby demonstrating that they participate in the coherence of tonal masterworks not only through their integration into linear–harmonic structure, but also through the unifying force of motivic cross-reference.[1]

1. It is necessary to clarify the use of the term "chromatic tonicization" in the present paper, *vis-à-vis* Schenker's own writings. Schenker's use of the term "tonicization" in itself reveals the development of his theories from *Harmony* to *Free Composition*. Having coined the term in *Harmony* to describe how "each scale-step manifests an irresistible urge to attain the value of the tonic for itself" (*Harmony*, p. 256), Schenker, in keeping with the increasing and eventually all-encompassing role that counterpoint was to assume in his work, by *Free Composition* ceases to use the term. The processes described earlier by "tonicization" now are explained under the umbrella of counterpoint and fundamental structure, and in specific techniques such as "the transference of the forms of the fundamental structure to individual harmonies," "the addition of a root," and the like (*Free Composition*, pp. 88ff.). Furthermore, even in *Harmony* Schenker does not use the specific term "chromatic tonicization"; he rather refers to the tonicization of chromatic scale steps, or of chromatically altered scale degrees. Complicating the issue further is the fact that writers such as Matthew Brown and Gregory Proctor have, combining important points in *Harmony* and *Free Composition*, identified "tonicization" and "mixture" as the two sources of chromaticism in Schenker's thought. Although I believe such an identification ultimately to be correct, the terminology is confusing, since chromaticized *Stufen* derived by "mixture" can be "tonicized" (*Harmony*, p. 288; although Schenker does not use the term "mixture" here, the concept of tonicizing the triad of opposite mode is explicit), and since the term "tonicization" disappears from *Free Composition* altogether. In consequence, the term used here, "chromatic tonicization," is not derived directly from Schenker. Yet I would argue that by preserving the term "toniciza-

However, Schenker's view of chromatic tonicization – and indeed, his view of key and tonal structure *in toto* – has recently been called into question. Leo Treitler has sharply criticized currently popular analytical systems, such as Schenker's, that concentrate only on the internal coherence of individual works, and thus are unconcerned with culturally encoded and historically determined aspects of those works, particularly those aspects concerned with tonal structure. He asserts that in "formalist analysis" one finds sophisticated theories of tonality, but little interest in the qualitative side of key relations, although this was an important instrument for the rhetorical and expressive functions of music in the era of common practice.[2] Treitler thus falls into line with Joseph Kerman[3] and other historical musicologists who have recently taken Schenker to task for dealing with music in a way that, to use an expression of Treitler's, "draws the blinds before music's expressive force."[4]

Schenker and Treitler in fact represent two opposing poles of thought regarding chromatic tonicization in the tonal music of the later eighteenth century and the nineteenth century. This opposition between the thinkers may be structured in three ways:

1. In terms of the degree to which individual works are considered synchronically or diachronically. Here Schenker concentrates on the internal, synchronic functioning of the individual work, and focuses on its inner coherence without regard for historical considerations, while Treitler argues that diachronic, historically based criteria are essential to analysis as well.

2. In terms of the degree to which keys are attributed independent status. Here Treitler considers keys as viable analytical entities that are crucial to an ongoing musical discourse, while Schenker subsumes all keys and modulations (at least in his later work) into an ultimate diatonic structure.

3. In terms of analytical scope. That is, in multi-movement works Schenker limits his analytical observations to individual movements, whereas Treitler is willing to deal with relationships that are operative across all movements.

We might reformulate these two categories of opposition in terms of the distinction "systemic/extra-systemic," such that systemic relationships are

---

tion," and by focusing on chromaticism in its harmonic rather than its linear sense, I am recuperating into Schenkerian theory a particularly harmonic point of view that was eloquently presented in *Harmony*, but gradually became overwhelmed in Schenker's thought by the privileging of counterpoint.

See Matthew Brown, "The Diatonic and the Chromatic in Schenker's Theory of Harmonic Relations," *Journal of Music Theory* 30/1 (1986), pp. 1–33; Gregory Proctor, "Technical Bases of Nineteenth-Century Chromatic Tonality: A Study in Chromaticism," (Ph.D. diss., Princeton University, 1977).

2. Leo Treitler, "'To Worship That Celestial Sound': Motives for Analysis," *Journal of Musicology* 1/2 (1982), p. 153.

3. Joseph Kerman, "How We Got into Analysis, and How to Get Out," *Critical Inquiry* 7/2 (1980), pp. 311–31.

4. Treitler, p. 153.

all those definable in Schenker's theory, while extra-systemic relationships involve all those that his theory does not address. Viewed in such terms, Treitler's approach to chromatic tonicization is extra-systemic in several ways: first, it brings historical criteria to bear upon the individual work; second, it is willing to consider keys as viable "things" in analysis; and third, in multi-movement works it invokes inter-movement relationships that exceed the boundaries of the single *Ursatz*, to which Schenker limited himself, in his mature theory, almost exclusively.

The present study will take this systemic/extra-systemic opposition as a springboard for a reconsideration of our theories of chromatic tonicization in tonal music. The argument will proceed in four stages: (1) an overview of the central features of Treitler's and Schenker's points of view concerning key relationships; (2) the proposal of an alternative way of considering chromatic tonicization, based on preserving important aspects of Schenker's point of view, but incorporating essential elements of Treitler's as well – here a careful review of Schenker's development of a theory of chromaticism will attempt to show that he occasionally came close to articulating a position that shares certain features of Treitler's work, but that his increasing focus on counterpoint and the theory of the *Ursatz* led him eventually to concentrate his observations on the contrapuntal unfolding of single movements; (3) an analysis of the opening measures of Beethoven's *Leonore* Overture No. 3, in the light of this review; and (4) an analysis of "Pause," the twelfth song of Schubert's *Die schöne Müllerin*, based on the same principles.

Treitler and Schenker on key relationships

When Treitler accuses "formalist analysis" of not taking into account the "qualitative side of key relations," he does not direct his criticism specifically at Schenker. He might as well have, however, for Schenker was simply not interested in such matters. One can search the entire corpus of his analytical essays and theoretical works and find not so much as a single statement in which he has recourse to qualitative aspects of keys as the basis of an analytical judgment. Just as Edward T. Cone parodies twelve-tone theorists by suggesting that their analyses work equally well if the pieces under consideration are turned upside down,[5] so might we assert that for Schenker, it makes no difference what key a piece is in, so long as it is in one, and so long as it conforms to the high standards of coherence posited by his system. Now to make such a claim, of course, overstates the case, just as Cone did; but to do so points out the extent to which Schenker's system excludes considerations of this sort.

Although Treitler applauds Schenker for his insights and his systematization of tonal language, he nevertheless argues that there are certain

5. Edward T. Cone, "Beyond Analysis," *Perspectives of New Music* 6/1 (1967), pp. 33–51, reprinted in Benjamin Boretz and Edward T. Cone, eds., *Perspectives on Contemporary Music Theory* (New York, 1972), pp. 72–90.

aspects of tonal music that Schenker's theory does not address. What Treitler claims to hear that Schenker does not – or at least that Schenker does not feel compelled to incorporate into his theory – involves an extra-systemic, long-standing and time-honored tradition of associating musical keys with affective states. If we take the tonal system, as it existed at a particular moment in the late eighteenth or in the nineteenth century, we would have to include, as a part of most competent listeners' mindsets, a complex baggage involving affective associations with particular keys: a cultural code, as it were, albeit an ill-defined one, that links key and affect.[6] Closely related to such a code is the association of affect with sharp and flat keys, often with the description "bright" for the former, "dark" for the latter. It is from such traditions that Treitler draws in his analysis of Beethoven's Ninth Symphony, in order to buttress his argument that there is more to the choice of tonicizations in that work than can be accounted for by "formalist" analysis.[7]

In his analysis of the Ninth Symphony Treitler uses the concepts of key and key affect in order to identify the ongoing rhetorical, expressive content of the work. For him, this content turns in large measure upon Beethoven's use of keys – not only tonicizations within individual movements, but the use of keys throughout the entire work. For example, he considers the roles of D major and D minor, and of B♭ major across the four movements of the piece, and he makes an attempt to account for the expressive and rhetorical roles that these keys play. In analyzing the work he invokes both the historically and stylistically based characteristics of keys and the "within-the-piece" meaning that these keys assume as the movements progress in order to show how tonal structure articulates expressive content.

Although his analysis is, of course, not concerned only with tonicizations or keys that are chromatic, his explanations of such tonicizations provide a telling point of comparison of his approach to that of Schenker. When Treitler encounters a chromatic tonicization, he tends to explain it in terms of key characteristics. Thus, in explaining the surprising tonicization of D♭ major toward the end of the third movement of the Ninth Symphony, he invokes the "atmosphere of religiosity" associated with this key in the nineteenth century.[8] Taking a broad view of Treitler's analysis of the Ninth Symphony, we might suggest that Schenker can make a more self-motivating, self-contained whole of individual movements, while Treitler can account better for inter-movement relationships, for why different keys are tonicized over the course of the work, and in general why the movements of the piece are in D minor/major and B♭ major, rather than, say, C♯ minor/major and A major.

6. For an excellent overview of the historical development of concepts of key characteristics, see Rita Steblin, *A History of Key Characteristics in the Eighteenth and Early Nineteenth Centuries* (Ann Arbor, 1983).
7. Treitler, pp. 159–70. See also Treitler's "History, Criticism, and Beethoven's Ninth Symphony," *19th-Century Music* 3/5 (1980), pp. 193–210.
8. Treitler, p. 167.

From a theorist's point of view, Treitler's analysis is provocative in that it deals with issues that contemporary theory has tended to avoid, and it brings these issues directly into analytical contact with an individual work. We may find his analysis lacking in rigor, and we may question his claim that he accounts for the expressive content of a work in a way that formalist analysis cannot. Nevertheless, we are at the very least challenged by a point of view that does not limit itself either to a purely synchronic consideration of a piece, that takes an anti-Schenkerian position on the issue of tonicization, and that is able to consider all movements of a multi-movement work.

Treitler's analytical use of the concepts of key and key characteristics, of course, contrasts strikingly with Schenker's. We can summarize the essentials of Schenker's theory of chromaticism in a few brief points. First, as Matthew Brown has recently shown in a valuable reconsideration of Schenker's views on the topic, his theory provides for an entire chromatic system to be generated directly from the triad through tonicization and mixture, and that chromaticism can penetrate all the way from the foreground into the deep middleground, even though the background is fully diatonic.[9] Second, tonicizations of chromatically derived triads are explained ultimately as linear phenomena. Even the most distant and most extensive uses of chromaticism are ultimately relatable to the diatonic background by being shown to be expansions of chromatic passing tones or chromatic neighbor tones. In his later work, the tonal flux, or the "tonality" (as opposed to "diatony"), as he calls it,[10] of the foreground is rigorously governed by the counterpoint of the background. Extended tonal areas, chromatic or not, are not to be perceived as keys as such, or even as modulations from a principal key, but as linearly derived prolongations of scale steps.

As a useful model of the Schenkerian approach to a chromatic tonicization, let us look first at a brief example from that class of later eighteenth- and nineteenth-century works in which a chromatic detail early in a piece is expanded to create a chromatic tonicization on a deeper level later in the piece. A classic example is Brahms's song, "Wie Melodien zieht es mir," Op. 105, No. 1. The crucial chromatic element in the song, pointed out eloquently in Edward Laufer's well-known analysis,[11] is the B♭ sixth chord of measure 4, which first appears as a relatively insignificant detail, but is later greatly expanded (measures 33–40) in an extraordinary musical realization of the poetic text.

The Schenkerian way of treating this chromaticism is to view it as an expansion of a linear element, as Laufer does in his analysis. At the initial

9. Brown, p. 25.
10. *Free Composition*, p. 5.
11. Edward Laufer, "Brahms, Op. 105, No. 1: A Schenkerian Approach," in Maury Yeston, ed., *Readings in Schenkerian Analysis and Other Approaches* (New Haven, 1977), pp. 254–72. I have reproduced neither the song nor Laufer's sketches here because they are readily available in Yeston's anthology.

appearance of the B♭ triad in measure 4, Laufer simply notes that "the flatting of the b neighbor note avoids the diminished fifth b-natural–f-natural[1]."[12] When the same triad returns in the climactic measures 33–40, he observes:

> The word *mild* is now associated with *leise* in m. 4. The same sound (B-flat-major triad) returns, and in a certain sense the b-flat of m. 4, only an embellishing neighbor note, is also "fulfilled" or "realized," having become the final note of the bass arpeggiation. . ."[13]

In other words, the return of the B♭ is an expansion of a voice-leading detail (the flatting of a pitch in a neighbor-note motive) into an event of greater structural importance.

An alternative view on chromatic tonicization

Having looked briefly at analytical examples from the points of view of Treitler and Schenker, we are now in a position to ask the fundamental question: Are these two points of view the only ones possible on the issue? Specifically, are we in the position of having to opt either for Treitler, thereby sacrificing Schenker's theoretical rigor and analytical power, or for Schenker, thereby sacrificing Treitler's claim that he can deal more adequately with expressive content and historical context? As Schenkerians, we are tempted to cast our vote happily for our mentor, pointing out, with considerable justification, that Schenker was marvelously sensitive to expressive effects of every sort. For when Schenker describes the moving effect of a chromatic tonicization in an analysis, he is content to relegate the sort of key-related phenomena in which Treitler is interested to descriptive adjectives, but he explains how such musical events actually occur with the theoretical rigor of nouns.

I tend to cast my vote with those forces that would reject the diachronic features of Treitler's point of view. Bringing diachronic questions of style and culturally encoded key characteristics into analysis raises difficulties with which music theory still copes only with limited success. I propose, however, that if we dismiss Treitler entirely, we shall lose an important opportunity to increase our understanding of tonal music in general, and the music of the late eighteenth century and the nineteenth century in particular. For I would argue that Treitler's concern for keys as keys, as perceptual and perceptible things in themselves, with a life of their own, captures a crucial feature of the music in question, even though the adoption of such a point of view seems to fly directly in the face of what we have learned from Schenker. At the very least, allowing ourselves to hear "keys" as such in a multi-movement work allows us to move beyond the individual movement and consider works as wholes. At the most, if we follow the deeper implications of Treitler's observations, they might help us to develop a theoretical framework that preserves the insights of

12. Laufer, p. 260.
13. Laufer, p. 265.

Schenker even in single movements, while at the same time adding another dimension that could supplement those insights.

Let us return, as an example, to the Brahms song analyzed by Laufer. Another way to look at the B♭ of measure 4 and its expanded return later in the piece is merely to note the strangeness of the B♭ major triad when it first appears – a strangeness that is purely harmonic rather than linear, for at the crucial moment in measure 4 we do not just hear a B♭ as a pitch, or as a neighbor-note; we hear a whole triad. Although we can analyze the piece outside of time and "read" the B♭ as an altered neighbor note, we are, perceptually speaking, more likely to "hear" a full triad – a triad that is marked for memory (that is, it seems strange) because (1) it is the first non-diatonic event in a hitherto entirely diatonic song, and (2) this initial chromaticism is not a predictable chromatically inflected leading tone to a diatonic scale degree; rather, it is the more distant flatted second scale degree.

Our second view of the B♭ and its associated triad focuses on how the triad, as a harmony, is marked for memory, and how that memory is recalled, expanded, "realized" (to use Laufer's language), and given deeper meaning in measures 33–40. Such a point of view does not question the validity of Schenker's view at all; indeed, it depends upon it, because the Schenkerian view explains the whole diatonic structure which enables us to perceive the B♭ triad as "strange" or "marked for memory" in the first place. Where the two points of view differ is precisely in the matter of the relative priority of voice leading. For Schenker, of course, voice leading is absolutely prior, and all chromatic events must be rooted in voice leading: as is clear in Laufer's analysis, voice leading generates chromatic expansions. Our alternative point of view, however, while by no means denying that such events are ultimately subsumable into a diatonic voice-leading structure, nevertheless claims for them a purely harmonic status; such events are unfolded through voice leading, but they are harmonic in character, and they do not necessarily originate in voice leading. I would argue that the B♭ triad of measure 4 in "Wie Melodien" is not generated linearly through the chromatic alteration of the B to avoid a diminished fifth, but rather that the B♭ triad is what measure 4 is really about, and that the voice-leading paradigm (the neighbor note) is what allows the triad to be worked smoothly into the musical discourse.

In this view, the B♭ triad is in fact a motive – not a linear motive, but a harmonic one. It is the basis of an association, of a cross-reference. As such, it is conceptually independent of voice leading. It requires voice leading to be worked into the musical structure, but it is "detachable" as a motive and cross-reference in a way that voice leading is not. To view the triad in this way brings up a critical issue: the relationship between the conception, described here, of a harmonic entity as a motive, and Schenker's conception of the motive as it relates to harmony and to voice leading.

It will be worth our while to trace in some detail the relationship of motive, harmony, and voice leading in Schenker's thought as it evolved from *Harmony* to *Free Composition*. As is well known, the fundamental premise with which *Harmony* begins is that music is based on the idea of association. After predicating imitation of nature and association of ideas as the bases of all the other arts, Schenker asks:

But whence should music take the possibility of associating ideas, since it is not given by nature? Indeed, it took a host of experiments and the toil of many centuries to create this possibility. Finally it was discovered. It was the motif.

The motif, and the motif alone, creates the possibility of associating ideas, the only one of which music is capable. The motif is a primordial and intrinsic association of ideas.[14]

Although, as Oswald Jonas points out in an explanatory footnote to the passage quoted above, Schenker would later make the principle of motivic association subsidiary to the principle of *Auskomponierung*,[15] prolongation and voice leading, his interest in the motive – in repetition, in association – is evident throughout *Harmony*. In the very beginning of Part II of this treatise, the *Praktischer Teil*, he notes, "In practical art the main problem, in general, is how to realize the concept of harmony (of a triad or seventh-chord) in a live content."[16] What that "live content" turns out to be, of course, is the motive, which he sees as an "interpreter of the harmonic concept."[17] Thus, clearly enough, the motive articulates and unfolds harmonic scale steps.

But how does he view chromatic aspects of the motive? Can a particular chromatically inflected scale degree be motivic in itself, or is the chromatic inflection always grounded in a purely linear event? A close reading of Schenker suggests the latter. Thus in the Brahms song, Laufer is, from a Schenkerian point of view, perfectly correct never to suggest in any way that the Bb itself is motivic. His procedure of showing the Bb as an altered neighbor which is then expanded later accords not only with Schenker's later views, but even to some extent with his theory in *Harmony*, where he derives the "Phrygian II" from motivic considerations – that is, "the motif is not always happy at the thought of possibly finding itself in the position of a diminished triad."[18] The closest that Schenker comes in *Harmony* to articulating the point of view of a harmony as itself motivic occurs toward the end of the long section on chromaticism. Here he writes:

The harmonies behave in this respect much like the motifs. If the latter, in order to crystallize in our minds, need an association such as a simple repetition, a contrast, or any juxtaposition whatever. . .the harmonies likewise welcome contrast as a most desirable means of association, and not only in the sphere of a small diatonic fragment. . .but also in larger form complexes. One should note, for example, the inserted E major passage in the midst of the long E-flat major complex in the Rondo of Beethoven's E-flat major Sonata, op. 7. How much greater is

14. *Harmony*, p. 4.
15. *Ibid*.
16. *Harmony*, p. 211.
17. *Ibid*.
18. *Harmony*, p. 110.

the effect of the E-flat major key here because suddenly we are, chromatically, in E major![19]

Here, interestingly, the concept of "harmony as motive" is not invoked as a principle of similarity, as we are suggesting in the Brahms, but as a principle of contrast: the return of E♭ is made more effective by the surprising detour into E. Schenker then points out similar examples of "motivically" contrasting tonicizations a semitone apart in Beethoven's Piano Sonata Op. 106 (B to B♭ major toward the end of the development in the first movement, and again in the Scherzo), in Beethoven's Ninth Symphony (B to B♭, first movement), and in Haydn's Piano Sonata in E♭ major (Hob. XVI/52), where the first and last movements are in E♭ major, but the slow movement in E major.[20] In all these cases, the operative principle is that of contrast and return, although it is significant that Schenker is willing to attribute to a harmony or key any motivic status at all, and that, in the case of the Haydn Sonata, he is willing to do so across movements.

Of course, as Schenker developed his theories, he became more and more intent on relating all musical phenomena ultimately to counterpoint, so that, by the time of *Free Composition*, the principles of repetition and association are clearly subordinated to the *Ursatz* and to voice leading. As Jonas points out in his introduction to *Harmony*, phenomena that are given harmonic or motivic explanations in the earlier treatise are given contrapuntal ones later.[21] Accordingly, in the later work, "chromatic tonicizations" are generated through the expansion of linear events, through mixture, and through various techniques of prolongation.[22] A typical example is his analysis of the first movement of Beethoven's Sonata in F minor, Op. 57, where the emphasis on G♭ near the beginning of the first movement is explained rigorously in terms of linear motive and voice leading (the neighbor motive c–d♭–c generates, through a 5–6–5 motion, the harmonic G♭) rather than in purely tonal terms.[23]

However, there are two fascinating instances in *Free Composition* in which Schenker comes tantalizingly close to suggesting that harmonies, or chromatically inflected scale steps, may indeed function motivically. The first of these instances occurs in the section on motivic repetition in the foreground, and concerns the first movement of Beethoven's Piano Sonata in E♭ major, Op. 81a:

Here $g♭^2$ and g^2 are engaged in a struggle with one another – only two single tones, certainly not a motive repetition in the usual sense. And yet the synthesis of the entire first movement circles around this conflict [see Example 1].[24]

What Schenker clearly recognizes here is a kind of motivic synthesis that

19. *Harmony*, p. 289.
20. *Harmony*, pp. 289–90.
21. *Harmony*, pp. ixff.
22. See *Free Composition*, pp. 88ff.
23. *Free Composition*, p. 59. For another of Schenker's analyses that interprets a large-scale prolongation of the "Phrygian II" as arising from a 5–6–5 motion, see his essay on Chopin's Etude in E♭ minor, Op. 10, No. 6, *Das Meisterwerk* I, pp. 148ff.
24. *Free Composition*, p. 100.

Example 1. Beethoven, Sonata Op. 81a, first movement
(from *Free Composition*, Figure 119/7)

turns not on voice leading, but on the cross-referencing and association of individual tones, as tones. Although we might subsume the play of G♭ and G into Schenker's broader theory by accounting for it as mixture, his recognition of the motivic repetition and association of individual pitches is telling.

The other example in *Free Composition* of Schenker's attributing motivic status to chromatic elements occurs not in the section on motivic repetition, but in that on chromatic tones in the foreground. Commenting on a brief tonicization of A♭ major in the Rondo of the Beethoven Violin Concerto Op. 61, he notes:

Occasionally an enharmonic tone can introduce a chromatic change. The insertion of an enharmonic situation provides opportunity for a small but beautiful prolongation: here one finds an allusion to what is to come [see Example 2].[25]

Example 2. Beethoven, Violin Concerto Op. 61, third movement, measures 247ff.
(from *Free Composition*, Figure 114/7)

From our point of view, the crucial comment here is not the description of the prolongation itself, but the comment on the "allusion" to come. That allusion is, of course, the much more extensive and much more dramatic tonicization of A♭ toward the end of the Rondo. Although Schenker's comment is elliptical, apparently it is the enharmonic change itself that will become the basis of the allusion – that is, the motivic cross-reference or association.

25. *Free Composition*, p. 92.

Looking back over our traversal of Schenker's writings, we can say that, although his theories, both early and late, tend to avoid attributing motivic status to harmony *per se*, there are, in both *Harmony* and *Free Composition*, observations and analyses that suggest a willingness to entertain such a notion when musical context supports it. If we cannot therefore claim that a point of view which focuses on the purely harmonic aspect of the B♭ in "Wie Melodien zieht es mir" and raises it to the status of a motive in and of itself is "Schenkerian" in the strict sense, we can nevertheless claim a Schenkerian precedent for such a position.

That Schenker ultimately rejected this point of view is surely due to his being utterly convinced of the power of his contrapuntally based theories to explain all aspects of tonal music. The two remaining examples in the present paper will endeavor to show that, although his linear theories are absolutely essential to our understanding of chromatic tonicizations in individual tonal works, the premise that certain aspects of such tonicizations are generated from outside the system – that they are "extrasystemic" – can also be analytically productive, particularly if we accept the notion that a given chromatic scale-step, harmony, or even pitch-class can assume a motivic role. Since I have presented three examples already of how a harmonic concept of motive can work in single-movement works, I shall choose for the remaining examples single movements of multi-movement works: precisely the area of interest to Leo Treitler, and precisely where we would expect to find situations where harmonic–motivic associations exceed the individual *Ursatz* and yet create motivic repetition and cross-reference over the course of a work as a whole.

Beethoven's *Leonore* Overture No. 3

A dramatic example of the process in question is the Adagio introduction to Beethoven's *Leonore* Overture No. 3 – a passage analyzed by Schenker in *Free Composition* (see Example 3).

Example 3. Beethoven, *Leonore* Overture No. 3, Adagio
(from *Free Composition*, Figure 62/2)

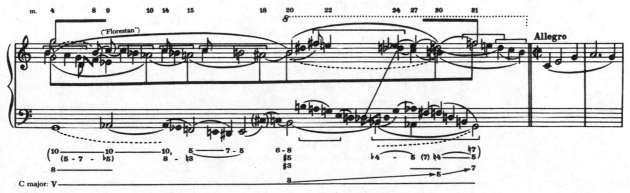

Because I shall consider his analysis in some detail, I shall quote his commentary upon it in full:

Only the first space of a third, g^1–b^1, is filled in by chromatic passing tones. The further course of the prolongation shows the arpeggiations b^1–d^2 and d^2–f^2. In measures 9–14 there is an event of marvelous beauty: the first passing tone, ab^1, undergoes a transformation into the interval of an octave, that is, into the $Ab \frac{8}{3}$ chord, and upon this harmony, the first four bars of the "Florestan Aria" are sounded; the chord shapes itself into a virtual stage, and on it Florestan, arisen from a dream, takes up his song. Evidently, Beethoven did not consider it sufficient to relate the overture to the opera by quoting those measures only in the course of the Allegro: hence he strove to make the quotation distinctly more logical by anticipating it with another in the introductory Adagio. Thus the circle of relationships within the overture is closed; it is as though the overture had no need of the opera. Beethoven achieved the effect of the vision in the Adagio by placing it in a passing tone of chromatic origin, which is more remote than the diatonic $a\natural^1$. It is this which makes the vision more distant, more visionary. To a genius, a simple prolongation can create who knows what unseen opportunity![26]

Schenker's sketch and discussion clarify beautifully the issue in question here. Although Schenker's perceptive analysis demonstrates elegantly how the chromatic tonicization of Ab is worked into the voice-leading structure, there is, it seems to me, a process at work here that he does not address. Yet we cannot criticize him on the grounds that he is insensitive to aesthetic effect, that he fails to note the symbolism whereby chromatic distance in the music represents psychological distance in the drama, or, of course, that he neglects to note how Beethoven creates a coherent musical structure in the overture itself. If we find his analysis less than completely satisfactory, it must be on three rather different counts: first, that he overlooks the associative connection of the Ab tonicization in the Adagio to the Ab key of Florestan's aria itself, in Act II of the opera; second, that he elevates voice leading to a level of importance that our perception of the piece does not justify; and third, that his inferences regarding the compositional thought process of the composer is counter-intuitive to us.

Let us look at these points in order. First, Schenker's sentence, "Beethoven achieved the effect of the vision in the Adagio by placing it in a passing tone of chromatic origin, which is more remote than the diatonic $a\natural^1$," correctly identifies the remoteness of Ab from C major as the source of the musical effect that he describes. Yet why did Beethoven achieve this effect of psychological distance precisely by introducing Florestan's melody in association with a tonicization of Ab major? Surely because the key of Ab major is as much a part of the motivic reference as is the tune. Florestan's aria in Ab major marks his first appearance in the opera, both in the *Leonore* version of 1805–06, for which the overture is intended, and the later *Fidelio* of 1814.[27] An analysis which limits itself solely to musical

26. *Free Composition*, p. 64. The figures from *Free Composition* reproduced in Examples 1–3 are used by permission of Schirmer Books, a division of Macmillan, Inc.

27. Alan Tyson has shown conclusively that the *Leonore* Overture No. 3, intended for the single, unsuccessful performance of *Leonore* in 1806, was in fact the second of the four overtures for the opera *Leonore/Fidelio* to be composed. The correct ordering for the over-

relationships within the overture itself necessarily overlooks this obvious tonal connection.

Second, by describing the passage in terms of Beethoven's working the Ab prolongation into a chromatic passing tone, Schenker implies that the voice leading was already there, and that the problem is simply to find the right place for a musical and dramatic cross-reference. Again, it seems to me, his priorities are reversed. At least in my perception, the force of the Ab tonicization unquestionably takes precedence over the voice leading, particularly when it is related to the opera as a whole. Beethoven's skill in voice leading undoubtedly makes the passage work smoothly, but I would argue that the voice leading is a way of making the stark juxtaposition of keys effective, rather than that the juxtaposition of keys grows out of a process of voice leading.

Third, Schenker seems to attribute a compositional priority to the quotation of the Florestan aria in the Allegro of the overture, where it occurs in the exposition in E major, and in the recapitulation in C major, as the second idea of the sonata form; for he notes, "Evidently, Beethoven did not consider it sufficient to relate the overture to the opera by quoting those measures only in the course of the Allegro: hence he strove to make the quotation distinctly more logical by anticipating it with another in the introductory Adagio." Yet it seems more reasonable, both musically and dramatically, to imagine that the idea of beginning the overture, and thus the opera as a whole (we must remember that this overture is the one that was performed in 1806, at Beethoven's second attempt to launch *Leonore*), with the music of the opera's central male character, in the right tempo, the right key, and even the right instruments, was central from the outset; and therefore that the unifying use of the motive in the Allegro arises from the original statement of the Florestan melody in the Adagio, rather than vice versa.

If we look at the passage from the overture in terms of the distinction systemic/extra-systemic, as developed above, we can see clearly the difference in points of view articulated by Schenker and Treitler. Although we do not have a Treitler analysis of the passage, we can hypothesize from his analysis of the Ninth Symphony that he would try to make tonal sense of the opera as a whole as well as the passage in question, and that he would bring historically determined concepts of key characteristics into the argument as they are relevant, so that his view of the beginning of the overture would be informed by evidence in the overture itself, in the opera as a whole, and in the musical culture at large. Schenker, however, limits his purview, for the most part, to the closed piece that is the overture. Although he does, of course, recognize the traditional motivic relation of Florestan's tune to the opera, he does not mention the tonal motivic

tures by date of composition is: *Leonore* Overtures No. 2, No. 3, No. 1, *Fidelio* Overture. See "The Problem of Beethoven's 'First' *Leonore* Overture," *Journal of the American Musicological Society* 28/2 (1975), pp. 292–334. Also, it is relevant to note that the Florestan aria is in the key of Ab major in all three versions of *Leonore/Fidelio*, and both *Leonore* Overtures Nos. 2 and 3 (that is, the first two to be composed) bring in the motivic reference in Ab in the first few measures of their opening Adagios.

relation incorporated in the A♭ prolongation. Thus he brings neither the tonal structure of the opera as a whole nor, needless to say, any concept of "key characteristics" into his analysis. In tonal terms, then, a Treitler-like analysis is extra-systemic with respect to Schenker in that it considers the tonal structure of the whole "multi-movement" piece as bearing on the analysis of a particular passage, and in that it invokes culturally and historically determined criteria as well.

The present paper argues for a position between Schenker and Treitler – one that maintains Schenker's rigor in analyzing voice-leading structure, and at the same time accepts Treitler's approach of considering multi-movement tonal structure in the analysis of single movements, yet does not accept Treitler's recourse to key characteristics. For neither Schenker's explanation of the Adagio, which works well as an analysis of a self-contained tonal piece (the overture), nor an approach which might relate the heroic C major of the Allegro and the gentle A♭ major of Florestan's aria to cosmic, culturally determined Cs and A♭s, and thus might work as an informal description of the piece, can tell the whole story. In Schenker's case, the scope of the analysis is too narrow (the overture, which bears a single *Ursatz*); while in the latter case, the scope is too broad (tonal music of a particular period, considered diachronically). It is only when we see the tonal plan of the Adagio as arising from tonal relations within the whole opera that we can fully understand why it works as it does.

Schubert's "Pause"

To see how a point of view that values both Schenkerian voice-leading paradigms and inter-movement tonal relations can work, let us look briefly at a familiar lied, Schubert's "Pause," the twelfth song of the cycle *Die schöne Müllerin*, which sets the poetry of Wilhelm Müller. The song is surely the most chromatic and harmonically complex of the twenty songs in the cycle, and its use of chromaticism bears directly on the issue of what is the proper scope of our analytical observations in multi-movement works of this sort.

Within the cycle as a whole "Pause" is both a point of repose and the crucial turning point of the narrative. At the beginning of the cycle, the protagonist, apparently a miller's apprentice, and a poet or singer, is in the open countryside, singing the praises of a life of wandering. We see him being led by a brook from his isolation in nature to a mill and its surrounding village, where he sees the miller's daughter and falls in love with her. The first eleven songs involve his being led by the brook to the mill, and his wooing the miller's daughter. The exuberant eleventh song, "Mein!", articulates the point at which he believes that he has successfully wooed and won the girl. It is upon the basis of this confidence in the success of his courtship that he dares to lay down his lute; for his lute, his art, has always been part and parcel of his life in isolation: if he wins the miller's daughter, he will not need the lute, since his isolation will be relegated to the past.[28] In the twelfth song, "Pause," he reflects upon his experience thus far; he sings of hanging his lute on the wall, for his joy at winning the miller's daughter is so great that "no song on earth can contain it." Yet he also has a premonition of things to come. Realizing that he has left the lute hanging for a long time, he imagines the wind stroking the strings lightly. Upon hearing that sound, as if from a distance, he asks himself:

> Is it the echo of my love's sorrow,
> or shall it be the prelude to new songs?

A straightforward interpretation of the poem here would read the "echo" as reflecting that time of uncertainty when the poet was courting the girl, and the prelude as anticipating new, and less anxious songs of love. Yet a more ironic interpretation is possible as well. That is, has he won the girl, thereby allowing him to leave the lute hanging on the wall? Or will his joy prove to be an illusion, and will he thus have to take it up again and sing "new songs"? The answer, for him and for us, is suggested in the next song, "Mit dem grünen Lautenbande," where he sings of the green ribbon wound around the strings of his lute, and thus unknowingly introduces the source of his own undoing, for the color green is not only the color of "nature," where we began his story, but also that of the *Jäger*, the hunter. Thus, beginning with the fourteenth song, "Der Jäger," in which the hunter appears as a strong rival for the *Müllerin*, the answer to our poet's question becomes more and more inevitable. He is constrained to return to his isolation in the countryside, and he eventually takes his own life by drowning himself in the very brook that once led him to the mill.

All the evidence, both in Müller's cycle of poems and in Schubert's cycle of songs on those poems, supports the view that the two songs "Mein!" and "Pause" articulate the central point in the larger dramatic structure. "Pause" not only ends with the questioning couplet that ties the entire cycle together, but it also, along with "Mein!", stands apart in terms of its poetic structure. "Mein!" and "Pause" are the only two songs in the cycle that are not strophic. Furthermore, "Mein!" avoids the regularity of meter and the common rhyme schemes of the other poems – abab, abcb, or aabb – and portrays the ebullience of the young lover by radically varying the length of the poetic line, and by rhyming the ends of all lines with the syllable "-ein." "Pause," on the other hand, in a sense suggests a strophic structure – the sentence structure works as 4 + 4 + 2, 4 + 4 lines, with rhyming couplets throughout – but Müller has arranged it not according to the sentence structure, but simply in the pattern 10 + 8 lines. More significantly, the long and metrically irregular lines, most of which employ the five stresses of pentameter rather than the more normal four of tetrameter, contrast strikingly with the short lines of "Mein!" In sum, Müller seems to have set apart, in terms of poetic structure, as well as

---

28. The discussion here of the isolation of the artist in society in the early nineteenth century draws upon the work of Robert Bailey.

narrative content, the two central songs in which the young poet sings of his triumph in love and questions the permanence of that triumph.[29]

Turning now to Schubert's setting of the poem, we can see that he has followed Müller's structure closely. Schubert's division of the song into two large parts – measures 1–41 and 42–81, both being articulated by the same opening material – parallels Müller's division of the poem into two sections of ten and eight lines. He also follows Müller's sentence structure in his formal subdivision of the song. Thus, Müller's 4 + 4 + 2, 4 + 4 organization of the poetic lines is reflected in the musical construction: after the piano introduction, measures 9–19 set lines 1–4, measures 20–32 set lines 5–8, measures 33–41 set lines 9–10, to make up the first section of ten lines; then, after an abbreviated return of the introduction, measures 46–55 set lines 11–14, measures 56–69 set lines 15–18, and measures 70–77 repeat and thus emphasize the crucial final couplet of the poem.

Surely the most puzzling musical passage in the song is the bizarre harmonic progression to which this final couplet is set; and it is this passage, which we already know to be central from a dramatic point of view, that will be the focus of our analytical discussion. From a circumscribed, intra-piece point of view, a Schenkerian linear analysis shows the passage to be far more organically motivated than its harmonic audacity might suggest upon first hearing. The middleground sketch in Example 4a shows that the entire song turns upon the conventional interrupted structure:

$$\hat{3}\ \hat{2}\ \|\ \hat{3}\ \hat{2}\ \hat{1}$$
$$\text{I\ V}\quad\text{I\ V\ I}$$

Example 4. Schubert, "Pause"

(a) middleground sketch

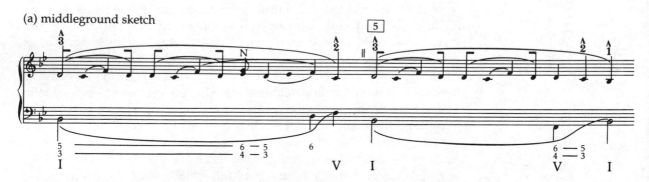

29. I have learned from John Rothgeb that the late Ernst Oster, in a paper presented to the Music Theory Society of New York State in 1975, also grouped "Mein!" and "Pause" together as a pair. While I did not hear the paper and am unaware of Oster's reasons for pairing the two songs, I am convinced of the validity of such an interpretation. In addition to the evidence adduced here on the grounds of dramatic meaning and poetic structure, there are important musical connections between the songs. "Mein!", in the key of D major, introduces into its contrasting middle section a prolongation of the flatted sixth scale degree, B♭, the key of "Pause." Also, an obvious motivic and rhythmic similarity links the opening measures of the two songs: compare the f♯[1]–a[1] in measures 1–2 of "Mein!" to the d[1]–f[1] in measures 1–2 of "Pause"; both motives involve a leap from the third to the fifth scale degree, and the rhythmic settings are identical.

Example 4 (*cont.*)

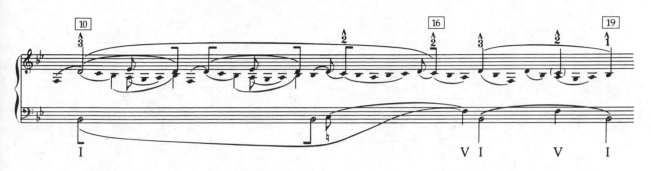

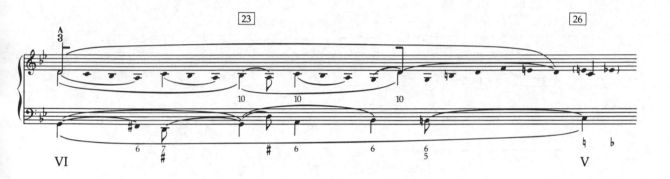

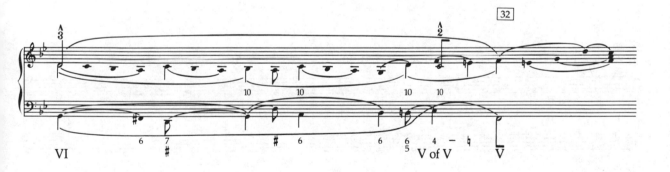

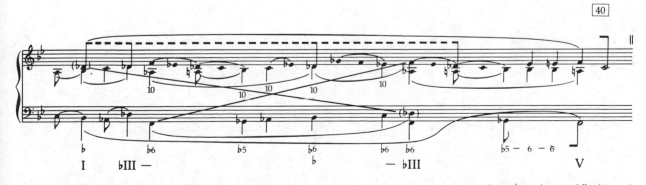

(*example continues on following page*)

Example 4 (*cont.*)

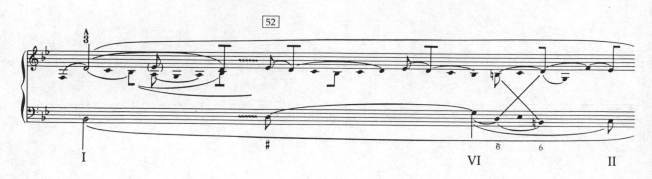

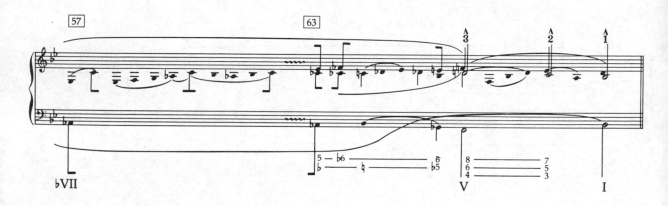

(b) measures 1–32   (c) measures 34–40   (d) measures 42–74

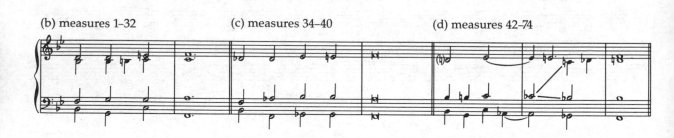

(e) hypothetical setting   (f) hypothetical setting   (g) hypothetical setting

Within this larger pattern, we can see that much of the large-scale melodic activity is directed toward the unfolding of an extraordinary motivic parallelism: that is, the prominent d^1–f^1 of the first measure of the accompaniment, there opened up as the unfilled minor third between the third and fifth scale degrees of B♭ major, is filled in slowly and inexorably, not once, but three times over the course of the song (measures 27–32, 33–41, and 42–67). Each time the harmonization is different, each time the path is slightly different, and each time the effect becomes more bizarre, more questioning. We can nevertheless see clearly enough that measures 33–41 are in a sense a variation of measures 27–32, and that the most puzzling harmonic progression of the piece, measures 63–69, is in turn a fascinating variation of measures 27–32, measures 33–41, and, ultimately, the d–f melodic interval of measure 1 as well (see Examples 4b–4d).[30]

Such a linear analysis is indeed powerful; it shows us, to use words rather like those that Schenker frequently used, how the most wide-ranging flights of compositional fantasy are anchored in a coherent diatonic structure. Yet a troubling question remains: why is there the striking emphasis on the F♭ major sixth-chord in measures 63–65 and 71–73? Our linear analysis has shown us how this chord fits into the linear–harmonic unfolding of the piece, but it has not explained why this particular chord is there – and, more significantly, why it, of all chords, is chosen to articulate the most dramatic moment of the song, and indeed of the whole cycle. All the rhetorical gestures of the passage point to this moment as the critical dramatic one in the song; the accompaniment comes to a total state of rest, and the singer floats over it in a free, almost recitative-like style – all on a triad whose root is a tritone away from the tonic! Why this particular chord, when many others, suggesting entirely different chromatic areas, are possible (see Examples 4e–4g)?

If we consider the text of the song, and especially if we keep in mind that this musical passage is an elaboration of measures 33–41, we can see immediately that the harmonic expansion here is a portrayal of the text. At the earlier passage, the poet sings how his joy is so great that no song on earth can contain it. Now, when he sings the words "Ist es der Nachklang meiner Liebespein?" we can see that a linear–motivic expansion has become a rhetorical device: the later music, being an expansion of the earlier passage, echoes that music, just as the text speaks of an "echo of my love's sorrow." Furthermore, the irony of having the "echo of love's sorrow" refer back to a moment of incomprehensible joy is captured perfectly by the harmonic distance of the F♭ triad from the tonic of B♭.

Yet we can understand the F♭ triad even more deeply if we consider the text not just in terms of "Pause" itself, but in terms of the entire cycle, for

30. I am grateful to John Rothgeb for providing me with a copy of Ernst Oster's analytical sketch of "Pause." Although Oster's interpretation of certain text–music relationships in the song – particularly with respect to the F♭ major triad in measures 63–65 and 71–73 – was apparently entirely different from mine, his linear sketch (which involves only measures 42–81) and mine agree in all essentials. Both sketches show a chromatic unfolding from d^1 up to f^1 in the upper voice, and a similar chromatic progression from B♭ down to F in the bass.

it is the structure of *Die schöne Müllerin* as an entire cycle that explains why the enigmatic F♭ chord is made into such an arresting dramatic moment. As we have seen, the passage in which the chord occurs is the center point, the fulcrum of the cycle. Upon it the poet looks back at what has been and questions what is to be. And just as his questions take us motivically – and ironically – back to his expression of joy halfway through "Pause" itself, so do they take us tonally – and again ironically – to the very beginning and end of the cycle. His looking back is symbolized tonally (see Example 4) by the fact that "Pause" is the first song since "Das Wandern," the opening song of the cycle, to be in B♭ major; it is thus a flashback, a return. At the same time his looking forward is symbolized by the F♭ chord itself; F♭ is the enharmonic equivalent of E, and it is in E major, in the song "Des Baches Wiegenlied," that we say farewell to the dead poet. The F♭ triad is thus not just part of a linear progression. From the point of view of the whole cycle it is in a very real sense the central feature of that progression; it is what the poet hears when the wind touches the strings of his lute and gathers time present, time past, and time future into a single moment. Of course, within the context of "Pause" itself, it must ultimately be heard as something on its way to B♭; but that does not prohibit us from hearing it as something else at the same time.

One last question remains, however. From a logical point of view, we would expect "Ist es der Nachklang meiner Liebespein?" (the echo) to refer back to B♭, and "Soll es das Vorspiel neuer Lieder sein?" (the fore-shadowing) to refer ahead to E. Here, as always, Schubert's magnificent sense of irony has the last word. That he doesn't compose the song this way is due, trivially, to the obvious need for the song to end in B♭ rather than E. But more substantively – and this is the most bitter irony of all – the "Liebespein" which began in "Das Wandern" in B♭ is not over: it is, tragically, not limited to the songs to which our poet looks back, but is destined also to include the songs that he has yet to endure on his way to "Des Baches Wiegenlied" in E.

"Pause" and the other examples used here embody the compromise between linear analysis and harmonic cross-reference that has been the focus of this paper. They show that linear analysis, which views chromatic tonicization as subsidiary to voice leading and motivic structure in single movements, and which generally limits itself to individual movements, to single *Ursätze*, is by no means incompatible with a point of view that finds tonal meaning echoing from moment to moment in a single movement, or from movement to movement in a multipartite work. Even if, as I have suggested, we as theorists will do better to find that tonal meaning within the confines of that multipartite work itself, rather than in the vast and nebulous world of key characteristics, we can see that the principles of linear analysis and of chromatic tonal cross-reference are not necessarily mutually exclusive. We must, of course, exercise caution in our analyses. We must not prescribe tonal cross-reference in situations where linear explanations are clearly adequate, and where there is no telling evidence for a particularly harmonic point of view. Nor should we assume that such principles are operative in all tonal works: they seem to be valid only in works beginning with the late eighteenth century, and only in selected pieces even then – particularly pieces in which features such as rhythm, texture, orchestration, or gesture lead us to hear a particular event more as a harmonic entity than as part of a linear progression. But when a pitch, triad, or tonal area impresses itself upon us with rhetorical emphasis, and when it recurs and develops in a way that suggests that it is harmonic–motivic rather than linear–motivic in character, we should feel justified in invoking principles that go beyond those of Schenker. Ultimately our doing so is a tribute to him, for it is he whose *Fernhören* has taught us to hear such broad relationships in the first place.

Departures from the norm in two songs from Schumann's *Liederkreis*

Charles Burkhart

It is well known that Schumann's song and character piece cycles frequently exhibit unusual features that depart markedly from normal compositional practice. Such features are often highly imaginative and worthy of special study since their purpose is nearly always to express a particular programmatic idea or, in the songs, a particular aspect of the text. These departures from the norm exist on many different levels of musical structure, both in Schumann's cycles generally and in the one in question here, the Eichendorff *Liederkreis*, Op. 39. But I shall discuss only the most drastic kind of departure I have found in that strange and wonderful work – the basing of entire songs on the incomplete progression V–I, that is, on a harmonic foundation that lacks the normal initial tonic. There are actually three such songs in the *Liederkreis*, but I shall treat here only two – the two that are most closely related to each other.

Schenker called an incomplete progression ending on the tonic an "auxiliary cadence" (see *Free Composition*, §244 and Figure 110), placing under this term not only V–I, but also the progressions IV–V–I, III–V–I, and II–V–I. (It is clear from his examples that he also considered I⁶–V–I to qualify in some cases as an auxiliary cadence.) He illustrated his discussion of this technique, as he did all others, with copious examples from the literature. Most of his examples are only portions of compositions, for auxiliary cadences much more often than not are only details within a work. A few of Schenker's examples, however, are, like the songs I am treating here, complete compositions.

Structuring an entire piece on an auxiliary cadence was a problem that interested many nineteenth-century composers. Brahms was particularly fascinated by it, judging from the number and variety of such pieces in his work. Most such pieces by any composer are short, for it is difficult to sustain a long piece without the aid of an opening tonic. But there are a few notable long ones, perhaps the most impressive being the finale of Brahms's Third Symphony, which is, in my view, an attempt to compose an entire movement in which a structural tonic is avoided until late in the last form section. Whatever its length, an auxiliary-cadence piece is always something of a tour de force. Beginning off the tonic is obviously a less natural procedure than beginning on it. Once such a starting point is chosen, the problem is to prolong it over most of the composition – to create harmonic motion *within* it while simultaneously subverting its natural tendency to resolve to a tonic. But only to a *structural* tonic, of course. One can prolong, say, V by means of *subordinate* tonic chords, e.g., V–(I–IV)–V.

Since auxiliary-cadence pieces are rare, it is rather surprising that of the twelve songs that make up Schumann's *Liederkreis* as many as three are pieces of this nature. It is also noteworthy that these pieces occur one after the other in the middle of the set (they are Nos. 5, 6, and 7). Of course their unusual structure has something to do with their being part of a larger entity (I will take this up again later), but it is much more interesting to me that one of the three cases is the song from *Liederkreis* that is most often performed alone. I refer to the celebrated "Mondnacht," Song No. 5 – a work that should dispel the suspicion, if any, that I am discussing oddities only.

"Mondnacht"

Eichendorff's poem has three short stanzas. The first two evoke a picture of nocturnal nature that is essentially static – a quality portrayed in the music by the motionless background dominant. In Philip Miller's rendering:[1]

> It seemed as though the heavens
> had kissed the earth to silence,
> so that, amid glistening flowers,
> she must now dream heavenly dreams.
>
> The breeze passed through the fields;
> the corn stirred softly;
> the forest rustled lightly,
> so clear and starry was the night.

The crucial third stanza introduces the speaker of the poem, as well as the typically Eichendorffian idea of Man's yearning to be one with Nature. Schumann composes the words

> And my soul spread
> wide its wings;

by means of a blossoming out to a neighboring subdominant (see measure 51). With the final lines,

> took flight through the silent land
> as though it were flying home.

the music regains the dominant and resolves to the long-awaited tonic precisely on the last word, "Haus." The poem seems almost to have been written for the very purpose of being recomposed in terms of an auxiliary cadence!

---

1. Philip Miller, *The Ring of Words* (New York, 1963; reprint edn, 1973), p. 39. Miller points out that in line 4 "nun träumen müsst" became "nur träumen müsst" in Schumann's setting.

Example 1. Schumann, "Mondnacht," early levels

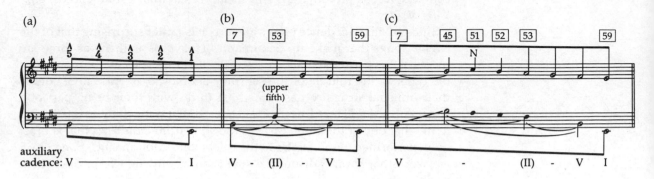

Example 1a shows the auxiliary cadence underlying "Mondnacht" – a formulation whose relevance to the music will grow, I hope, more apparent in the course of the following discussion. Examples 1b and 1c present the earliest harmonic and melodic elaborations of this structure – a prolonging II harmony (or "upper fifth," as Schenker would call it), and the neighbor tone C♯ – elements that will themselves be richly elaborated and will also reappear on many levels of the composition.

The essential sections of the form of "Mondnacht" may be schematized as follows:

	A¹		A²			B	
	a	a	a	a		b	a¹
measures	7–14	15–22	29–36	37–44		45–52	53–60

Each capital-letter section is commensurate with one stanza of the poem, and each lower-case section with two lines. The four statements of section a are virtually identical. In the sense that A¹ is therefore identical to A², the entire form consists basically of just two rather than three large sections. The lower-case sections, which I call "phrases," are all eight measures in length, dividing as 4 + 4. A constant duple meter (strong–weak), undisturbed by phrase expansion or any other special procedure that would alter the number of measures in a group, operates at every hypermetrical level. (Example 2 makes clear the metrical scheme.) Duple pulse is especially obvious to the listener at the 4 + 4 measure level, and is also readily experienced at the level of 8 + 8. To me these large steady rhythms, particularly since they are realized through, so to speak, "beautifully monotonous" reiterations of the same music, suggest an idea relatable to the text – something like the slow, silent rhythms of Nature.

The rhythmic regularity of "Mondnacht" would become truly monotonous if ways were not found to counteract it. One such way is the repetition of the six-measure introduction (measures 23–28), but more interesting are the many rhythmic shifts, particularly anticipations, that occur on several levels near or in the foreground. Some of these are indicated in my graphs, and the reader may well discover others. Though I will return to this subject later, I will mention now just one example – the C# $^6_5$ chord in measure 14. This measure belongs basically to the first vocal phrase, a, and its basic harmony is the B major chord begun in measure 13. The C# $^6_5$ is an anticipation of the start of the second vocal phrase. I single this example out because it seems to compose the very syntax of the approaching line of text – that is, to suggest the mental shifting of gears, often accompanied by an intake of breath, that one makes before uttering a subordinate clause. I make bold to claim that a singer's awareness of it can make a subtle difference to the way he sings the words "dass sie."

The first vocal phrase (measures 7–14) and its repetitions

The first phrase of "Mondnacht" (measures 7–14) is surely one of Schumann's most atmospheric creations. We should not be surprised, therefore, that the basic tonal material of this passage receives a very subtle and unusual diminution. To understand it, one must first realize that the piano introduction has already established the initial structural elements of the composition proper: the dominant harmony and, as the top voice of this harmony, the tone b^1, ready to serve as $\hat{5}$.

Examination of the music will show that the vocal melody of the first phrase is essentially static, being based on a two-note figure, c#–b, the first note an appoggiatura to the second. The right-hand part of the accompaniment duplicates this appoggiatura figure, and also presents a second melodic element just beneath it – a falling fourth-progression b^1–f#^{1}. Both these important elements, which will intertwine throughout the repetitions of the phrase, are represented in Example 2a, which shows the chief components of the first phrase in their most normal register, voicing, and rhythm. The reader will note that the tones of the vocal part unexpectedly appear here in the "tenor" register, and that the falling fourth, whose b^1 is held over from the introduction, is shown here as the top voice. Though the chief harmony is the background V, as noted, a middleground II–V progression prolongs this V. (Such a II–V might be termed an "auxiliary semi-cadence.") The II chord turns the held-over b^1 into a suspension, thus initiating the falling fourth.

Example 2b, a further stage of elaboration, shows that the addition of the bass tone e (measures 11–12) transforms the formerly dissonant g#^{1} and e^1 into consonances. The resulting E major chord does not damage the appoggiatura character of these tones. We still hear them as passing tones on the way to their goal, f#^{1} and d#^{1}. The E chord, since it belongs to the middleground V, basically functions like the $^6_4$ shown in Example 2a. But it is supported by a preceding dominant of its own. This is not to be confused with the background dominant, but is strictly local, applying to the E chord only. The insertion of this subordinate V–I progression has certain rhythmic concomitants. Among them are a foreground chord rhythm of steady half notes, and, on the lowest level, the *anticipation* of

Example 2. Schumann, "Mondnacht," later levels

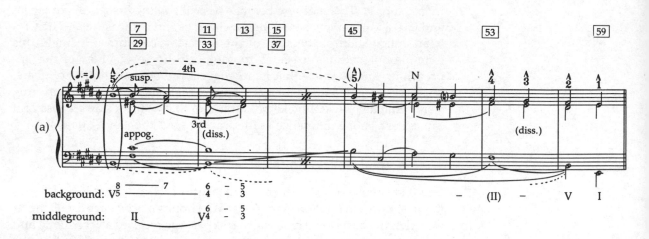

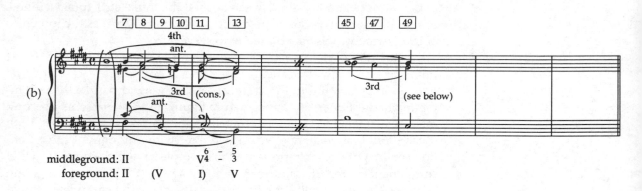

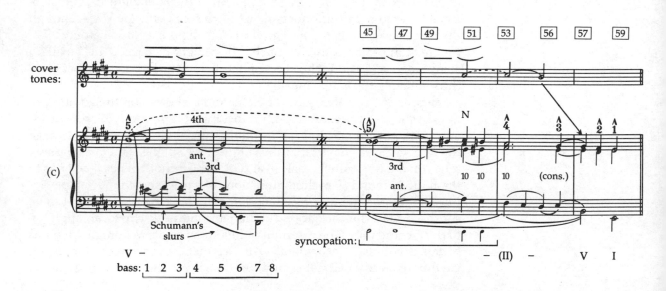

the g#¹ and e¹ (measure 10). I ask the reader to keep this anticipation in mind.

Some may balk at my assertion that a II–V progression undergirds the entire eight-measure phrase, since on the surface the literal II is present for only one measure (measure 8) and the V for only two (measures 13–14, or, better, measures 21–22). I can only refer such readers to measures 53–58, where a somewhat clearer and more explicit form of the same progression occurs – then continues on to I. (See also Examples 2a and 2c, for these measures.)

Example 2c brings us to the threshold of the composition. Most notable is the lifting of the c#–b from the "tenor" to the "soprano," where it is actually composed. The c#² "reaches over" the held b¹, causing it to move down, then moves itself to b¹, thus restoring the original starting point and making possible the repetition of the entire process in the next phrase. I have said that the c#–b lies most naturally in an inner voice. Since it is composed in the topmost register, the b¹ (with its appoggiatura c#²) is to be taken as a cover tone. The voicing here is unusual. Very rarely in music is the II–V progression voiced with scale-degrees 6̂ and 5̂ on top, as in Example 3. The reason for this is not merely the parallel fifths, but that such a top line does not readily serve the purpose of forward motion toward a goal. Its effect is static. In "Mondnacht," however, that is precisely the effect desired (until the very end, of course). The essentially static vocal melody hovers over the more active accompaniment – like the soul contemplating the twilit world.

Example 3. Concerning voicing in "Mondnacht," first phrase

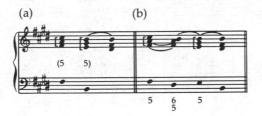

The b¹ in measure 7 represents the 5̂. The subsequent falling fourth (b¹–f#¹) replicates the conduct of a structural top line that is interrupted at 2̂. Though a middleground element, it prefigures the eventual background descent 5̂–1̂, an event that will likewise take place in the piano part.

Example 2c also brings some of the expressive details of the phrase into focus, most obviously the momentary suspension of the bass register, which imparts a weightless, floating quality. This example also reproduces Schumann's two large bass slurs that, spanning the entire phrase, contradict the natural articulation of the bass tones d#–e (measures 9–10).

They also contradict (in the bass) the normal 4 + 4 measure grouping with 3 + 5, an effect promoted still further by the descending left hand arpeggio spanning measures 10–12. The shifting of the E major chord from measure 11 back to measure 10 is the subtlest of the song's many anticipations. Schumann highlights it with his second bass slur, an articulation that demands the most sensitive performance. Clearly the pianist is not to play measures 7 through 10 as though they were merely a 2 + 2-measure sequence – $\frac{6\,5}{5\,3}$, $\frac{6\,5}{5\,3}$.

The anticipation of the E chord lengthens this sonority to three entire measures (measures 10–12), during which the voice leading, previously so active, is suddenly quiet. I suggest this is a depiction of the German word "still." This word can mean still (i.e., calm, motionless), silent, or soft. Miller has translated "die Erde still geküsst" as "kissed the earth to silence," which may be more accurate than "softly kissed the earth." The absolute motionlessness – stillness – of the voice leading during the E major chord suggests that Schumann may have read this line in the same way.

Example 4 (which takes Example 2c one level closer to the surface) shows the vocal melody's highest tones to be superpositions of tones from the inner-voice third-progression f#^{1}–e^1–d#^{1}. Even the embellishing e#^{1} of the inner voice (measure 7) is repeated in the vocal part in measure

Example 4. Schumann, "Mondnacht," foreground

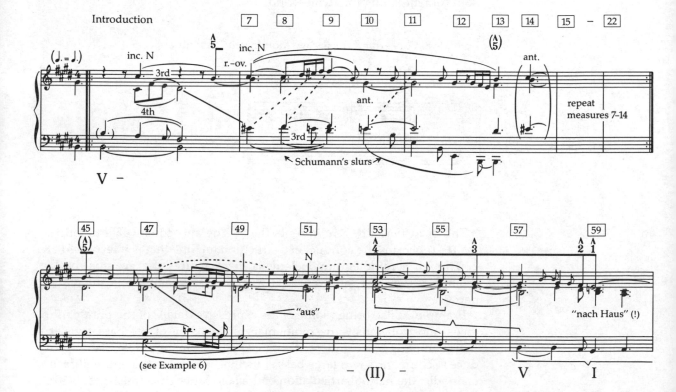

Example 4 (*cont.*)

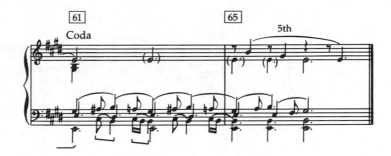

8 (as a member of one of the most famous, not to say poignant, dissonant intervals in the literature). The succession e♯–f♯–e♮ of the piano (left hand) is almost repeated "canonically" by the voice. Then the left-hand arpeggio (embraced by Schumann's second slur) gradually restores the bass register all the way down to low B_1, the very first pitch of the composition, charmingly arriving at this goal one eighth note "too soon."

The introduction

The extent to which the evocative piano introduction encapsulates the ideas of the song to come is astonishing. (See Example 5a for its main elements in their simplest form.) The c♯–b figure, the falling fourth (even with its opening suspension implied), the third-progression (now on top), and the two-tiered harmony (II–V under V) – all are here. As I have demonstrated, these elements will all blossom out in measures 7–14, a time span that is essentially twice as long. The reader will discover still further correspondences between the introduction and the song proper. I will add only that the II harmony will receive its most significant expression at measure 53 (recall Example 1b), where, like the II of the first phrase, it will serve a larger V – the largest of all.

Example 5. Schumann, "Mondnacht," Introduction

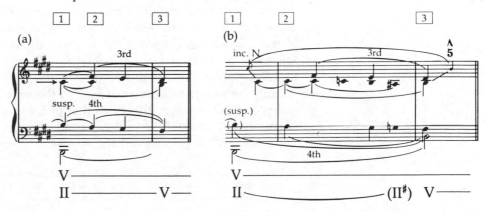

(*example continues on following page*)

Example 5 (*cont.*)

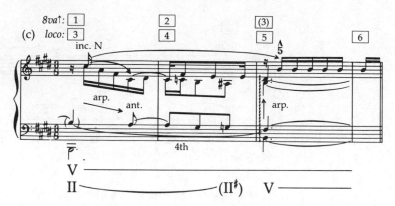

In the introduction (unlike the first phrase) the background V is present on the surface from the very first note. The opening right-hand arpeggiation of the II, though it sounds over the low B_1, does not coalesce with V to form a V^9_7 chord. To keep the two harmonies distinct Schumann carefully avoids using d# chordally. The II endures through measures 1–2 (the g# and e are passing tones within the II), resolving to (middleground) V in measure 3.[2]

The introduction covers six measures, but it is essentially a four-measure phrase extended through repetition to six, thus:

$$\text{measures} \quad \begin{array}{cccc} 1 & 2 & (3) & \\ 3 & 4 & 5 & 6 \end{array}$$

The repetition causes the two middleground harmonies, II and V, to be superposed in measures 3–4, thus:

measures

The successful articulation of measure 3 requires great skill. For example, in measure 3, beat 1, the left-hand b is simultaneously both the root of the V and a dissonance against the II. As a dissonance it resolves to the following a. Thus the initial b of the falling fourth-progression b–f# literally appears here, thanks to the repetition.

From the strictly local point of view of the introduction alone, the normal voicing of the introduction is that of Example 5a. In this sense the c#²–b¹ shown in small notes in Example 5b are superpositions of the inner-voice c#¹–b. (Thus even the cover-tone aspect of the song is pre-

2. I am indebted to Edward Aldwell and Carl Schachter, *Harmony and Voice Leading*, Vol. 2 (New York, 1979), pp. 130–31; 2nd edn (San Diego, 1989), pp. 448–49, for this view of the harmony of the introduction. The "II#" is my addition.

figured!) But from the point of view of the entire composition the $c\#^2$–b^1 is a *large* event, for it prepares the $\hat{5}$ and also establishes the primary register.

The last section: measure 45 to the end

How can a piece structured almost entirely on a single dominant nevertheless create a sense of continuous forward motion? What keeps it from dying of inertia? In the first half of "Mondnacht" Schumann solves this problem through recourse to the II harmony – backing up before the V, as it were, and progressing into it. The second half (the B section, or measures 45–60) prolongs the V by a long motion from V to II and back.

Large-scale melodic factors also contribute to the forward drive, notably the diminution of $\hat{5}$ by means of neighboring $c\#^2$. Example 2c shows that in the first half of the song the incomplete neighbor $c\#^2$ occurs in the strongest possible metrical position. In the second half, by contrast, the *complete* neighbor $c\#^2$, with its following b^1, occurs in the weak half of a weak hypermeasure (at measures 51–52). This brings $\overset{4}{\text{II}}$ on the next hypermetrical downbeat (measure 53) – a crucial turning point. Freed at last of its often-reiterated $\hat{5}$, the structural top line now swiftly falls to its conclusion.

Another large-scale rhythmic feature of the B section is the "slowing down" caused by the syncopation in the bass at measures 45–50 (indicated in Example 2c). The syncopated E generates the need for the following quarter notes (measures 51–52) – as in fifth species counterpoint – which intensify the drive toward $\overset{4}{\text{II}}$. The energy thus built up keeps the quarter-note motion going in the bass for another hypermeasure (measures 53–56).

One small detail yet deserves mention, though it has no bearing on the auxiliary-cadential structure. The poem presented a built-in difficulty to Schumann at the beginning of its third stanza:

> Und meine Seele spannte
> Weit ihre Flügel aus,

where the words "spannte weit" (spread wide) obviously belong together. Of course Schumann could have contrived to connect them, but he chose (wisely, I think) not to. He did not wish to disturb the hypnotic effect of the constantly repeated rhythm:

Therefore he repeated this rhythm once again in measures 45–48, including the expected rest, thereby creating a phrase notorious among singers, who must make a special effort to "think across" the awkward break between "spannte" and "weit." But Schumann remarkably managed to smooth over this awkwardness to some extent, not only by means of the piano's beautiful allusion to the introduction, but in the very voice leading. As shown in Example 6, there is a long third-progression b^1–a^1–$g\#^1$

Example 6. Schumann, "Mondnacht," "spannte weit"

(a) basic voice leading

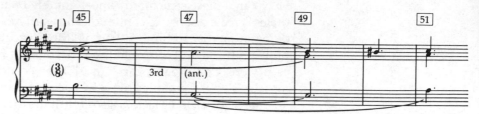

(b) vocal part

(c) piano part

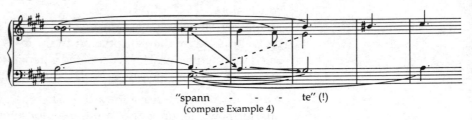

(d)

spanning measures 45–49. Both the vocal and piano parts have this third, but they complete it at different times. The vocal part resolves the dissonant a^1 to $g\#^1$ on the word "spannte" in measure 47. But the piano does not let go of the a just yet, but *extends it over the singer's rest* (the g♯s in the piano at measures 47–48 are all passing and neighbor tones), and over an exchange of voices, to resolve it in the bass at measure 49 precisely on the word "weit." In this ingenious way Schumann achieved something like the "solution" pictured in Example 6d.

The question of a cover tone does not arise in the opening measures of the B section, i.e., from measures 45 to 51. But at measure 51, while the piano moves down in parallel tenths toward the $\frac{4}{\text{II}}$ (measure 53), the voice, taking advantage of the common tone c♯ (measures 51–53), soars out over the piano's descent for the last time. The voice part must ultimately surrender to the more powerful line, but resists doing so – resists being drawn "nach Haus" – until the last possible moment.

Example 2 makes clear that the background $\hat{1}$ occupies only measures 59–60. The background ends at this point. But in the foreground the tonic harmony is extended so as to produce an eight-measure coda (see Example 4, measures 61–68). The long retention of the unresolved dominant has created the need for a similar retention of the tonic when it finally arrives.

"Schöne Fremde"

Unlike "Mondnacht," Song No. 6 *is* something of an oddity, though it ends with a "typical outpouring of Romantic ecstasy," as Eric Sams says.[3] Not as great a song as "Mondnacht," and too short to succeed outside the cycle, it has, nevertheless, a viable structure that warrants being considered in isolation.

Again Schumann confronted a three-stanza poem. In Philip Miller's English:[4]

> The treetops rustle and quiver
> as though at this hour
> about the ruined walls
> the ancient gods were making their rounds.
>
> Here beyond the myrtle trees
> in the quiet shimmer of twilight,
> what are you telling me, confused as in dreams,
> fantastic night?
>
> The stars all shine upon me
> with the glow of love;
> the far horizon speaks ecstatically
> as if of great happiness to come.

How did Schumann's reading of this poem, as we find it expressed in his song, lead him to structure the composition as he did? I propose that the key to Schumann's reading is in the poem's second stanza. The speaker hears a message in the voices of nature – a kind of enchanted nature – but the meaning of the message is as yet uncertain, "confused as in dreams." In the third stanza the message comes through somewhat more clearly: "The far horizon speaks ecstatically (intoxicatedly) as of great happiness to come." How is this progression from vagueness to relative clarity composed in the music?

The peculiar opening of this song gives the impression of something already in progress, as though begun before the first written measure. This impression seems confirmed from measure 11 on, where we begin to realize we are hearing the first several measures again. (The metrical position of measure 11 implies that measure 1 is to be taken as weak – as the

3. Eric Sams, *The Songs of Robert Schumann* (London, 1969), p. 100.
4. Miller, p. 40.

second measure of a two-measure hypermeasure.) What is the implied, uncomposed point of departure that "begins" the progression that we catch in mid-stream, as it were, at the first sounding notes?

The answer begins to emerge when we realize that the opening measures have a remarkable surface similarity to the first vocal phrase of "Mondnacht." (Compare measures 7–14 of "Mondnacht" with measures 2–5a of "Schöne Fremde.") Schumann composed the two songs just seven or eight days apart, incidentally. He wrote "Mondnacht" first, and its opening may still have been echoing in his memory.[5] Unlike "Mondnacht," "Schöne Fremde" has no explicit dominant at the outset, but its first phrase (measures 1–7) composes out the space of a third, $a\#^1$–$f\#^1$, and ends with a tonicization of F# major. The background of the first phrase, therefore, would seem to be the dominant harmony of the tonality.

The second phrase (measures 8–16, with pick-up) starts from a higher point, $c\#^2$, but then continues in a manner very similar to the first, moving to inner-voice $f\#^1$ and ending again on an F# major chord. The last phrase (measures 17–24) starts on an unequivocal $\overset{\hat{5}}{V}$ (just like "Mondnacht") and ends, of course, on I. All this seems to build a strong case for a background V from the beginning, and for an auxiliary cadence spanning the whole. This interpretation seems to me true to the spirit and sense of the poem. Schumann has composed into the music the poem's overall progression from confusion to clarity and joy by means of a background V–I whose V does not resolve to I until the poem's last word.

Example 7 shows the auxiliary-cadential structure. It also shows the background V composed out by means of a top-voice arpeggiation of three notes, $a\#^1$–$c\#^2$–$f\#^2$. Now there are just three phrases in the song, one for each stanza. The $a\#^1$ of the arpeggiation covers the setting of the first stanza, the $c\#^2$ the second, and the $f\#^2$ (which is the $\hat{5}$) is reached in the third. This arpeggiation is another way, this time in the middleground, that the music composes the general idea of the poem – a gradual progression to a distant goal.

Example 7. Schumann, "Schöne Fremde," background

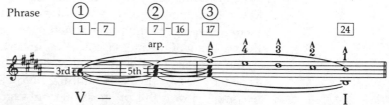

The rhythmic structure of "Schöne Fremde" is intimately connected with the metrics of the poem. The same is true to some extent of many lieder, but the particular procedure here is unusual. The poem's first two stanzas are fitted to phrases whose basic rhythmic structure issues from the meter of just two poetic lines, that is, *half* a stanza. What is unusual is

5. The complex chronology of the cycle's composition is fully discussed by Herwig Knaus in *Musiksprachen und Werkstruktur in Robert Schumanns "Liederkreis"* (Munich, 1974); see especially p. 14.

that both phrases 1 and 2 employ "phrase expansion" to accommodate their respective *complete* stanzas.

To explain: phrase 1 rapidly traverses the third a#^{1}–f#^{1} (measures 1–3), leaving, as it were, nowhere to go except back to a#^{1}, a move finally made at the phrase's end (measure 7). The basic length of this phrase is just four measures, as shown in Examples 8a and 8b – a length that would cover

Example 8. Schumann, "Schöne Fremde," later levels

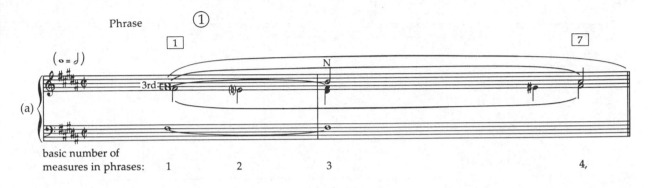

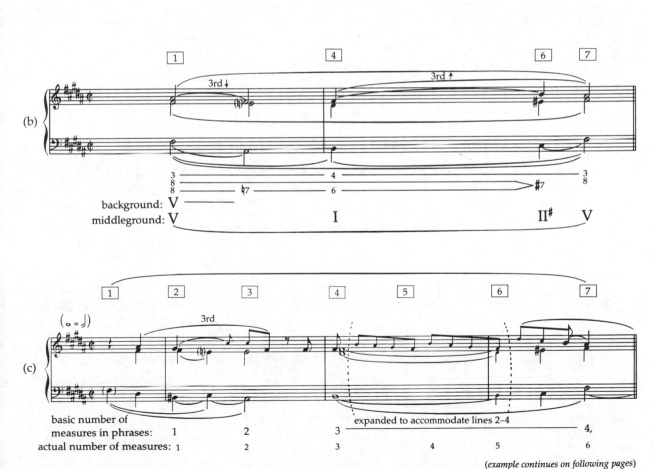

(example continues on following pages)

Example 8 (*cont.*)

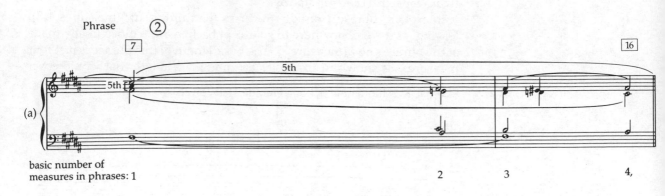

basic number of
measures in phrases: 1   2   3   4,

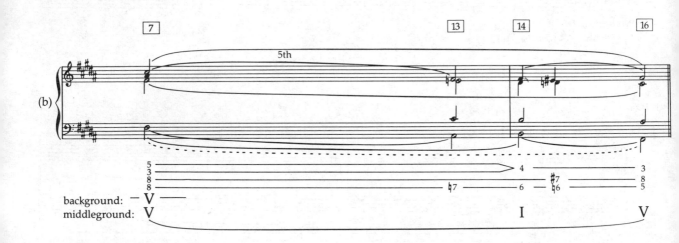

background: — V —
middleground: V   I   V

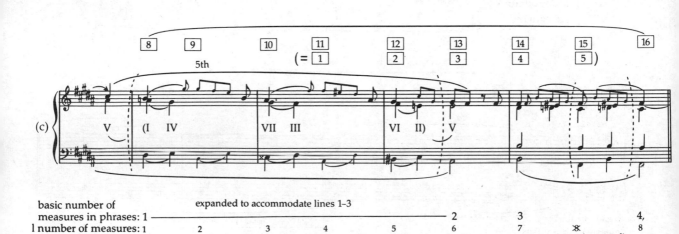

basic number of
measures in phrases: 1 ——————— expanded to accommodate lines 1–3
l number of measures: 1   2   3   4   5   2/6   3/7   ✻   4, 8
                                                      7 (repeated)

Example 8 (*cont.*)

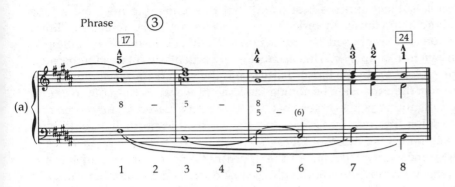

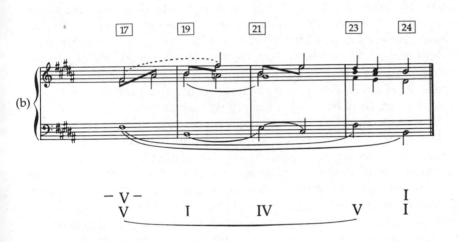

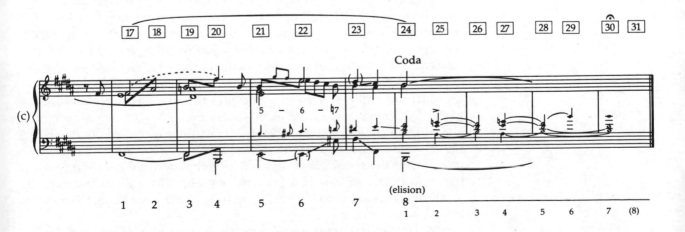

only the first two lines of the stanza (see from the pick-up to measure 2 to the downbeat of measure 5). We now observe that line 1 of the stanza is a simple subject and predicate, and that the remaining lines are a long subordinate clause. In order to make room for these remaining lines, Schumann composed an expansion (Schenker's term is *Dehnung*), as shown in Example 8c. This expansion is particularly interesting because the prolonging of the B chord articulates the sentence's very grammar. To prevent the expansion becoming too long, however, Schumann *contracted* the durations of the notes that set the words placed in measures 5–6, crowding into two measures of music words that normally would have taken four. One has the uneasy feeling that the plethora of syllables in these measures necessitated the "poco rit." in measure 5, and that the overall rhythmic effect of the phrase just escapes being cumbersome. On the other hand, these seeming local shortcomings contribute to the larger effect the composition is building.

More tonal space – that of a fifth– is available for setting stanza 2, as noted; this interval will eventually be composed out as a falling fifth-progression. Examples 8a and 8b show that the basic voice leading of phrase 2 is very similar to that of phrase 1 (see the figured bass for both phrases that is written under Example 8b), and that the basic length, by analogy with phrase 1, is again just four measures. Therefore, another expansion is needed to accommodate the entire stanza. This time the expansion occurs at the start of the phrase (see Example 8c), prolonging the opening V chord by means of a complete journey through the diatonic circle of fifths, and stretched out sufficiently long to cover lines 1–3 of the stanza. It is interesting that the complete phrase now has essentially eight measures, giving it a superficial impression of metrical normalcy. We may compare the effect of phrase 1, where the expansion is more obvious and the total number of measures only six. (The slight extension at measure 15 does not disturb the overall sense of regularity. I leave for the reader the discovery of the charming role played by this "extra" measure.)

Phrase 2's falling fifth (measures 7–13) is traversed at a slower rate than was the falling third of phrase 1. The tones $c\#^2$–b^1–$a\#^1$ cover four measures (measures 8–11, with pick-up), leaving the remaining four for the reiteration of the song's beginning. What can one say about this mysterious repetition? What does it mean? We know that the "fantastic night" is "speaking" to the speaker of the poem through various images of the landscape – the rustling treetops, the flowering myrtles (emblem of love), the splendid twilight. Then the question that the speaker puts to the night – "Was sprichst du. . .zu mir?" – sums up, as it were, these scattered images in an attempt to grasp their meaning. Setting this question to *new* music would have had the rhetorical effect of separating the nature images from the speaker. But setting it to a repetition of the opening gives the impression that the speaker's experience mingles with nature itself – and the further impression of bringing us full circle, of ending where we began: in uncertainty.

Since phrase 3 must obviously bring the composition's structural close, and complete the dramatic course of the text, it is not surprising that its procedures differ from those of the first two phrases. The music now simply parallels the metrics of the poem in a phrase of normal eight-measure length. Again unlike the first two, this phrase will end forcefully. We should note that it also does not start out at once on its main tone (f#^{2}), but, as shown in Example 8b, diminutes this tone during the first half of the phrase (measures 17–20) by means of an upward octave transfer (f#^{1}–f#^{2}), and, further, that these measures contain the slowest chord rhythm of the entire song – one chord per two measures. All this will make the second half of the phrase that much more emphatic when, starting in measures 21–22, the speed of chord change markedly quickens as the vocal line, in a complex of motivic references to what has gone before (see the arrows and brackets in Example 9), rushes down toward its conclusion.

Example 9. Some "hidden repetitions" in "Schöne Fremde"

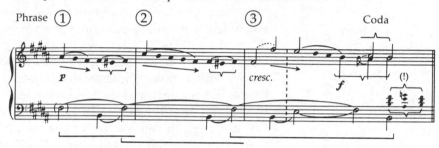

When expanded phrases occur in songs, much more often than not they will be at or near the song's end to create a kind of climax or sense of fulfillment. "Schöne Fremde" proceeds in the opposite manner, starting with expansions and ending with normalcy. This is the final way in which the music composes the general sense of the poem – the gradual progression from confusion to presentiments of joy. Upon arriving at this goal, the composition celebrates with an eight-measure coda.

Example 9 also calls attention to the "motivic" nature of the bass, particularly how F# repeatedly moves down to B and back. These Bs tantalize the ear, so to speak, for none of them function primarily as tonics – until the last.

While I certainly am not advocating that "Mondnacht" and "Schöne Fremde" form a diptych within the cycle, I believe that they share, in addition to many technical similarities, certain broad poetic themes.[6] The texts of both songs feature nature images that create a milieu in which the speaker moves toward a new state of being or a deepening of experience – toward union with nature in the first case, toward future happiness in the

6. For another and much fuller discussion of thematic relationships among the songs of the cycle see Jürgen Thym's excellent dissertation, "The Solo Song Settings of Eichendorff's Poems by Schumann and Wolf" (Ph.D. diss., Case Western Reserve University, 1974).

second. This general similarity may seem so very broad as to be virtually meaningless, for the theme of nature, very pervasive in Eichendorff's poetry to begin with, figures in no less than seven of the other poems Schumann chose to include in *Liederkreis*, and of these at least four likewise portray movement toward a new awareness or state. But it is noteworthy, I think, that with one exception all of the seven other nature poems differ from "Mondnacht" and "Schöne Fremde" in that they associate nature with evil, death, or some earthly woe. The exception is "Frühlingsnacht," the last song in the cycle. That it sees nature as friendly relates it to the two songs I have treated here.

A more specific relation exists between just "Schöne Fremde" and "Frühlingsnacht." First of all, both are among the several poems that treat of happy love; most specifically, these two songs are the fastest and most ecstatic of the entire set of twelve. Therefore their placement as Nos. 6 and 12 strongly tends to divide the cycle in half. But in "Frühlingsnacht" there is, of course, no auxiliary cadence to keep the listener in suspense, for here there is no longer *movement toward* a future goal. The goal has been reached. We are in the present as the voices of nature proclaim: "She is thine! She is thine!"

Three of the nine songs set to nature poems, then, treat nature as benign, and in two of these an auxiliary-cadence structure promotes this theme. But Schumann does not reserve this structure for the portrayal of this theme only. (Since music has no objective meaning, a good composer can use a given musical technique to portray almost anything.) He employs it yet a third time in Song No. 7, the cryptic "Auf einer Burg," which treats nature within a view of life that is essentially tragic. Here the auxiliary cadence is composed out in a manner wholly unlike that of its two predecessors. Discussion of this strange song's features, together with several other and less drastic departures from the norm in *Liederkreis*, awaits another forum.[7]

---

7. As a postscript to this article I would like to credit two recent treatises on tonal rhythm: Carl Schachter's set of three articles, "Rhythm and Linear Analysis," in Vols. 4–6 of *The Music Forum* (New York, 1976, 1980, 1987), Vol. 4, pp. 281–334, Vol. 5, pp. 197–232, and Vol. 6, Part 1, pp. 1–59; and William Rothstein's dissertation, "Rhythm and the Theory of Structural Levels" (Ph.D. diss., Yale University, 1981). I do not know if I have applied their ideas as the authors would have, but their writings, which grow directly out of Schenker's own theory and practice, have deeply influenced the way I think about rhythmic analysis.

Either/or

Carl Schachter

I shall begin by citing a brief excerpt from that recent masterpiece, Italo Calvino's *Invisible Cities*. It is one of the passages in which Marco Polo converses with the Emperor Kublai Khan:

Marco Polo describes a bridge, stone by stone.
    "But which is the stone that supports the bridge?" Kublai Khan asks.
    "The bridge is not supported by one stone or another," Marco answers, "but by the line of the arch that they form."
    Kublai Khan remains silent, reflecting. Then he adds: "Why do you speak to me of the stones? It is only the arch that matters to me."
    Polo answers: "Without stones there is no arch."[1]

Detail and context

As a parable of the relation between detail and context in music, Calvino's little conversation could hardly be surpassed. It is of course a truism of Schenkerian analysis and, largely thanks to Schenker's work, a generally accepted idea these days that a compositional detail, like the stone in the arch, derives its meaning from its context; the same note, chord, or melodic succession will "mean" different things in different surroundings. But it is also true that the larger shape manifests itself to the listener only after he has correctly understood certain crucial details, for unlike the curve of an arch, the underlying shape of a musical line is not always immediately evident to the person perceiving. The descending fourth shown in my Example 1, for instance, can be heard and recognized without any problem if all four notes occur in immediate succession. But if the fourth stretches over eight, or twenty, or sixty measures, as well it might, only through certain telling details will even the most skillful and experienced listener be able to hear that it forms the guiding idea of its context. And even after having perceived the fourth, the listener has obtained only a very incomplete and preliminary understanding, for as the example shows, even such a simple structure can mean many different things.

1. Italo Calvino, *Invisible Cities*, trans. William Weaver (New York, 1974), p. 82.

Example 1. A descending fourth: some possible interpretations

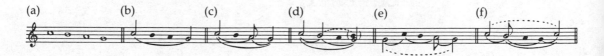

Everyone with a little experience in Schenker's approach learns that certain successions and combinations of notes inevitably create a forked path for the analyst, who must search for clues about which of two or more possible interpretations is the correct one, or about which of two or more "correct" ones is the truest artistically. With a bit more experience he may begin to be able to predict the direction of some of the forks, for an important but little discussed feature of the tonal system is the way that certain tonal configurations evoke specific clusters of possible interpretations. The descending fourth of Example 1 is one such configuration, and the example shows the likeliest interpretations; many other melodic figures make similar demands upon the analyst's judgment.

Harmonic interpretation

It is probably in the sphere of harmony, however, that the most frequent and difficult problems arise, and it is mainly questions of harmonic interpretation that I shall discuss in this paper. A problematic character is inherent in the very nature of harmony, whose fundamental unit, the functional chord, or *Stufe*, exists not as a combination of particular sounds, but only as a kind of Platonic idea that can realize itself in many such combinations. There is no such "thing" as a I chord in C major, but only an idea that can find expression through the notes C, E, and G in any kind of simultaneous blending, through intervals created by two of these notes, through the note C alone, through such combinations as C–Eb–G, C–E–G–A, and C–E–G–Bb, through melodic lines of the most various shapes, through whole constellations of contrapuntal lines and chord successions controlled by the note C. As Schenker so beautifully expresses it in the Preface to his *Harmony*, "In contrast to the theory of counterpoint, the theory of harmony presents itself to me as a purely spiritual universe, a system of ideally moving forces born of Nature or of art."[2]

In this paper I shall discuss some of the ways context can illuminate detail and detail can clarify context with respect to harmonic interpretation and to questions of voice leading that impinge on harmony. I shall point out some of the kinds of clues to large structure that an examination of details can yield, though it is far from my intention to offer a "method for the reading of diminutions" or, God help us, a "theory of reduction."

2. Schenker, *Harmony*, p. xxv.

I strongly doubt that such methods or theories can be made to work, for I believe that the understanding of detail begins with an intuitive grasp of large structure, however imperfect or incomplete, a process that is ultimately resistant to rigorous formulation.

IV (II) or I?

Example 2a illustrates, in schematic form, a particularly frequent and sometimes troublesome problem in harmonic analysis: is the governing chord of a given stretch of music a I or a IV? For this problem to arise, the IV (or perhaps II) must precede the I within the span in question, and a strong V must appear thereafter. In our abstract example, the "I" of the second measure can be heard either as a continuation of the initial (and obviously structural) tonic harmony or as a subordinate element connecting IV and V. As the little two-part progressions of Examples 2b and 2c suggest, both of our harmonic interpretations rest on a foundation of logical and coherent voice leading. If we infer a IV, the e^2 of the melody is basically a passing seventh transformed into a consonance by the C chord under it. If we infer a I, the f^2 is a neighbor note shifted to the downbeat where it takes on the guise of a 4–3 suspension; here the F chord provides the consonant support. Which of the two readings is correct? The arid surface of our abstract example can provide decisive confirmation for neither interpretation; therefore one is as good or as bad as the other. This illustrates, incidentally, why the study of harmony must, to a large extent, involve itself with the analysis of compositions and with the writing of quasi-compositional exercises; to study the endless formulas in white notes that disfigure so many harmony texts is to learn almost nothing about the ways chords can be prolonged and, therefore, to learn too little about harmony.

Example 2. IV or I?

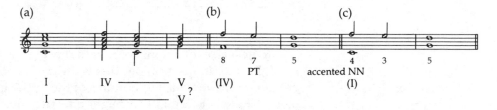

How different is the picture that emerges from a study of the opening phrase of a Chopin Mazurka, quoted in Example 3. Here too we can question whether measures 5 and 6 continue to express the prolonged tonic of measures 1–4 (Example 3a) or introduce IV as a new harmony (Example 3b), but unlike the abstract example, the Mazurka can give us reasons for our choice. On the basis of harmony and voice leading alone, we could hardly decide, for the setting is a spare and unpretentious one in which the beautiful melodic line receives a bare minimum of contrapuntal and harmonic support. The Mazurka, however, has a particularly refined and intricately worked out motivic design, which begins to unfold in these opening measures. The basic figure of this design is the neighbor-note figure D#–E–D# that I have sketched in above the music in Example 3a. Indeed it is largely this figure (an age-old "lament" motive) that carries out the "Mesto" character of the Mazurka. But to infer its presence requires that we hear a composed-out tonic in measures 2–6; reading a IV in measure 5, for instance, leads us to hear the d#² as a supported passing note rather than as the resolution of a neighbor note and destroys the integrity of the figure, as can be seen in Example 3b. (A third reading, inferring a I in measure 5 and a IV in measure 6 is possible, and it would not affect the D#–E–D# figure in the soprano line. But the two measures are so clearly parallel that this reading seems rather capricious and arbitrary.)[3]

Example 3. Chopin, Mazurka Op. 33, No. 1

If we hear an overarching tonic harmony in measures 2–6 of our Chopin example, and, in my opinion, that is the only tenable interpretation, it is because of the motivic implications of the upper line and for that reason alone. The other factors that might influence our reading – phrase contour, rhythm, texture – would as easily (but no more easily) support our hearing a IV as governing the measures in question. That design often gives us a key to large-scale structure is hardly news; but the often crucial role of motivic details in specifying the governing harmony of a passage is, I think, not sufficiently acknowledged.

Such acknowledgment leads to another important insight. The possibility of interpreting our abstract example in two different, mutually exclusive, and equally valid ways might lead one to conclude that the same tonal configuration is just as ambiguous when it appears in a composition. And this conclusion, in turn, would lead one to believe that the three alternative analyses of Example 3, for instance, are equally good. But this belief would be erroneous. One of the three readings is truer to the Mazurka as a unique and individual work of art than are the other two, which can be considered valid only from a perspective that takes in general aspects of tonal structure but that excludes the specific features of the piece's design.

This is not to deny the possibility that ambiguity and multiple meanings might exist in tonal music; they certainly do exist. But their function, in my opinion, is more narrowly circumscribed than some analysts, perhaps misled by false analogies to language, seem to believe. It is just as much a part of the composer's art as it is of the sculptor's or painter's to be able to create clear and distinct shapes; the more clearly and vividly the listener perceives these shapes, the more fully and deeply will he live the life of the composition as he hears it.

Motivic factors are just as decisive in Example 4, the beginning of the slow movement of Haydn's Symphony No. 99. Here the fork in the road leads, on the one hand, to the inference of a prolonged II in measures 9–11 or, on the other, to interpreting the G chord of measure 10 as a I that completes a tonic prolongation begun in measure 7. Only the first alternative deserves serious consideration. The way measure 11 repeats the beginning of measure 9, with its dotted turn and rising third, points to a connection in voice leading (see the brackets marked "x" in Example 4b). In addition, the rhythmic emphases and the inner articulations of the phrase – factors that were not decisive in the Chopin excerpt – support the inference of a prolonged II. Note, incidentally, that the melodic structure of measures 9–11 uses most of the same scale degrees – indeed almost the same notes – as measures 5–6 of the Mazurka (E–D–C–B here and D#–E–D#–C#–B in the Chopin), but that contextual differences lead to interpretative ones.

This excerpt contains a wonderful motivic parallelism – subtler than any in Example 3 (though not subtler than some that occur later on in the Mazurka). The unstemmed notes on the staff above the graph in Example 4b show that the seemingly insignificant link of parallel thirds played by the bassoons at the turn of measures 6/7 reappears in fantastic enlargement in the violin melody of measures 9–12. This parallelism also suggests that II, not I, must govern measures 9 and 10, though in the absence of other supporting evidence so subtle and seemingly tenuous a connection would not determine the outcome. Apropos of its being tenuous I might mention that just this figure – a descending third and second combining into a fourth (or in this case a pseudo fourth) – serves as the primary agent of continuity in this movement, binding whole sections together (note that it already appears in measures 2/3).

Example 4. Haydn, Symphony No. 99, second movement

Problems in locating boundaries

In this excerpt, more strikingly than in the Mazurka, the rival analyses differ significantly with regard to the boundaries that they establish between prolongational spans. In both, a I moves to a II⁶, but each establishes the frontier at a different point. Questions of boundary lines between prolonged chords arise all the time; their proper solution is a necessary step toward understanding the rhythmic shape of a passage – if you will, toward understanding its "harmonic rhythm" more fully than in the usual superficial way. In the Haydn excerpt, the boundaries are located with great precision, yet the effect is that of a continuous song, far removed from anything mosaic-like or segmented. Part of the reason lies in a kind of unity of color resulting from the very economical chordal vocabulary; there are G chords within prolongations of A minor, and A minor chords within prolongations of G. The A chord of measure 8, for instance, should be heard as passing within a G major harmony (G inflected to G♯ to lead to the A minor prolongation of the next measure); it would spoil the rhythmic effect to hear the prolongation of II already beginning in measure 8. Even more significant than the pervasive use of G major and A minor sounds are the ever-present suspended sevenths and their derivatives, which culminate in the climactic suspended ninth of measure 15 (compare measure 15 with measure 2, out of which it grows).

The apparent tonic

The G chord in measure 10 of the Haydn example might be termed an "apparent tonic" – that is, a chord constructed like a tonic but without a tonic's function. It does not form the beginning or goal of a significant prolongational span, and it does not connect convincingly with another similar chord that does function as beginning or goal. Therefore it represents a relatively low-level event within the span of measures 9–11, whereas a true tonic is, in principle, the highest-level harmony within its span, ultimately generating all the others.[4] Deciding whether to read a chord as a true or only an apparent tonic is a very frequent analytic problem. Its solution is sometimes decisive for understanding the form of a piece.

Formal divisions

Boundaries between prolongational spans – especially between those spans governed by structural harmonies – often coincide with points of formal articulation. In a sonata movement, the boundary between the interrupted V and the resumed structural I is also usually the boundary between the development and the recapitulation. Sometimes, however,

4. A seeming exception to this statement: interpolated or parenthetical passages and some instances of interruption-like segmentation may involve true tonics that belong to a lower level than do one or more of the adjoining harmonies, but these tonics are displaced representatives of chords that are structural within a previous time span.

the extension of a prolongational span bridges over the formal division. There are two beautiful instances of this in the Gavotte en Rondeaux from Bach's E major Partita for unaccompanied violin; Example 5 shows one of them.

Example 5. Bach, Partita No. 3 for unaccompanied violin, Gavotte en Rondeaux

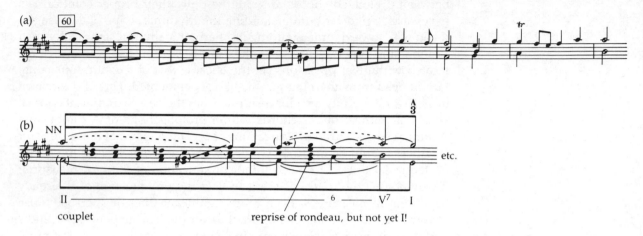

Example 5 quotes the end of the third couplet and the beginning of the fourth rondeau section; the couplet gravitates to and strongly cadences in F♯ minor (II), while the rondeau, of course, returns to E major.[5] One might be tempted to hear this return to E as occurring at the usual spot – the beginning of the reprise (measure 64, second half), but this interpretation would be most unconvincing here. Since II lacks a direct harmonic relationship with I but has one with V, and since V appears prominently at the head of measure 66, it makes more sense, on harmonic grounds alone, to infer a connection II–V. Furthermore, that connection is composed out in the voice leading of the passage, whose "bass" passes by step from II through II⁶ to V. The reprise, then, begins with an apparent tonic – a passing chord between II and II⁶. Note how Bach, to achieve this stepwise bass, transforms the opening chord of the reprise from a $\frac{5}{3}$ to a $\frac{6}{3}$.

Because of its position in the form, the apparent tonic of this excerpt has an effect very different from that of the one in the Haydn movement. By unmistakably signalling a return to the rondeau, it simultaneously signals an imminent return to tonic harmony, though it does not embody that return. Here we have a true double meaning: the E chord does not function as a tonic but, almost like some negative formulations in

5. From a perspective that takes in the entire Gavotte, even the E major that is stabilized later in the return is not to be taken quite at face value, for large-scale tonal connections between the framing episodes take precedence over it. The issues are too complex for discussion here; I discuss the piece in some detail in a separate article, "The Gavotte en Rondeaux from J. S. Bach's Partita in E Major for Unaccompanied Violin," *Israel Studies in Musicology* 4 (1987), pp. 7–26.

language, it asserts the existence of that which it is not. Furthermore it acts upon the F♯ harmony that it prolongs in a most important way: it transforms it from the local tonic of measure 64 to the II on the way to the V of measure 66. Incidentally, one ought to reformulate the valuable notion of the "pivot chord" in the light of modulating passages like this one. In such passages one would find pivots on two levels. Here, the "background pivot" is the prolonged F♯ minor chord itself, which changes in function from a local I to a II. But it is the E major passing chord (the "foreground pivot") that effects this change in function.

One might imagine that the presence of a formal division within a harmonic and voice-leading continuity would tend to break up that continuity, but here, I think, the opposite turns out to be true. The sense of harmonic arrival at the V of measure 66, and the sense of directed linear motion in the passage leading to that goal are, if anything, intensified by their play against the opposing force of sectional articulation.

Before leaving this example, I should like to mention one point of general significance. A fundamental difference exists between an apparent tonic, like the one that begins this reprise, and a chord of any other harmonic function consigned to a lower structural level than its position in the piece's form might at first seem to warrant. A dominant, say, at the double bar of a movement in a Bach suite can function as a relatively low-level divider rather than as part of the fundamental structure without necessarily ceasing to function as a dominant. But by definition a tonic is the highest-level harmony within any prolongation of which it forms a part; a demotion in rank necessarily strips it of its tonic insignia (but see footnote 4).

One inclusive structure or two successive ones?

With our next example we come to a very different fork in the road (or perhaps a fork in a very different road). The choice here is between understanding the harmonic background of an extensive passage as comprising two large cadences or combining the two into a single, still more inclusive structure. As in the Bach Gavotte, the harmonic interpretation impinges upon our understanding of the piece's form, only here the problem involves the meaning of a whole section, not just a point of articulation. The piece in question is the Larghetto movement from Mozart's Piano Concerto in C minor, and it is illustrated in the graphs of Example 6. The movement is composed as a rondo in five parts; its two episodes are in C minor and A♭ major – VI and IV of the E♭ major tonality of the movement. The rondo theme itself has an ABA design, and a length of nineteen measures at its first appearance. The second return corresponds closely to the original statement, but the omission of a four-measure repeat reduces it to fifteen measures instead of nineteen. The first return, however, appears in drastically curtailed form, for it is represented by a mere four-measure phrase.

In his brief discussion of five-part rondo form in *Free Composition*, Schenker explains it as the combination of two three-part forms: ABA and ACA combine to form ABACA.[6] Schenker specifies that neither the variation nor the abbreviation of the A section in one or more of its later appearances effects a fundamental change in the rondo principle; abbreviation and variation, of course, both occur in this movement. According to Schenker, the B and C sections of a rondo have as their tonal basis the same elements as the middle sections of ternary forms: modal mixture, neighbor notes, sevenths above the V chord, and so forth. In our Mozart movement, both episodes lead back to the rondo theme through retransitions composed around very strong dominant seventh chords; both times the seventh is in the soprano, forming an upper neighbor to the G of the movement's fundamental line. In the A♭ section, the melodic A♭, seventh of the coming dominant, is prepared as a consonance. Example 6a, a middleground sketch of the entire movement, accords with Schenker's explanation of rondo form. Accordingly it shows two large cadences, I–VI–V–I and I–IV–V–I, before the structural I–V–I that supports the descent of the fundamental line in the third A section.

Example 6. Mozart, Piano Concerto K. 491, second movement

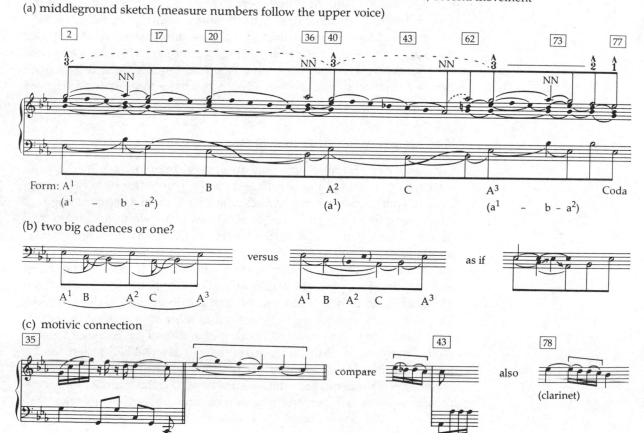

(a) middleground sketch (measure numbers follow the upper voice)

(b) two big cadences or one?

(c) motivic connection

6. Schenker, *Free Composition*, p. 141.

This interpretation makes a good deal of sense, and it is certainly a defensible reading of the movement. Still, I find it less than completely satisfying, for I miss in it something that I hear in the music – a connection that is more than a casual, associative one between the C minor and the Ab episodes; like many common-sense explanations, this one fails to match the complexities of experience. Why must I hear the two episodes as closely connected? First of all, *pace* Schenker, the brevity of the second A section influences my hearing. Although the elaborate retransition effects a return to tonic harmony, that return seems to me to be too fleeting to match the weight of the first and third statements. Secondly, the orchestration – dominated in both episodes by the wind nonet – provides a strong coloristic link, a link reinforced by the piano, which both times provides a varied repeat of the wind parts. Third, the foreground keys, if heard as linked, fuse into a coherent progression: I (first A section) arpeggiating through VI (first episode) to IV (second episode), V^7 (retransition), and I (third A section). Example 6b diagrams the two readings.

The second reading in Example 6b receives confirmation from a most beautiful and refined motivic link: the upbeat that introduces the Ab section is a reminiscence – disguised but recognizable – of the melodic figure that closes the C minor episode (Example 6c). Thus the second episode begins where the first one had left off, as though the brief intervening reprise had been a mere digression. Note that the coda begins with still another transformation of this same figure.

If the two episodes are linked (as I think they are), what then, would be the harmonic meaning of the second A section? Surely it is no merely apparent tonic; the elaborate V^7 that prepares it precludes any explanation of that kind. Indeed when the reprise begins, one hears the Eb major as a fully stable tonic that forms the goal of the large harmonic motion developed in the episode and retransition. But when it breaks off after only four measures, and when a new section begins that connects in tonal motion, orchestral color, and motivic design with the first episode, sensitive retrospective hearing will modify that initial impression of stability. This tonic return will be understood as a brief parenthetical statement that brings into momentary consciousness the tonal motion's point of departure just before it continues on to its next important goal.

As the third diagram in Example 6b points out, this incidental tonic return can be regarded as a special instance of the retained tone. The Eb that begins the bass line is retained conceptually through the C minor and Ab major episodes, becoming the third and fifth of their respective "tonics." Not infrequently, middleground structures – linear progressions or arpeggiations – that compose out a prior verticality (as this Eb–C–Ab composes out the fifth Eb–Ab) will be segmented in a way that allows the background structure to "peer through"; thus Eb–C–Ab becomes Eb–C–(Eb)–Ab.

Both/and

If my reading of the Mozart movement is correct, it reveals a genuine double meaning: the large-scale bass motion traverses a descending arpeggio Eb–C–Ab; within the same time-span, (but less significantly) it also encompasses a return to Eb. That these two events can coexist without contradiction is due to the implicit presence of the Eb throughout the arpeggiated motion. On the foreground, "polyphonic melodies" often reveal small-scale segmentations of a similar nature: the subject of Bach's two-part Invention in F major embodies both a rising arpeggio and an initial note (f[1]) that persists in returning.

Our final piece shows a double meaning of a different sort, one that involves a motivic association that persists in the face of a changed harmonic meaning. Everyone who has worked for a while with Schenker's approach will have run into bass lines that fill the gap from I up to V with both the third and fourth notes of the scale (and possibly with the second as well). Such lines pose an analytic problem: is the basic progression I–III (or I⁶) –V with the fourth scale degree passing between III and V, or is it rather I–IV (or II⁶) –V with scale-degree 3 as the passing note? (If the line is completely stepwise, there is a third possibility as well: I–II–V–I, but it does not bear on the present discussion.) Example 7 shows the two possibilities.

Example 7. I–III (I⁶)–V or I–IV–V?

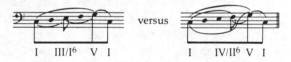

Schenker addressed himself to this issue in *Free Composition*, in the section where he begins to show how the bass arpeggiation of the fundamental structure can be prolonged; indeed, my Example 7 is based on his Figure 14.[7] His explanation is most interesting. He begins by showing an arpeggiation 1–3–5, the most "natural" division of the rising fifth between tonic and dominant. He then indicates that the thirds formed by the arpeggio can be filled with passing notes, producing a stepwise motion through the fifth; one or two of these stepwise notes will possibly fall away (basses tend to disjunct motion). And because of some emphasis built into the composition, one of the passing notes (scale-degrees 2 or 4) can become a focal point of sufficient importance to reduce scale-degree 3 to a lower rank.[8] The type of emphasis that Schenker mentions is the one caused by the coincidence of the bass note in question with one of the notes of the fundamental line. Of course the same harmonic situation will often occur at lower levels where there is no question of supporting a note of the fundamental line; other kinds of emphasis (some of

---

7. *Free Composition*, pp. 29–30 and Figure 14.
8. I have discussed this issue in slightly more detail in "A Commentary on Schenker's *Free Composition*," *Journal of Music Theory* 25/1 (1981), pp. 130–31.

them related to the one Schenker cites) will then influence the analytic interpretation.

In Schubert's song, "Auf dem Flusse," the broken chord E–G–B functions as a basic motive, linked both to the frozen river that forms the central image of the poem and to the protagonist's heart, whose icy crust and painfully seething interior are explicitly likened to the river. Rising figures that embody or reflect the motive permeate both the bass and the vocal line at middleground and foreground levels; changes in the motive follow the poem's imagery as it unfolds. The song is too long and too complex for me to discuss in its entirety here; in any case, many of its most interesting features do not bear directly on the topic of this paper.[9] Example 8a shows the basic motive, stated simultaneously in two forms: without elaboration in the bass and filled in with the briefest of passing notes in the upper voice. (At the beginning of the song, the vocal line is merely an embellished doubling of the bass. Not until measure 23 does an independent top line begin to develop.) And Example 8b quotes the postlude and sketches the way the motive dissolves into the final arpeggiated chord; the river becomes a mere blur on the horizon as the protagonist trudges on to new encounters.

Example 8. Schubert, "Auf dem Flusse"

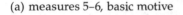

(a) measures 5–6, basic motive

(b) postlude

9. There is an incomplete middleground sketch in *Free Composition*, Figure 40/2; the sketch reveals clearly the extent to which arpeggiated figures dominate the texture. Oswald Jonas, without mentioning the basic motive as such, discusses briefly some of its most fascinating transformations in his *Introduction to the Theory of Heinrich Schenker*, trans. and ed. John Rothgeb (New York, 1982), p. 48. For a very different, but interesting and thought-provoking approach to the song, see David Lewin, "Auf dem Flusse: Image and Background in a Schubert Song," in *19th-Century Music* 6/1 (1982), pp. 47–59; reprinted in Walter Frisch, ed., *Schubert: Critical and Analytical Studies* (Lincoln, 1986), pp. 126–52.

Example 8 (*cont.*)

(c) measures 23–30, foreground
(upper 10ths)

(d) measures 23–30, middleground sketch
(upper 10ths)

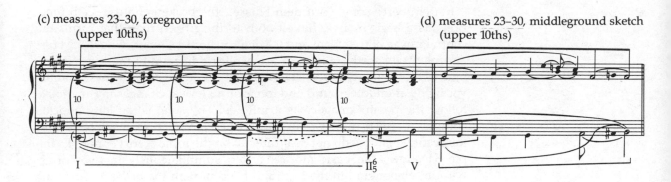

With the change to major in measure 23 (Examples 8c and 8d), the arpeggio figure begins to undergo new transformations. The bass line of measure 23, E–G♯–A♯–B, remains close to the original form of the figure despite the upward register transfer of the first note. In particular the time frame – from downbeat to downbeat – remains the same. This one-measure statement, however, is nested within a larger bass motion whose contents, the linear progression E–F♯–G♯–A–A♯–B, stretch over the entire eight-measure phrase (see especially Example 8d). This structure traverses the same ground as the stepwise form of the basic motive (vocal part, measures 5–6), and it represents the biggest expansion and most significant transformation of the motive thus far in the song.

In the course of this expansion and transformation, one note of the line – the fourth scale degree (measures 28–29) – receives a double emphasis: it supports both the culminating note (c♯²) in a series of parallel tenths above the bass and f♯¹, the note that connects most closely with the initial g♯¹. The third scale degree, by contrast, recedes in importance; the harmonic structure of this phrase is surely I–II⁶₅–V rather than I–I⁶–V. Here the emphasis on the active fourth scale degree mirrors the text, in which the narrator stops addressing the river and begins, however ineffectually, to act. The triadic arpeggiation 1–3–5, a Nature symbol, gives way to the dissonant passing tone that better expresses the world of human feeling and action. (In an almost uncanny way, Schenker's theoretical description of the prolonged bass line is embodied in the motivic design of this masterpiece.)

And yet this bass line, despite its changed harmonic meaning, grows out of the same higher-level structure as the 1–3–5 arpeggiation, and it must be regarded as a manifestation of the same underlying compositional idea. Unlike our earlier illustrations, where one and the same passage presented the listener with a choice between conflicting interpretations, here we encounter two distinct passages each with only one plausible interpretation. The difference in harmonic structure is far from negligible, but we can remain aware of it while also acknowledging the validity of a perspective from which the similarity in linear contour and over-all direction outweighs it. How important it is not to reify a theoretical construct like I–I^6–V (remember Schenker's characterization of the theory of harmony as a "purely spiritual universe, a system of ideally moving forces"). Otherwise we run the risk of becoming imprisoned in our vocabularies and ways of thinking; without vigilance on our part, these can all too easily block our access to the music we wish to make our own.

Introduction

In this section, Jonathan Dunsby and William Rothstein offer their perspective on past and present Schenker studies in Great Britain and in America. (Jonathan Dunsby has supplemented his conference presentation with a bibliography of recent British writings related to Schenker, compiled by John Rink.) The 1985 symposium included a third report, a survey of Schenker studies in Australia given by Kay Dreyfus of the University of Melbourne.[1] Schenkerian activity is spreading to regions very remote from Schenker's Vienna, and the future charted by Dunsby and Rothstein is very different from what Schenker could have imagined.

In his words of farewell at the 1985 Schenker symposium, Robert Cuckson, then Dean of The Mannes College of Music, also looked toward the future. Quoting the words of the Medieval monk John Scotus Erigena, "Diffusion is goodness; reunion is love," he expressed the following hope: that the knowledge and understanding gained by the symposium's participants would prompt them to reunite in the enjoyment and discussion of the music they love. We can do no more than hold the same hope for the readers of this book.

---

1. For a comprehensive discussion of Schenkerian work outside the United States, see David Beach, "The Current State of Schenkerian Research," *Acta Musicologica* 57 (1985), pp. 279–81. Studies on the reception of Schenker's thought may be regarded as an aspect of historical writing on Schenker; see William Pastille's review of Hellmut Federhofer's *Heinrich Schenker* in the *Journal of the American Musicological Society*, 39/3 (1986), p. 668.

Schenkerian theory in Great Britain: developments and responses

Jonathan Dunsby

Until recently the impact of Schenker's writings and teachings in Britain was minimal. Why this was so has been explained well enough by Britain's senior theorists Ian Bent and Arnold Whittall in various sources. I estimate that it resulted from a combination of inevitability and accident. On the one hand, British empiricism, with its antipathy to explanatory theory, not only survived the war but was probably nourished by it, so that a deep mistrust of German idealism lingered long into the fifties and sixties, as it lingers still, in the cherished view that free counterpoint and functional harmony are the best explanations of what motivates tonal music. On the other hand, in the musical community there was little to counteract this trend, since few Viennese musicians, let alone Schenkerians, made their home in Britain in the thirties and forties. Some, of course, did arrive in America, and it is notable how essentially American Schenkerian studies have become and how different matters might have been but for the accidents of war. In Britain, it would have been in the conservatories rather than in the universities that Schenker's pupils might have found a voice. Their achievement might have been, not textbooks for theory courses, but a living institutional tradition that would have enriched the development of performers and composers. But the American understanding of Schenker has lapped the shores of Britain to all intents and purposes as hard-core music theory, in print, at second hand in various forms, as a specialist area of learning representing concerns apparently far removed from the sphere of conservatory education and much university education, and also removed from the sphere of professional musical performance. My first point, then, is that the neglect in Britain until recently of what one can call the American Schenker is comprehensible and partly justifiable – in a way that the German rejection of Austria's greatest modern theorist, of his pupils who stayed there, and of his writings in their native tongue, is neither easy to understand nor easy to justify, even allowing for the strength of the Riemann tradition. It should be pointed out too that Britain before the war had little to offer in the way of professional musicology. "Systematic musicology" was virtually unknown, hardly any writers on music worked in the universities, and in any case British scholarly life as a whole was markedly distinct from that of Europe and America: as David Fallows pointed out in his history of recent British musicology, British culture has been unusual even to the extent of omitting philosophy from the standard education of the well-bred citizen.[1]

In the 1960s a wind of change – for some, a bitter wind – blew through British academic music. There was a rapid proliferation of universities and an expansion of existing universities, in which a young generation of academic musicians, fired by the optimism of American and Continental musicology, and inspired by the opulent resources on offer to scholarly initiative, set out to define a new image for their discipline. They succeeded, though the old amateur journalistic approach survives alongside Britain's new, tougher musicological face. And not only did they succeed, but somewhere in this development thinking that could be traced back ultimately to Schenker emerged, peripherally, often as the object of deep suspicion, but inexorably for all that. The main initial area of inquiry was twentieth-century music, yet a separate identity for theory was beginning to be accepted. So dramatic has this development been that the intentions motivating it have rather outstripped the reality of its achievement. If you consider yourself an analyst of tonal music in Britain now, you are *assumed* to be a Schenkerian, if not only a Schenkerian; yet security of knowledge and technique is still not all that common, and good teachers of Schenkerian theory are few and far between, faced as they are with the difficult compromise of working within existing curricula devised with other means and ends in view. In fact, in that peculiarly British way of, as it were, letting other cultures do the work while fixing one's eyes on a misty horizon, Schenkerian practice is increasingly considered ideologically sound but limited and limiting. The main focus of attention, when it is not new music, is often early twentieth-century music or pre-Baroque music. This bias is fueled by undergraduate educational priorities in universities, where knowledge and understanding of Classical and Romantic music are more assumed than nurtured, and where the most pressing need is perceived to be the broadening of students' experience of early and modern music. And from a research point of view, our brightest young writers can find the concerns of Schenker's own work to be rather out of date, a turn of events which will be mentioned again toward the end of this paper.

I intend now to elaborate on some of these points and, where possible, cast them in a transatlantic light.

First, how did Schenker emerge in Britain? Ironically, it was partly to do with the post-war assimilation of new music, with the preoccupation of a new generation of composers with Second Viennese repertory. Working in these areas, musicians who avoided the deathly grip of British Romanticism found theoretical self-awareness to be vital, and it was found too that this would not automatically weaken the creative innocence of a composer's soul. Those who had studied in Paris or Princeton legitimized the disciplined approach to music-making and, vicariously in most cases,

1. David Fallows, "Musicology in Great Britain since 1945," *Acta Musicologica* 52 (1980), pp. 38–68.

legitimized the inherently disciplined approach to tonal theory and analysis offered, more than anyone else, by Schenker. This was not always a vicarious process either, to which the direct influence of the Manchester school, including Harrison Birtwistle, Peter Maxwell Davies, and Alexander Goehr, testifies.

Institutionally, Schenker's work was disseminated primarily through the University of London, where some of the first experiments at systematic graduate schooling were attempted. And on this score theory and analysis seem to owe a major debt to historical musicology. Without going into a parochial history, one may at least observe that the main impulse in the development of London as a center of excellence in musical scholarship was the desire to establish a body of comprehensive undergraduate education and specialist graduate education in musicology. The emphasis was on breadth as well as discipline, with, for instance, hopes of a place for ethnomusicology, and language skills. And it followed that theory and analysis may as well form the tail end of this development, if not as the central discipline, then at least as an identifiable aspect of musical research. I suppose the architects of this grand scheme hardly anticipated that one day the tail might threaten to wag the dog.

Technically – and it has already been mentioned how the war did not throw up a real Schenkerian tradition in Britain – it wasn't Schenker who took hold, but Felix Salzer, whose textbook *Structural Hearing* was for several years the source of Schenkerian analysis to most British research students and undergraduates.[2] Though teachers here and there may have studied *Der Tonwille*, *Das Meisterwerk*, and *Der freie Satz*, classroom teaching had to be from Salzer's book. Schenker's *Five Graphic Music Analyses* were available, but seemed too advanced and in places obscure to form the basis of a rational pedagogical exercise. On the basis of a Salzerian education, although stimulating research articles in *The Music Forum* or the *Journal of Music Theory* could break into the British consciousness, American research that appealed directly to Schenker's own work, reflecting it notationally, investigating it theoretically, naturally seemed a little alien to – if I may call them this meaning no offence to any parties – British Neo-Schenkerians. It is also true that rather few were able to see the potential and seemingly obvious value of *Structural Hearing*. There were brilliant young musicians ready to give serious attention to Katz and Salzer – notably Wilfred Mellers, who wrote in 1953 with unusual insight about the place of Schenkerian theory, which he found "a tonic and a civilized achievement," although he experienced "a certain elegiac gloom" at this symptom of "our relatively uncreative age."[3]

Nowadays, the average undergraduate at a British university is unlikely to complete a program without having at least heard of Schenker, but will usually have come across him only in a short series of lectures slotted into an overview of tonal analysis. This does little more than validate Schenker

2. Felix Salzer, *Structural Hearing* (New York, 1952; reprint edns, 1962, 1982).
3. See Mellers's review of *Structural Hearing* in *Music and Letters* 34/4 (1953), p. 332.

in the student's eyes, placing the bulk of his actual work in a long and honorable list of matters which would be studied if only there were time in a three-year specialist program. In an increasing number of departments, however, some attempt is made to go further into the subject. The publication in English of *Free Composition* has been a significant stimulus in this respect, and has had the further effect of stimulating teachers to assess how much Schenkerian theory was already available in English in various sources. The subsequent publication of Allen Forte and Steven Gilbert's textbook[4] is likely to promote, in my view, a minor revolution, as authoritative information on questions of recognizably Schenkerian theory and technique is no longer in Britain the preserve of an unwilling cartel of academic musicians: indeed, the beginnings of this revolution are already detectable as one hears people discussing Schenkerian matters – recent literature, research development and the like – with much more confidence and commitment. It is through this textbook in particular that practice is likely to catch up with purpose. Yet the Forte/Gilbert introduction is certainly provocative, given the habits of the British mind, with its preference for comparative and speculative inquiry supported by full consideration of the related literature, of which, in this case, there is virtually no indication – as is appropriate to its particular aims.

As for British publication, it has been understandably slow to emerge. Only in the last few years have indigenous monographs appeared – and I shall return to this as to other points – which reflect and exploit Schenkerian ideas; and only in the last few years have theorists been able to turn away from American publication to their own British journal. The record is both good and bad, an ambivalence symbolized by that British flagship, *The New Grove Dictionary*, a flagship for which many of the weapons were supplied from America. At last Schenker began to figure in the mainstream of British musicology, in name and in discipline, though rarely in spirit in *The New Grove*'s general view of tonal music.

What cannot so easily be overcome by these advances in the spread and understanding of Schenkerian theory is the bedrock of resistance in secondary or high school education, not to Schenker's own concept of free composition which doesn't even arise at that level, but to the preliminary part of that "Great Teaching" which he urged as a substitute for false theory. In Britain, professional musicians, and students who go on to other careers, and amateurs right down to those hundreds of thousands of children who take instrumental lessons for at least a few years, all take examinations controlled by an Associated Board of the Royal Schools of Music. This Board publishes a theory book, the common heritage of all British musicians, however distant a childhood memory it becomes. And one proceeds through eight grades with virtually no contrapuntal information and with a misconceived, but mercifully brief account of thorough bass, where one is given such valuable hints as this, for

4. Allen Forte and Steven Gilbert, *Introduction to Schenkerian Analysis* (New York, 1982).

instance: "The notes can be arranged in any order." And while children are benefiting from such advice, they are also studying repertory for performance grades from special authorized editions of music published by the Associated Board. It need not be described what these editions have been like over the years and what the Board believes they are for; suffice it to say by way of comment that they perpetrate a much wider scheme of musical nonsense than just the phrase marks Schenker wanted to see banished.

None of this is unique to British music. It represents the kind of nineteenth-century legacy that has to be dispelled in America too. But there is a lasting point to be made about this great divide between Schenkerian tenets – in many senses, the tenets of eighteenth-century music theory – and the practices of musical life in the 1980s; and it is that Schenkerians have yet to fully confront the educational challenge implicit in this discipline. Aware as they are of the dangers of glib misuse of graphic analysis and of the difficulties in its mastery, which can often quickly demoralize a student, leading figures in this field have tended to stress what daunting knowledge and skills have to be amassed. How often has it been written and said that Schenkerian theory and analysis demand years of patient study. If even in Britain this is now a commonplace slogan, one can be confident that the message, a commendable message in an absolute sense, has been made strongly and permanently. But what of the further issue, an "allegation" as Schenker called it, that the "inherent difficulties" of his work make it "unsuitable for large-scale exploitation in the schools"?[5] Has this problem really been addressed? In Britain, it has not, and the development of Schenkerian theory in higher education in fact serves to widen the musical gulf which it is supposed that musicians may be able to cross in their late teens. While the tradition of research provided from America is needed and appreciated, its idealism seems to know no bounds. This is not to undervalue some excellent American sources which start from rudimentary factors and develop a voice-leading approach through levels of greater complexity. Yet there doesn't seem to be much concern in the world of Schenker nowadays, or at least that part of it which crosses the Atlantic, about musical education in its entirety and especially at its roots. If this issue has gone a little cold in America, it is also a loss to Britain.

A further area I propose to discuss briefly is an aspect of the relation of Schenkerian theory to musicology and to criticism. In Britain there is more interest in analytical practice than in theory and the history of theory, so the belief of historians that Schenkerians are scholastically lightweight is perhaps even more widespread than in America. And in a country where a systematic approach to musical explanation is undervalued in favor of the record of one's personal response to music, there is no need of a campaign for the humanistic and the idiosyncratic – in Britain, this battle can be won almost without being fought. In fact, there

5. Schenker, *Free Composition*, p. xxii.

is no keen interest even among what might be regarded as respectable theorists in Britain in the everyday world of Schenkerian work, in the kind of familiar routines making modest discoveries which are a necessary part of the pedagogical process but which are really private matters rather than statements of general interest: after all, such regular exposition can be found everywhere in American publications and does not carry any more weight if it happens to be devised by a British musician; and in Britain Schenkerians are constantly on their guard, having observed the challenges in the development of American theory, against the accusation that they may just be applying familiar techniques to familiar repertory to prove points known in advance, in principle if not in practice. The reaction to this situation has been intriguing, and takes the form that British exponents of voice-leading analysis seem to me to have been pushed to the fringes of Schenkerian development, opening up areas of study which, in their self-evident importance, increasingly silence the sceptical musicologist and critic.

To illustrate this, there is no avoiding the somewhat invidious procedure of giving particular examples. In the article literature, I would single out Christopher Wintle's essay on Corelli's tonal models. As he notes, the great line of development from Palestrina through Domenico Scarlatti is "untouched by the contemporary analytic movement,"[6] yet

every one of [Schenker's] most important concepts can be rediscovered through the Italian instrumental music of the late seventeenth century, whose dissemination played so vital a part in establishing the *lingua franca* of the late Baroque, [which] points to the fundamental historical importance of this music.[7]

Wintle's technical illustration of this in one of Corelli's Trio Sonatas is firmly based in Schenkerian theory, yet it offers a critically wider view than, as it happens, Schenker suspected or, perhaps, got around to investigating. Such an important broadening of critical perspective is also pursued in Wintle's recent comparative studies of Beethoven analysis by Riemann, de la Motte, Tovey, Schenker, and Federhofer.[8]

Among dissertations, I suppose I must mention my own 1976 study of Brahms, one of the first modern analytical presentations in Britain, and one which, significantly, more or less avoided using Schenkerian method (despite a studied awareness of its significance), since I had sufficient respect for Schenker not to want to distort his theory by applying it partially and probably inaccurately, as I thought likely of work conceived to all intents and purposes in a Schenkerian vacuum and certainly not within a confident, ramified, even organic Schenkerian tradition.[9]

6. Christopher Wintle, "Corelli's Tonal Models. The Trio Sonata Op. III, n. 1," in *Nuovissimi Studi Corelliani: Atti del Terzo Congresso Internazionale, Fusignano, 1980,* ed. S. Durante and P. Petrobelli (Florence, 1982), p. 30.
7. *Ibid.,* p. 31.
8. Wintle, "Kontra-Schenker: *Largo e Mesto* from Beethoven's Op. 10, No. 3," *Music Analysis* 4/1–2 (1985), pp. 145–82.
9. See Jonathan Dunsby, *Structural Ambiguity in Brahms: Analytical Approaches to Four Works* (Ann Arbor, 1981).

Among the book literature, I would mention Julian Rushton's recent monograph on Berlioz,[10] which, though it is not in any sense an orthodox Schenkerian study, would be inconceivable without the backdrop of Schenker's accounts of tonality and musical structure. Especially in Britain, with its tradition of the critically informal "life and works" on popular composers, this volume is conspicuous for its technical commitment. Who, one wonders, in the next serious account of a major composer's works, will dare to pretend that we can now do without the insights of voice-leading analysis and the technical issues of organic tonal structure? Plenty of people will, of course; indeed some already have, and they may take the strong position that the allusion to and general guidance offered by Schenkerian organicism is in the end more meaningful than doubtful attempts to present taxing voice-leading inquiries to the general musical public. As Arnold Whittall puts it in the Prologue to his study of Britten and Tippett:

it seems inescapable that any serious discussion of structural harmonic issues should seek to make use of the insights consequent on the application of Schenkerian methods. Yet the most radical aspect of those methods is not the conclusions they draw about harmonic relationships in music, but the fact that they demand presentation in graphic, non-verbal form: they therefore tend to the rejection of the book "as we know it."[11]

As for the journal literature, *Music Analysis* is not in fact or intention a Schenkerian publication, yet in its first years of remarkably disparate material it has published several articles of an avowedly Schenkerian stance in one form or another, and this is apart from discussions and reviews also reflecting Schenkerian matters. From America, it has occasionally taken canonical expositions of a kind that would certainly have pleased Schenker, but not surprised him. From British writers, stranger fare is on offer, all the way from the three-voiced *Ursatz*, via harmonically ambivalent voice leading in Wagner, to the paradigmatically referential voice-leading graph. This type of work may sometimes be so specialized as to seem to leave the general concerns of musicology and criticism far behind. It may even leave behind, with a raised eyebrow, the American theorist used to more conventional development of a discipline from within. Yet of the various factors which are contributing to this extraordinary wave of creative thought – a wave that I have termed a process of "disciplinary deconstruction" – the intense study by younger musicians of Schenker's own analytical, theoretical, and musicological legacy is, in my diagnosis, the primary impetus.

Now I want to consider the future, from two points of view – a future that is mapped out in no small measure by senior research students in a handful of institutions. It is striking how, enriched by their experience of Schenker, they turn one after another – though not exclusively – to the music of the late nineteenth and early twentieth centuries, or to new

10. Julian Rushton, *The Musical Language of Berlioz* (Cambridge, 1983).
11. Arnold Whittall, *The Music of Britten and Tippett* (Cambridge, 1982), p. 9.

music, or occasionally to early music. There are reasons for this which have nothing to do with Schenker, but there is one reason which has everything to do with him. A growing appreciation of Schenker's insights often results in a growing realization on the part of the research student that there is little hope of following his example, and if Schenker can't possibly be matched on his own ground, one has to move elsewhere. Yet the issues of the Viennese masterpieces have certainly not been exhausted, and some have hardly been raised to the extent of becoming general questions. I look forward in particular to the publication in English of all Schenker's writings in his periodicals and yearbooks, and of the Beethoven monographs, which more than any other step could dispel the notion that Classical tonal music is a relatively easy repertory, and more than any other step, in its exposure of such a rich variety of speculation on many different aspects of music barely covered in *Free Composition*, would fire the imagination of young researchers once again. It may be a pity that more musicians don't read German, but to allow Schenker's wider research, into editorial practice, performance practice, music and text, or the interpretation of nineteenth-century criticism – to go on allowing these achievements to be a casualty of linguistic borders is highly undesirable, whatever the causes may be. The further investigation of works already glossed by Schenker, the completion of his partial graphs, the elaboration of Schenkerian premises as regards orchestration, interpretation, editorial matters, and many further topics – such inquiry within the ground staked out by Schenker is as essential as are the fringes in the evolution of this field.

Finally, I do find it striking that Schenker's philological approach to his inherited musical literature has had apparently little effect as a model for modern scholars. From across the ocean, American scholarship seems to be at the mercy of a kind of social strife, which I mention as obliquely and quickly as possible. Whereas I can point out to a student where Schenker himself evaluates the opinions of one or another commentator – his discussion of Mozart's A minor Piano Sonata, for instance, is fascinating and exemplary in this respect[12] – I'm at a loss to advise on where the concepts of, say, contrapuntal structure or double function are compared with Schenkerian, perhaps also Fortean accounts of music that might display these features covertly; just as I'm at a loss to know what literature to advise to the student who seeks reasoned comparative critiques of the principles of rhythmic reduction, or indeed of the distinction and possible interaction between rhythmic reduction and durational reduction. Some intrepid comparative study in David Beach's collection has begun to point the way in this respect,[13] as has the work in Germany of Hellmut Federhofer[14] and Karl-Otto Plum.[15] Yet it does not seem from the outside

12. Schenker, *Der Tonwille* 2 (1922), pp. 7–24.
13. David Beach, ed., *Aspects of Schenkerian Theory* (New Haven, 1983).
14. Hellmut Federhofer, *Akkord und Stimmführung in den musiktheoretischen Systemen von Hugo Riemann, Ernst Kurth und Heinrich Schenker* (Vienna, 1981).
15. Karl-Otto Plum, *Untersuchungen zu Heinrich Schenkers Stimmführungsanalyse* (Regensburg, 1979).

that the American climate of opinion has decided to take on board a thorough, frank, comparative appraisal of fifty years of Schenkerian work. I doubt whether it will come from Britain, and I commend it to American academe as a significant objective.

Select bibliography of literature related to Schenker by British authors or in British publications since 1980

compiled by John Rink

* The following selection is designed to show some of the depth and range of Schenkerian influence in British music theory of the 1980s. It is not comprehensive and aims rather to be representative. The author of this article and the compiler of the bibliography apologize in advance for any glaring omissions.
   Entries by the same author are listed in chronological order.

Ayrey, Craig. "Berg's 'Scheideweg': Analytical Issues in Op. 2/ii," *Music Analysis* 1/2 (1982), pp. 189–202.
   Review of David Beach, ed., *Aspects of Schenkerian Theory*, in *Music and Letters* 65/1 (1984), pp. 83–87.
Bent, Ian. "Heinrich Schenker, Chopin and Domenico Scarlatti," *Music Analysis* 5/2–3 (1986), pp. 131–49.
Bent, Ian, trans. "Heinrich Schenker, Essays from *Das Meisterwerk in der Musik*, Vol. 1 (1925)," *Music Analysis* 5/2–3 (1986), pp. 151–91.
Bent, Ian, with William Drabkin. *Analysis*, London: Macmillan; New York: Norton, 1987.
Cavett-Dunsby, Esther. "Mozart's Variations Reconsidered: Four Case Studies (K. 613, K. 501 and the Finales of K. 421 [417b] and K. 491)," Ph.D. diss., King's College London, 1985.
   "Schenker's Analysis of the *Eroica* Finale," *Theory and Practice* 11 (1986), pp. 43–51.
Chew, Geoffrey. "The Spice of Music: Towards a Theory of the Leading Note," *Music Analysis* 2/1 (1983), pp. 35–53.
Chittum, Donald. Review of Eugene Narmour, *Beyond Schenkerism: The Need for Alternatives in Music Analysis*, in *The Music Review* 41 (1980), pp. 154–55.
Cook, Nicholas. *A Guide to Musical Analysis*, London: Dent; New York: Braziller, 1987.
Drabkin, William. "Characters, Key Relations and Tonal Structure in *Il Trovatore*," *Music Analysis* 1/2 (1982), pp. 143–53.
   Review of Felix Salzer, ed., *The Music Forum*, Vol. 5, in *Music Analysis* 1/2 (1982), pp. 203–9.
   Review of Karl-Otto Plum, *Untersuchungen zu Heinrich Schenkers Stimmführungsanalyse*, in *Music Analysis* 2/1 (1983), pp. 102–5.
   "Felix-Eberhard von Cube and the North-German Tradition of Schenkerism," *Proceedings of the Royal Musical Association* 111 (1984–85), pp. 180–207.
   "A Lesson in Analysis from Heinrich Schenker: The C major Prelude from Bach's Well-Tempered Clavier, Book 1," *Music Analysis* 4/3 (1985), pp. 241–58.
   "Building a Library, 1: The Beethoven Sonatas," *The Musical Times* 126 (1985), pp. 216–17ff.
Dunsby, Jonathan. "Heinrich Schenker and the Free Counterpoint of Strict Composition" (review of Heinrich Schenker, *Free Composition*), *RMA Research Chronicle* 16 (1980), pp. 140–48.
   Review of Karl-Otto Plum, *Untersuchungen zu Heinrich Schenkers Stimmführungsanalyse*, in *Music and Letters* 62 (1981), pp. 212–15.
   "The Multi-piece in Brahms: *Fantasien* Op. 116," in *Brahms: Biographical,*

Documentary and Analytical Studies, ed. Robert Pascall, Cambridge: Cambridge University Press, 1983, pp. 167–89.

"A Bagatelle on Beethoven's WoO 60," *Music Analysis* 3/1 (1984), pp. 57–68.

"The Formal Repeat," *Journal of the Royal Musical Association* 112/2 (1986–87), pp. 196–207.

Dunsby, Jonathan, and John Stopford. "The Case for a Schenkerian Semiotic," *Music Theory Spectrum* 3 (1981), pp. 49–53.

Dunsby, Jonathan, and Arnold Whittall. *Music Analysis in Theory and Practice*, New Haven: Yale University Press, 1987; London: Faber Music, 1988.

Ellis, James. Review of Julian Rushton, *The Musical Language of Berlioz*, in *Music Analysis* 5/2–3 (1986), pp. 270–80.

Evans, Richard. Review of Heinrich Schenker, *Free Composition*, in *Tempo* 136 (1981), pp. 37–38.

Finlow, Simon. "The Piano Study from 1800 to 1850: Style and Technique in Didactic Virtuoso Piano Music from Cramer to Liszt," Ph.D. diss., University of Cambridge, 1986.

Harvey, Jonathan. Review of David Epstein, *Beyond Orpheus: Studies in Musical Structure*, in *Music Analysis* 2/2 (1983), pp. 225–27.

Howell, T. B. "Jean Sibelius: Progressive Technique in the Symphonies and Tone Poems," Ph.D. diss., University of Southampton, 1985.

Keiler, Allan. Review of David Beach, ed., *Aspects of Schenkerian Theory*, in *Music Analysis* 3/3 (1984), pp. 277–83.

Leech-Wilkinson, Daniel. "Machaut's *Rose, Lis* and the Problem of Early Music Analysis," *Music Analysis* 3/1 (1984), pp. 9–28.

Marra, James. Review of Allen Forte and Steven Gilbert, *Introduction to Schenkerian Analysis*, in *Music Analysis* 2/3 (1983), pp. 281–90.

Marshall, Christopher. Review of David Beach, ed., *Aspects of Schenkerian Theory*, in *Brio* 21/1 (1984), p. 27.

Marston, Nicholas. "Trifles or a Multi-Trifle? Beethoven's Bagatelles, Op. 119, Nos. 7–11," *Music Analysis* 5/2–3 (1986), pp. 193–206.

Miller, Malcolm. "Schenkerian Analysis: A Practical Introduction, at Nottingham University, 21–2 September 1985" (conference report), *Music Analysis* 5/1 (1986), pp. 119–21.

Musgrave, Michael, Review of Heinrich Schenker, *Free Composition*, in *Music Analysis* 1/1 (1982), pp. 101–7.

Musgrave, Michael, and Robert Pascall. "The String Quartets Op. 51 No. 1 in C minor and No. 2 in A minor: A Preface," in *Brahms 2: Biographical, Documentary and Analytical Studies*, ed. Michael Musgrave, Cambridge: Cambridge University Press, 1987, pp. 137–43.

Parish, George. "Tonality: A Multi-levelled System," *The Music Review* 41 (1980), pp. 52–59.

Parker, Roger. "The Dramatic Structure of *Il Trovatore*," *Music Analysis* 1/2 (1982), pp. 155–67.

Pople, Anthony. "Serial and Tonal Aspects of Pitch Structure in Act III of Berg's *Lulu*," *Soundings* 10 (1983), pp. 36–57.

Puffett, Derrick. "The Fugue from Tippett's Second String Quartet," *Music Analysis* 5/2–3 (1986), pp. 233–64.

Rink, John. "The *Barcarolle: Auskomponierung* and Apotheosis," in *Chopin Studies*, ed. Jim Samson, Cambridge: Cambridge University Press, 1988, pp. 195–219.

Review of Heinrich Schenker, *J. S. Bach's Chromatic Fantasy and Fugue: Critical Edition with Commentary*, in *Music Analysis* 7/2 (1988), pp. 225–33.

Rushton, Julian. *The Musical Language of Berlioz*, Cambridge: Cambridge University Press, 1983.

Samson, Jim. *The Music of Chopin*, London: Routledge and Kegan Paul, 1985.

"The Composition-Draft of the Polonaise-fantasy: The Issue of Tonality," in

Chopin Studies, ed. Jim Samson, Cambridge: Cambridge University Press, 1988, pp. 41–58.

Sharpe, R. A. "Two Forms of Unity in Music," *The Music Review* 44 (1983), pp. 274–86.

Sutcliffe, W. Dean. "Haydn's Piano Trio Textures," *Music Analysis* 6/3 (1987), pp. 319–32.

Swanston, R. B. Review of Heinrich Schenker, *Free Composition*, in *The Royal College of Music Magazine* 78/2 (1982), pp. 199–201.

Tobin, E. M. J. "Aspects of Form in Schumann's Piano Music," Ph.D. diss., Trinity College, Dublin, 1982–83.

Wen, Eric. "A Disguised Reminiscence in the First Movement of Mozart's G minor Symphony," *Music Analysis* 1/1 (1982), pp. 55–71.

"A Tritone Key Relationship: The Bridge Sections of the Slow Movement of Mozart's 39th Symphony," *Music Analysis* 5/1 (1986), pp. 59–84.

Whittall, Arnold. "Schenker and the Prospects for Analysis," *The Musical Times* 121 (1980), pp. 560–62.

Review of David Epstein, *Beyond Orpheus: Studies in Musical Structure*, in *Journal of Music Theory* 25/2 (1981), pp. 319–26.

"The Music," in *Richard Wagner: Parsifal*, ed. Lucy Beckett, Cambridge: Cambridge University Press, 1981, pp. 61–86.

"The *Vier ernste Gesänge* Op. 121: Enrichment and Uniformity," in *Brahms: Biographical, Documentary and Analytical Studies*, ed. Robert Pascall, Cambridge: Cambridge University Press, 1983, pp. 191–207.

"The Theorist's Sense of History: Concepts of Contemporaneity in Composition and Analysis," *Journal of the Royal Musical Association* 112/1 (1986–87), pp. 1–20.

"Two of a Kind? Brahms's Op. 51 Finales," in *Brahms 2: Biographical, Documentary and Analytical Studies*, ed. Michael Musgrave, Cambridge: Cambridge University Press, 1987, pp. 145–64.

Williamson, John. "Strauss and 'Macbeth': The Realisation of the Poetic Idea," *Soundings* 13 (1985), pp. 3–21.

"The Structural Premises of Mahler's Introductions: Prolegomena to an Analysis of the First Movement of the Seventh Symphony," *Music Analysis* 5/1 (1986), pp. 29–57.

Wintle, Christopher. "Corelli's Tonal Models. The Trio Sonata Op. III, n. 1," in *Nuovissimi Studi Corelliani: Atti del Terzo Congresso Internazionale, Fusignano, 1980*, ed. S. Durante and P. Petrobelli, Florence: Olschki, 1982, pp. 29–69.

"'Humpty Dumpty's Complaint': Tovey Revalued," *Soundings* 11 (1983–84), pp. 14–45.

"Kontra-Schenker: *Largo e Mesto* from Beethoven's Op. 10 No. 3," *Music Analysis* 4/1–2 (1985), pp. 145–82.

"'Skin and Bones': The C minor Prelude from J. S. Bach's Well-Tempered Clavier, Book 2," *Music Analysis* 5/1 (1986), pp. 85–96.

"The 'Sceptred Pall': Brahms's Progressive Harmony," in *Brahms 2: Biographical, Documentary and Analytical Studies*, ed. Michael Musgrave, Cambridge: Cambridge University Press, 1987, pp. 197–222.

The Americanization of
Heinrich Schenker

William Rothstein

In a memorable passage at the beginning of his book *Suicide of the West*, the philosopher James Burnham meditates on the rise and fall of empires, using the image of an old historical atlas in which series of maps tell the tale of one imperium after another.[1] For example, there is the old Islamic empire, starting as a tiny spot in the Arabian desert and spreading irresistibly, map by map, until it extends from India to the heart of Europe; then it recedes.

Now it may be an example of what the rhetoricians call anticlimax to compare political or military history with intellectual history, and particularly with the history of one movement or fashion in musical thought. But I believe, at least half-seriously, that such a comparison can illuminate the spread of what some call Schenkerism in the American academy over the past several decades. Rather than rehearse the factual history involved in any great detail, I will seek some patterns behind the facts, that being an eminently Schenkerian enterprise. Like any analysis, mine will be rather personal – more personal than most, in fact, because it deals with experiences and ideas rather than with music itself.

To return, then, to my militaristic metaphor: I do not really imagine that there exists a secret room – somewhere at the Mannes College in New York, for example, that being the Mecca of our movement – in which fanatical Schenkerians plot new conquests. Nor do I really believe that there is a map in that room with pins stuck in it, each pin representing a music department or conservatory at which Schenkerism is propagated. But it is at least not too difficult to imagine what such a map would look like; and, wherever it might be, it is certain that the number of pins in it is steadily increasing. Clearly, the Schenkerian empire is still in its expanding phase.

For empires and intellectual movements alike, certain moments may arrive in which the full extent of the movement's power becomes suddenly clear. Napoleon's moment must have been his first night in Moscow, before his fortunes turned finally and desperately sour. (See Part 13 of *War and Peace*.) For me, a lowly noncommissioned officer in the Schenkerian army, it came sometime in 1984, when I was visited by two representatives from one of the major publishers of music textbooks. These worthies were

1. James Burnham, *Suicide of the West* (New Rochelle, N.Y., 1964), pp. 13–16.

scouring the country looking, naturally enough, for people to write text-books for them. Along the way, they were searching out members of the advisory committee to the 1985 Schenker Symposium, the list of which had been widely published. As they explained it, what they wanted was a new and up-to-date textbook in elementary harmony, something along the lines of the very successful text by Aldwell and Schachter – something, in their words, "Schenker-flavored."

Here I must digress to recount some more of my own experiences. I first encountered Schenker's ideas in a serious way in the middle 1970s at the New England Conservatory, where I studied for two years under the late Ernst Oster. From that encounter, I came away with the strong impression that Schenker's "approach" – to use the word that Oster himself preferred for it – held a tenuous and embattled position within the academy; that it was a fighting faith out of necessity, since opposition to it was so strong and so widespread; and that the motives of its opponents were defensive and self-interested at best.

Sitting in my office in Ann Arbor ten years later with the publisher's representatives, all that remained of this original vision – a vision which was enormously strengthened by the force of Oster's personality and by the difficulty of his own circumstances – was the idea of self-interest, which is to say, economic interest. Only now the interest was on the side of Schenker rather than against him. Now Schenker had become so fashionable that he was being paid the ultimate American compliment: he was being vulgarized. Once an arcane and difficult thinker, quite beyond the reach even of most university professors of music, he had become a "flavor," a whiff of which would help to sell textbooks to undergraduates.

Of course, I didn't really need this little epiphany to see what was going on with Schenkerism in America. It is one of the glories of American culture that it so readily absorbs foreign influences – at least, some foreign influences. But those foreign elements that it adopts, it adapts in the process, often changing them in essential ways. America is the country, after all, of the ham-and-cheese croissant and the pizza bagel. It is also one country in which European dialectical thinking has never really taken root. The moral is that foreign ideas and innovations must be ready to change, to be flexible enough to fit certain basic American preconceptions, in order to be widely accepted. This is of course the old idea of the melting pot, but applied to the intellectual rather than the sociological realm.

Nobody in America is more skeptical of the melting-pot concept than a New Yorker, for the New Yorker sees the "unmeltable ethnics" every day, and may in fact be one himself. As it is with people, so with ideas. It has proven possible, in New York, for foreign schools of thought, from Trotskyism to Freudianism to Schenkerism, to flourish in purer forms than has been the case elsewhere in the country. The predominance of New York-centered émigrés among the adherents of these schools, in their formative stages at least, is no doubt largely responsible for this phenomenon. One of the inevitable results – typical, apparently, of émigré cultures everywhere – has been an unnaturally intensified, hot-house atmosphere characterized by intense loyalties, internal squabbling, and a certain degree of paranoia with respect to the outside world. The attitude of mistrust very soon becomes mutual: the outside world views the foreigners, along with their ideas, as hostile, condescending, over-heated, and slightly ludicrous, all at the same time. It is in this context that one can begin to understand the view that has so often been taken, especially in earlier years, of the New York-centered Schenkerian move-ment. The resentment directed at it, in truth, has been pretty impressive. It has been seen as an exclusive and dogmatically minded cult, speaking an impenetrable jargon, whose members proselytize ceaselessly while constantly bickering among themselves over the proper tending of the sacred flame. Once an image such as this has been established in the popular mind, enormous effort is required to overcome it. American Marxists have never really succeeded in this, and Janet Malcolm has recently set the Freudians back considerably with her *New Yorker* series "Trouble in the Archives."[2] We Schenkerians are doing better, I think, but there is still much left to be done. I will suggest some paths for the future at the close of this essay.

First, let us identify those elements of Schenker's thought which clash most spectacularly with the American mind. Most of these unassimilable elements are readily apparent in Schenker's writings and have been fre-quently pointed out by friends and foes alike. Briefly, then, there is Schenker's pan-German nationalism; his sometimes explicit identifi-cation of the laws of God with the "laws" of art; there is, consequently, his unbending absolutism, which necessarily sees any deviation from revealed musical law as a symptom of cultural and even moral degeneracy. Less horrifying, but still unacceptable to the American ethos, is his shamelessly aristocratic attitude in artistic matters – and, incidentally, in political matters as well.[3] His notions concerning the supreme role of the German genius in musical history, and the correspondingly unim-portant if not actually harmful role of the non-genius, are well known. By comparison with these attitudes, Schenker's hatred of twentieth-century music is a minor matter indeed, for it is shared – if only in a reflexive way – by more people than many commentators care to admit.

Until the publication of Hellmut Federhofer's recent biography, the most concentrated repository of Schenker's objectionable opinions was probably the infamous Appendix 4 of *Free Composition*, that translation of passages excised either by Oswald Jonas or by Ernst Oster from *Der freie Satz*.[4] There, on a mere five pages, is a whole storehouse of ammunition

2. Malcolm's series of articles has also been published as a book, *In the Freud Archives* (New York, 1984).

3. See the discussion of Schenker's politics in Hellmut Federhofer's book *Heinrich Schenker: Nach Tagebüchern und Briefen in der Oswald Jonas Memorial Collection* (Hildesheim, 1985), pp. 324–30.

4. See Schenker, *Free Composition*, pp. 158–62. The passages in Appendix 4 are translated by John Rothgeb.

for the anti-Schenkerian. But there, too, is another illustration of the cultural clash between Schenkerism and America. The inclusion or exclusion of that appendix was a matter of intense controversy behind the scenes when *Free Composition* was about to be published. Those who argued for its omission were generally those most loyal to Schenker, who feared for the public reaction to his supposed indiscretions, and who most partook of the defensive mentality associated with the émigré group of orthodox disciples. They feared, apparently, that the core of Schenker's thought might be discredited along with his peripheral ramblings.

On the other side stood those whose loyalties were more immediately directed toward the canons of the American academy, according to which such suppression as was being contemplated was tantamount to falsification. This view, which ultimately prevailed, held that no disciple has the right to conceal the words of his master from the scrutiny of the scholarly community, or to prettify them. Therefore, in this view, what the editors of *Free Composition* sought to do to Schenker was unethical. Furthermore, it was thought, the knowledge that skeletons were being purposefully hidden would be far more damaging to Schenker's reputation than the airing of some reactionary remarks, which were really not so heinous anyway. On this last point – that a coverup would be more damaging than full disclosure – I think that this group was entirely right.

In fact, I have come to think that they were basically right on all points. Schenker can no more be exempt from the history of ideas than any other thinker; and, to the historian of ideas, context is paramount. Fortunately, today we have people – William Pastille is an example – who can write Schenker's intellectual history with real understanding.[5] Further, I think it is clear by now that the fears of rejection – rejection of Schenker's theories – which the suppressionists harbored were largely unfounded. If anything, the expansion of the Schenkerian empire has accelerated since the publication of *Free Composition*, and among the newly sympathetic have been some notable former opponents. American musicians, by and large, are not stupid, and they do not need to be patronized or shielded from unpleasant facts.

Yet there are limits. The fears of the suppressionists were not based on paranoid fantasies, even if they were perhaps misplaced in this instance. The rules of the American academy do not exclude Schenker's most significant ideas, but they do exclude certain kinds of behavior on the part of his adherents. Schenkerism may have become the dominant American theoretical tradition where tonal music is concerned, but it cannot be gainsaid that the acceptance, by the academy, of Schenkerians themselves is still in part an uneasy one. Naturally, Schenkerians must follow the rules like everyone else. Where we differ from "everyone else," however, is that *our* creed, in its original form at least, is inherently antipathetic to those rules.

5. See William Pastille, "Heinrich Schenker, Anti-Organicist," *19th-Century Music* 8/1 (1984), pp. 29–36. A fuller exposition is given in Pastille's "Ursatz: The Musical Philosophy of Heinrich Schenker" (Ph.D. diss., Cornell University, 1985).

Rule One, the most fiercely held tenet in the American academy, is – that no tenet should be too fiercely held. This is the anti-dogma rule. It is a peculiarly Anglo-Saxon cultural artifact, I think, but it seems to be more ironclad in America even than in Britain. I cannot imagine, for example, that the late Hans Keller, who was lionized in Britain for so many years,[6] would even have been tolerated on the other side of the Atlantic – especially not in a university.

In short, Schenkerians in America may not claim exclusive possession of the truth. Such a claim – even the perception of an implied claim – is greeted with hostility, suspicion, and unfavorable tenure decisions. Every truth, in the academy, must be provisional; it must be partial, not comprehensive; it must acknowledge the meritorious aspects of competing ideas; and it must be ready to adapt or even give way to new discoveries. For Schenker to swear by this code of ethics is for Schenker to change in a subtle but nonetheless fundamental way. Schenker is accepted in the academy only to the extent that he is cleansed of the taint of dogma. Even though it can be argued that there is at present no seriously competing theory in the field, we are obliged to assume that there could be – that other theories will soon catch up with ours – and are required to hold ourselves in readiness for the ensuing debate. Thus, we must treat Schenkerian theory as one theory among potentially many, even if not as one among actually many. Otherwise – and the implied threat is unmistakable – the sufferance under which we operate will be withdrawn.

Rule One has enormous consequences for the Schenkerian, affecting almost every phase of academic activity. Most important are the subtle but binding restrictions on how we may speak and write. Our rhetoric must be carefully modulated. We must master some form of the American academic dialect, which is sober and dispassionate. (Excessive enthusiasm is considered unseemly and intellectually suspect.) The poetic flights so characteristic of the writings of Schenker, Jonas, and Oster are discouraged. An occasional, slight rise in the emotional temperature is considered useful to inspire a class or a reader, but too frequent or too intense such rises will lead us to be regarded as feverish, unobjective, even fanatical. Rhetorical absolutism may have served German professors of a century ago well enough, but in present-day America it comes across like Adolf Hitler.

It is instructive to survey the various ways in which Schenkerians have attempted to deal with the problem of rhetoric. The best way to do this is actually to compare passages by various authors, preferably on the same general topic. Compare, for example, Schenker himself writing on the nature of the linear progression in *Free Composition*; Jonas on the same subject in his *Introduction to the Theory of Heinrich Schenker*; Felix Salzer's comments on the "structural line" in *Structural Hearing*; and, finally, Allen Forte and Steven Gilbert's discussion of the linear progression in Chapter

---

6. See the memorial symposium devoted to Keller in *Music Analysis* 5/2–3 (1986), pp. 341–440.

19 of their recent textbook.[7] There are of course numerous other authors whom one could add to this list, but these represent some of the major trends of the past half-century. One trend, however, namely the "scientific" view of Schenker inspired by Milton Babbitt and since taken up by others from Kassler to Lerdahl and Jackendoff, I have omitted as being incommensurate with the other, more traditional approaches.[8]

Very generally speaking – and my characterizations here will naturally be oversimplified – Schenker's voice is that of the prophet, pronouncing sacred mysteries from on high. In this mode he seems to me far more effective than Schoenberg, who more explicitly identified himself with the prophetic tradition. (But the kinship which outsiders often sense between the two surely resides partly in this congruence of personae.)

Jonas only rarely reveals the same prophetic fire. In general he is the poet of the group, although his convictions are as rock-hard as Schenker's. I have been surprised at how difficult students find him to read; he is too flowery and philosophical for many of them, and this makes them uncomfortable. It also leads them, sometimes, to question his intellectual solidity. On the other hand, he makes a more genial companion than Schenker, and the more sensitive student cannot help but find him inspiring at his best.

Salzer is an entirely different matter. I am convinced that the great impact which *Structural Hearing* had, years ago, was due in considerable part to its tone, its rhetoric, rather than merely to its chronological position, or to its still controversial expansion of Schenker's techniques. Salzer's tone is one of kindly authority, and I would stress the kindliness as much as the authority. The organization and comprehensiveness of the book make the student feel that he is in competent hands; while its reassuring tone – the tone of a wise and patient schoolmaster, confident of his own ideas yet liberal in spirit – eases the student's mind as he enters an unfamiliar world. The fact that Salzer can point to those whom he calls "narrow-minded and short-sighted," "those who still cling with the spirit of orthodoxy to every word Schenker has pronounced,"[9] allows him to appear even more liberal and benevolent by comparison.

As for those expansions of Schenker's techniques to what has been called the "post-Schenkerian repertory," that was entirely in tune with a dominant ideology of the fifties and at least the early sixties. At that time,

7. *Free Composition*, pp. 43–46 (see especially p. 44, §116); Oswald Jonas, *Introduction to the Theory of Heinrich Schenker*, trans. and ed. John Rothgeb (New York, 1982), pp. 62–89; Felix Salzer, *Structural Hearing* (New York, 1952; reprint edns, 1962, 1982), pp. 41–45; Allen Forte and Steven Gilbert, *Introduction to Schenkerian Analysis* (New York, 1982), pp. 237–45.
8. Babbitt has written relatively little on Schenker, but see his important review of Salzer's *Structural Hearing* in the *Journal of the American Musicological Society* 5/3 (1952), pp. 260–65. Babbitt, in his writings, has enthusiastically supported the work of Michael Kassler; see the latter's "A Trinity of Essays" (Ph.D. diss., Princeton University, 1967). For Lerdahl and Jackendoff, see their *A Generative Theory of Tonal Music* (Cambridge, Mass., 1983). The connection of the last two authors with Babbitt is my own, not theirs; they share Babbitt's scientific bias, although they diverge sharply from him on the "nature versus nurture" debate regarding the cognitive status of tonality.
9. *Structural Hearing*, p. xvii.

Bartók's music had become widely popular, and Hindemith's influence as a teacher (not to mention Boulanger's) was still strong in America. There was a fairly widespread attempt to demonstrate that, whatever Schoenberg and Webern might have been up to, this neo-tonal music was really not that different from the music of the tonal masters. This attempt may strike us oddly now, as a watering-down of essential distinctions, even as special pleading for a certain class of contemporary composers, but a glance at some of the textbooks of the time – from Hindemith's own *Traditional Harmony* to Wallace Berry's *Form in Music* – will quickly confirm my point.[10] (From this point of view, it is interesting to note, Adele Katz's *Challenge to Musical Tradition* was far ahead of its time.[11]) One of the products of this ideology was Allen Forte's first book, *Contemporary Tone-Structures,* although Forte was much more circumspect than Salzer about connecting modern music with older music.[12] Nevertheless, the fact that Forte himself no longer stands by that book is one indication of what has happened since then. Salzer and the revisionists allied to him may have won the rhetorical battles, back in the fifties; but the pendulum was eventually to swing the other way, and the ostensibly "narrow-minded" disciples such as Jonas and Oster were to gain parity and finally ascendancy within the fractious community of Schenkerians.

Allen Forte is a pivotal figure in the history of American Schenkerism. His 1959 article "Schenker's Conception of Musical Structure" introduced many readers to Schenker's basic concepts for the first time.[13] More important, it was Forte who, along with Milton Babbitt, was instrumental in bringing Schenker firmly into the Ivy League. This accomplishment was probably *the* major turning point for Schenker's fortunes, comparable to the conversion of Constantine. Ever since, Yale and Princeton, with the Mannes–CUNY axis directly between them and roughly equidistant from both, have formed the extrema of the great symmetrical set of Schenkerism.

Forte's rhetoric, and later Forte/Gilbert's, is extremely reserved in tone. Neither prophet nor poet, he is the cool taxonomist, concerned above all with rationalism and clarity. In his 1959 article he compares Schenker to the ideal scientist, thus possibly showing the influence of his friend Babbitt (to whom he dedicated his next book, *The Compositional Matrix*).[14] Forte's lack of passion is in line with American academic writing generally. From the point of view of the student, however, I think that he and Gilbert go rather too far in the direction of dryness, although I would not say the same about Forte's 1959 article. On the whole I think that Salzer

10. Paul Hindemith, *Traditional Harmony* (New York, 1943–53); Wallace Berry, *Form in Music* (Englewood Cliffs, N.J., 1966).
11. Adele Katz, *Challenge to Musical Tradition: A New Concept of Tonality* (New York, 1945; reprint edn, 1972).
12. Allen Forte, *Contemporary Tone-Structures* (New York, 1955).
13. This article, originally published in the *Journal of Music Theory* 3/1 (1959), is reprinted in Maury Yeston, ed., *Readings in Schenker Analysis and Other Approaches* (New Haven, 1977), pp. 3–37.
14. Allen Forte, *The Compositional Matrix* (Baldwin, N.Y., 1961; reprint edn, 1974).

struck a better rhetorical balance, whatever his shortcomings on the theoretical side.[15]

Although the objective, scholarly tone of Forte and the scientific bias of Babbitt were not motivated entirely by academic politics, they certainly had political consequences. Babbitt has been remarkably candid in declaring that his disposition to speak of music in terms derived from the philosophy of science was partly intended to secure music's place as a field of advanced thought within the academy. He wanted theoretical physicists to grant co-equal status to theoretical musicians, including composers. (In this he certainly failed, as he is the first to admit.[16]) Forte, in a work like *The Compositional Matrix*, tried to demonstrate that a Schenkerian theorist could be just as thorough, as scholarly, and as dispassionate as any historical musicologist.[17] Between them, these two trail-blazers – both entirely American, and both unscarred by the Wars of the Schenkerian Succession – completed the first and most difficult phase in the Americanization of Schenker.

Having now surveyed some of the past, I would like briefly to discuss the challenges of the present moment, and to suggest some paths for the future.

On the question of how Schenkerians present themselves, it seems to me that the most promising trend of recent years has been the synthesis of fairly orthodox Schenkerian thought with a more relaxed rhetoric, achieved in the writings of some younger scholars such as Carl Schachter and Charles Burkhart.[18] Schachter in particular sets a new standard, for his writing is lively, elegant, and unfailingly musical. An important landmark, in my opinion, was reached with his keynote address to the 1983 National Conference of the Society for Music Theory. Beyond his engaging style of presentation and the brilliance of his analyses, his thoughtfully critical remarks on Schenker's sometimes excessive background orientation – in *Der freie Satz* especially – showed a sense of fair-mindedness and a lack of defensiveness which have not always come easily to Schenkerians.

I would propose that we go even farther in this direction – not necessarily the direction of criticizing Schenker, although that should be done where appropriate, but in that of reaching out to other musicians. I

---

15. For Babbitt's reservations about Salzer (which are shared by others in the Schenkerian community), see his review of *Structural Hearing*. See also the controversy between Roy Travis (a student of Salzer) and Ernst Oster (a student of Jonas) in the *Journal of Music Theory* 3/2 (1959), pp. 257–84 and 4/1 (1960), pp. 85–98. Oster's blistering reply to Travis is a classic in the polemics of music theory.
16. See Jeffrey G. Hirschfield, "Milton Babbitt: A Not-So-Sanguine Interview," *High Fidelity/Musical America* 32/6 (1982), pp. 16–18, 40.
17. But see Nicholas Marston, "Schenker and Forte Reconsidered: Beethoven's Sketches for the Piano Sonata in E, Op. 109," *19th-Century Music* 10/1 (1986), pp. 24–42.
18. See, for example, articles by Schachter in *The Music Forum*, 6 vols. (New York, 1967–) and the following articles by Burkhart: "Schenker's 'Motivic Parallelisms,'" *Journal of Music Theory* 22/2 (1978), pp. 145–75; "Schenker's Theory of Levels and Musical Performance," in David Beach, ed., *Aspects of Schenkerian Theory* (New Haven, 1983), pp. 95–112.

think it notable, for example, that the journal *19th-Century Music*, a bastion of urbane humanism within the academy, has taken to printing articles about Schenker by Schenkerians. I think it at least equally noteworthy that Schenker has made such inroads into British musical life as Jonathan Dunsby describes in his article included in this collection. If we can win over both those who are trying to get into music analysis, and those who are trying to get out, the potential for winning many more skeptical musicians would appear to be almost unlimited, if only we go about it in the right way.

The right way, in my opinion, is never to force more of Schenker's approach onto anyone than can be truly absorbed and truly heard. If this means that most students and non-theorists generally are taught only how to interpret the foreground, well and good; that's more than most of them can do now, and, besides, it's in line with Schenker's own ideas on musical education. Backgrounds and even middlegrounds are simply not for everybody. Recall that even Wilhelm Furtwängler and Roger Sessions either could not or did not care to follow Schenker all the way to the background; so why must our students?[19]

Furthermore, we should conduct our outreach program in terms that musicians can readily understand wherever possible, and we should write in such a way that people will want to read us. Our British friends have much to teach us in this latter regard: a great deal of British musical writing – in *Music Analysis* and elsewhere – puts us Americans frankly to shame. I recall, in this connection, the British reviewer of Maury Yeston's *The Stratification of Musical Rhythm* who, while noting the book's positive contributions, complained politely about its "modicum of American academic jargon."[20] That reviewer was right on target, although Yeston is far from being the only or the worst offender. Now that our position within the academy is secure, we can and should dispense with the defensive posture of trying to appear more scientific than we really are. And we can do this without degenerating into genteel dilettantism, as the British have unfortunately often tended to do.

Of course it may be said that I am neglecting truly advanced research, scientific or otherwise, and that I certainly do not mean to do. Although I have only limited sympathy for the various attempts to "formalize" Schenker's ideas – because I don't believe it can be done beyond a fairly primitive level – it is at least an honest attempt, and it obviously requires a formal language. Similarly, psychological research into the perception of musical structures must involve scientific method. This is also an honorable enterprise, although it too has so far failed to cope with the real complexities of tonal music. (It is still in its infancy, however.)

19. See the articles by Furtwängler and Sessions in *Sonus* 6/1 (1985), pp. 1–5 and 6–14. Furtwängler's article originally appeared in his *Ton und Wort* (Wiesbaden, 1955), pp. 198–204. Sessions's article first appeared in *Modern Music* 12/4 (1935), pp. 170–78; it is reprinted in *Roger Sessions on Music: Collected Essays*, ed. Edward T. Cone (Princeton, 1979), pp. 231–40.
20. Bayan Northcott, in *Tempo* 123 (1977), pp. 41–43.

Other, less exact research – into rhythmic structure, for example, but also into orchestration, performance, the history of tonality, and any number of other areas – remains almost as open today as when Allen Forte raised some of these issues back in 1959. Depending on the inherent complexity or abstractness of the subject, much of the original research in these areas will of necessity be more or less beyond the reach of the average musician, even of the above-average theory teacher. This cannot be helped, but at least there should be no intentional obfuscation or pretentiousness, as is still too often the case today.

On the other hand, the challenge posed by the "scientific" theorists must eventually be met. To Milton Babbitt's insistence that only that theory which conforms to the standards of exact science can legitimately be called theory, there is an easy answer: if you don't want to call what Schenkerians do "theory," call it something else.[21] But someone ought to take up the thread left dangling by the late Victor Zuckerkandl, and investigate more thoroughly not only the psychology but also the epistemology of Schenkerian analysis.[22] To paraphrase both Zuckerkandl and Salzer, what must the human mind be like for structural hearing to exist? What kind of knowledge do we have when we hear music in the way that Schenker described? What kinds of thinking do we use? And how do we communicate our knowledge?

Another item which should be added to the list of topics for research is the nature and history of musical style *within* the tonal era. In my opinion, Schenkerians do not talk enough about style. This is not, as our opponents sometimes claim, because we do not recognize its existence. It is rather a matter of emphasis. Schenker demonstrated the unity of the tonal *language* over some two hundred years, and this was one of his most essential contributions. As for us, however, we should not only acknowledge but investigate the differences between individual idioms, between genres, and between historical periods. Only those informed by Schenker can do this with the requisite insight, I believe, because only they seem fully able to make the essential (though not absolute) distinction between language and style. The traditional guardians of styles and periods, the historical musicologists, have mostly fallen down on the job – just as Schenker maintained.[23]

There are many other areas of academic life which I will not go into here: the American tenure system, for example, which I think imposes special burdens on Schenkerians – burdens related to the slow tempo of the analytical process, but also to the mania for theoretical originality

21. My reference is to Babbitt's 1965 essay "The Structure and Function of Musical Theory," reprinted in *Perspectives on Contemporary Music Theory*, ed. Benjamin Boretz and Edward T. Cone (New York, 1972), pp. 10–21.
22. Zuckerkandl's principal books are *Sound and Symbol: Music and the External World* (Princeton, 1956) and *Man the Musician* (Princeton, 1973).
23. See the account of Schenker's relations with the musicologist Guido Adler in Federhofer's *Heinrich Schenker*, pp. 49–55. See also Sylvan Kalib, "Thirteen Essays from Three Yearbooks *Das Meisterwerk in der Musik* by Heinrich Schenker: An Annotated Translation" (Ph.D. diss., Northwestern University, 1973), Vol. 1, pp. 361–402 and 439–43.

at all costs. The academic calendar and prevalent curricular structures also conflict badly with the more leisurely Schenkerian rhythms. David Beach and John Rothgeb, among others, have addressed some of these pedagogical issues in recent articles.[24] The conflict is most strikingly apparent, however, in the introduction to the Forte/Gilbert textbook and in Larry Laskowski's review of that book in *Music Theory Spectrum*.[25] Forte and Gilbert have surrendered completely to the academic status quo in suggesting that, after only one year of basic harmony and counterpoint, analysis itself can be taught in just one year. Laskowski prefers to let the nature of the subject itself dictate the pace of instruction. Unfortunately, however much one may sympathize with Laskowski's position (and I sympathize with it very strongly), most schools at present simply will not allot the amount of time required to teach analysis adequately; so compromises are necessary – though capitulation, I think, is not.

Compromises are necessary all along the line for the Schenkerian in academia. We face problems that Schenker himself, who was estranged from the Viennese academy, never had to face – or, to put it differently, never had the opportunity to face. But through living the academic life as it actually exists, in this country and at this moment, we have gained unprecedented influence. The prospects for the young Schenkerian today could hardly be more different from those which faced Hans Weisse, Felix Salzer, Oswald Jonas, Ernst Oster, and the other refugees from a decaying Europe. A price has been paid for our success, of course: we have had to sacrifice something of Schenker's world-view as a token of acceptance – our acceptance of the standards of the academy, in exchange for the academy's acceptance of us. The exchange has not been easy for either side, and it continues to cause friction. But the reward has been an expanding Schenkerian empire which as yet shows no signs of decline, and which is finally mature enough to end its partly self-imposed isolation. Therefore my final piece of advice is directed to the keeper of the map, who is advised to lay in an extra supply of pins for the busy season ahead.[26]

---

24. See David Beach, "Schenker's Theories: A Pedagogical View," in his *Aspects of Schenkerian Theory*, pp. 1–38; John Rothgeb, "Schenkerian Theory: Its Implications for the Undergraduate Curriculum," *Music Theory Spectrum* 3 (1981), pp. 142–49.
25. *Music Theory Spectrum* 6 (1984), pp. 110–20.
26. A slightly different version of this article was published in *In Theory Only* 9/1 (1986), pp. 5–17.

INDEX